CRANSTON

CRANSTON
the Senator from California

ELEANOR FOWLE

JEREMY P. TARCHER, INC.
Los Angeles
Distributed by Houghton Mifflin Company
Boston

ACKNOWLEDGMENTS

All those who helped me with their memories, insights, and skills are too many to name. Yet I would especially like to thank a few whose help came when it was especially needed—George Pfeiffer, Dick Smart, Dick Keeble, Carolyn Baer, Doris Atkinson, Teddy Muller, Ann Fitz, Beverly Hemingway, Dave MacDonald, Megan Skelding-Eros, Pat Kollings, Ginny Combs, Lu Morris, and Frances Ketman.

There were also a few without whose help the book could not have come into being. There was the wise advice of Mary Stegner, the thoughtful teaching of Wallace Stegner, the remarkable seminars of Catherine Elwood and Marie Mudra, the creative typing of Gaye Passell, the vision, talent, and craftsmanship of my editor, Adele Horwitz, the warm support and encouragement of my family, Michael and Charyl Fowle, and Linda and Kevin Burke, and above all my husband, Jack Fowle, who makes so many things possible.

In writing this book I have used as source material family records, letters, taped interviews. I have occasionally used direct dialogue for dramatic effect which is always based on source material but is not necessarily a verbatim account.

Quotations from *Memoirs of a Man: Grenville Clark.* Compiled by Mary C. Dimond and Norman Cousins, Norton, 1975, with permission from the publisher.

Fowle, Eleanor.
   Cranston: the senator from California.

   Includes index.
   1. Cranston, Alan MacGregor. 2. Legislators—United States—Biography. 3. United States. Congress. Senate—Biography. 4. California—Politics and government—1951–   5. United States—Politics and government—1945–   I. Title.
E840.8.C72F68 1984   328.73'092'4 [B] 83-24232
ISBN 0-87477-320-2

Jeremy P. Tarcher, Inc.
9110 Sunset Blvd.
Los Angeles, CA 90069

Manufactured in the United States of America
D 10 9 8 7 6 5 4 3 2 1

TO JACK
WITH LOVE

PUBLISHER'S NOTE:

Cranston: The Senator from California was originally published in 1980. In this new edition the book itself remains unchanged, except for the addition of the "Foreword to the New Edition, by Alan Cranston" and the "Postscript," written by Eleanor Fowle, which brings the reader up to date regarding the Senator's 1984 election campaign for the presidency.

Contents

★ ★

Foreword to the New Edition

★ ★

This book was first published in 1980 while I was in the midst of a successful campaign for an unprecedented third term as Democratic U.S. Senator from California.

No one would have predicted then that when a new edition was published just four years later, I would be in the midst of a campaign for the presidency.

Certainly I at the time had no such expectations or plans.

But in thumbing again through the pages of my past, I find that my remarkably perceptive sister detected early on the overriding concerns that would later propel me into a presidential race.

Indeed, she almost foresees the very theme of my current campaign: Peace and Jobs.

Eleanor writes, among other things, of my discussions in 1945 with a group of prominent scientists and other leading Americans on how to avert the holocaust we saw looming on the horizon at the dawn of the Nuclear Age; of my meeting with Albert Einstein, who told me that nuclear war could destroy the environment that sustains life on this planet and who warned that "the unleashed power of the atom has changed everything save our modes of thinking, and we thus drift toward unparalleled catastrophe"; of my uphill efforts to get the Senate to ratify the Strategic Arms Limitation Treaty (SALT II); of my battle as a freshman senator to save the Job Corps from dismemberment by Richard Nixon and his cohorts.

And, speaking of a sisterly sixth sense about the future, near the end of the book proper Eleanor includes a quote by then Vice President Walter Mondale, a friend but presently a rival in the race for the White House, describing me as "the most decent and gifted member of the United States Senate" and calling me "the saint of the Senate"!

I love the Senate (though, as a sister would know, I'm no saint). I had hoped to devote the rest of my life—as I have devoted the past fifteen years—trying to make it more effective and more compassionate, as well as more democratic (with both a small and a capital "D").

One can accomplish a great deal in the Senate. I think I do. But much more needs to be accomplished—that can only be done from the Oval Office. The years of drift toward a U.S.–U.S.S.R. nuclear collision (a drift that Ronald Reagan and the Soviet leadership have whipped into dangerous rapids) along with Reaganomics and its deliberate and heartless use of unemployment as an economic tool have convinced me of that.

Under every American president and under every Soviet leader since 1945, we have slipped closer and closer toward the abyss. We blame the Soviets. They blame us. We cannot look to them for new leadership. We must look to ourselves.

No president has ever given the threat of nuclear war the absolute priority attention it requires. I will. No one else within reach of the presidency has the background on the issue that I have.

Thirty-eight years after Hiroshima and Nagasaki the modes of thinking of most political leaders have not changed. Before it is too late, we must change if we are to cope with the danger nuclear weapons pose to humankind's survival. Coping requires more than just a small adjustment in our rhetoric. It requires a fundamental change in our view of the world. And it requires a national commitment to the nuclear issue.

It is, unfortunately, inevitable that the radical differences in the U.S. and Soviet systems—our different values, principles, and purposes—will lead again and again to dangerous disagreements. We must protect U.S. national interests. At the same time we must prevent U.S.-Soviet disagreement from leading to Armageddon.

We cannot rely on routine negotiations to reverse the vicious cycle of the arms race. We have left arms control to arms control experts. And they have failed us. They have become bogged down in concepts of megatonnages, throw weight, surgical strikes, overkill, and theories such as Mutual Assured Destruction—the acronym for which is, appropriately, MAD.

Where are moral principles and ethical values in all this?

Where is common sense?

And wisdom?

I am running for president because now, while we yet have time to prevent the ultimate catastrophe, we need a president who is dedicated in his mind and heart, in his whole soul, to an all-out effort using all the vast powers of his office to halt the arms race. My first step would be to undertake to negotiate a mutual and verifiable nuclear weapons freeze with the Soviet leaders. I would follow that step with a determined drive to achieve mutual and comprehensive arms reductions in both strategic and conventional weaponry. The goal must be to banish nuclear weapons from the face of God's earth.

If I am elected president, it will be because the American people have said they want an end to the threat of nuclear war.

The strength of that mandate will enable me to deal from strength with the Soviet Union. And the peace agreement that will result from our negotiations will have the full approval and support of the American people.

The crucial task before us requires the active involvement of the American people—aroused to the need to avert a nuclear holocaust that could end all our lives in a flash, destroying all we have created . . . our children, our families, our homes, our communities, our nation.

It demands a president capable of negotiating successfully with the Soviet leaders and a citizenry able and willing to open a dialogue with Soviet society as a whole—in the areas of trade, travel, professions, education, and culture—to the maximum degree Soviet authorities will permit. Wider, deeper communications between our people are essential if we are to reduce misunderstandings that could lead to catastrophe. We must seek common cause not only with the Russians but with the people of other countries if we are to overcome the myriad of economic and social problems that face us in the years ahead.

Nothing less will suffice.

We, as Americans, cannot develop our full potential as long as we are spending trillions of dollars on military matters. Only when we have the arms race and its shameful costs under control will we be able to offer the world a positive vision of what an America at peace can be. At the center of that vision must be our determination that, at last, after years of unfulfilled promises, we will attain an economy of full employment and full production, without runaway inflation—an economy of plenty with a job for every American who wants and needs one.

Only when we lift ourselves out of the dark shadows of the arms race will we be able to devote the full force of our human capital and natural resources to the task of building a better America of equality and justice for all.

Alan Cranston
1984

★ ★ ★ ★ ★ ★ ★ ★

Foreword

★ ★ ★ ★ ★ ★ ★ ★

This memoir of Senate Majority Whip Alan Cranston by his sister is frankly intra-family—anecdotal, personal, affectionate, and supportive. Nevertheless, all the principles, policies, strategies, campaigns, and alliances that have marked Senator Cranston's political life are here, chronologically developed and displayed, the triangulation points of a significant and distinguished, if deliberately low-keyed, career.

The record is illuminating, for it shows Senator Cranston to be what few politicians are: one whose politics derive from principles rather than one whose principles depend on politics. As a boy in the idyllic California town of Los Altos, as athlete and apprentice journalist at Pomona and Stanford, as shoestring foreign correspondent in Mexico, France, Italy, and Germany just before World War II, Alan Cranston comes off his sister's pages with complete consistency. The boy was an unusual combination of curiosity, confidence, and commitment, and though he was born lucky and grew up safe, his life became a sort of Horatio Alger story. The student had a gift for being where important things were happening, and for knowing people who could teach him things. The correspondent had a nose for the news that mattered.

Very early, Senator Cranston developed interests that in some people have been far from compatible: peace and human rights. More and more, after he left a Europe whose fuse was burning toward war, he was drawn toward the politics of reconciliation rather than the politics of intransigence and confrontation. He has had a belief in politics as a means of accommodating the apparently irreconcilable.

Mrs. Fowle's narrative shows him moving directly from wartime service with the OWI in Washington — a service that gave him an intimate view of the capitol and an acquaintance with many of its movers and shakers — to involvement with the world government movement, and eventually to the presidency of the World Federalists. He has to a high degree the quality that literary critics know as "negative capability," an instinct for putting himself in other people's shoes and understanding and respecting their points of view even when he disagrees with them. Even civil rights, which enlisted him early because of his affection for Japanese friends sent to relocation centers at the outbreak of the war, never became for him the confrontationist issue that the 1960s made of them. His greatest gifts have been openness, reasonableness, friendliness, the desire to bring opposing factions together in workable compromises. He has a smile that cuts Gordian knots, and a patience that, if the smile fails, can untie them. It seems possible for him, as Mrs. Fowle's anecdotes demonstrate again and again, to have a genuine liking for many individuals with whom he profoundly disagrees.

Mrs. Fowle chronicles the ups and downs of California politics in detail and from a privileged inside position, with many glimpses into her brother's ambitions, hopes, and disappointments. His lowest hour, brought about by political rivalries that even he had been unable to heal, came when Pierre Salinger beat him out for the Democratic senatorial nomination in 1962, with the effect of throwing power back to the Republicans. His greatest triumph was his election to the Senate in 1968.

In a body notorious for showboats, he has been a workboat and sometimes a fire-boat. He has concerned himself with forwarding a program, not creating an image. He has been an instrument, not a self-conscious Identity suffering from television-deficiency. Of the hundred members of the Senate there is hardly a senator more useful or less conspicuous. There is surely none with a voting record more consistent with principles held from early youth.

In the character of those principles, in his complete lack of pretention or side, in his exuberant energy, in his faith in work, organization, and reasonableness, even in a certain boyish ingenuousness, Alan Cranston is American in ways that seem at once characteristic and healthily old-fashioned. If he has any of the angst and anomie that afflict many of his countrymen, his sister's affectionate story does not touch on them. He himself cut the clothes he wanted to wear, cut them very young and grew into them, and he wears them, it seems to many of us, with a special quiet distinction.

Wallace Stegner
January 1980

On the concept of leadership:

> A leader is best
> When people barely know
> That he exists.
>
> Less good when
> They obey and acclaim him.
>
> Worse when
> They fear and despise him.
>
> Fail to honor people,
> And they fail to honor you.
>
> But of a good leader,
> When his work is done,
> His aim fulfilled,
> They will all say:
> "We did this ourselves."
>
> —Lao-tzu

Alan Cranston has carried this quotation in his wallet for the past thirty-five years, as an ideal—perhaps never absolutely attainable—and a guide.

★ ★ ★ ★ ★ ★ ★ ★
Prologue
★ ★ ★ ★ ★ ★ ★ ★

In November 1976, just after President Carter's election, my brother Alan Cranston came to stay overnight at our home in Los Altos, California. I hoped he would have time to answer some questions about my book. He had arrived late the night before.

"Could I turn off the phone?" I asked in the sunny guest room upstairs.

"No," he said, smiling a little contritely.

I prayed that it wouldn't ring.

The room was in cyclonic disorder, the morning papers spread over the bed, his huge battered briefcase spilling open on a chair.

Wearing his red running suit, he stretched out in an easy chair, put his feet up on Mother's old rocker and crossed his legs. His tanned face glowed from running three miles on our country roads. His dark eyes, deep-set over prominent cheekbones, danced and shone. With his usual indifference to appearances, he hadn't shaved. He was happily comfortable.

He retrieved a dog-eared file from the bureau top and handed me clippings from the eastern press. "Thought you might like to have these."

"Thank you!"

I was poised with a pencil and question-filled pad, conscious the time was short, when the telephone rang.

It was Roy Greenaway, Alan's chief of staff in Washington. Alan listened carefully as Roy talked.

"Well!" he exclaimed. He looked at me, angled his eyebrows up-

1

ward, nodded his head from side to side and shrugged, indicating that Roy's news was extremely engrossing. "Hm . . . yes. . . ." Once he said sharply, "It's just a rumor." Moments later he said, "That's pleasant."

Then he said tersely, "There's no reason to think about it or wait. We'll issue a statement right away, not let things get any farther. I'll draft something along the lines of my veep statement and call you back. Meanwhile you get to work on it too."

He hung up and sprawled on the double bed, piling pillows behind him. He picked up a pencil and yellow pad.

"Roy's heard from an 'unimpeachable source' that I'm high on the list being considered for secretary of state."

"Secretary of state! I can hardly believe it," I said.

"I can't either. I'm going to send word to Carter that I'm not interested."

"Why?"

"Because it could interfere with my race for whip. And if I became Carter's final choice and turned him down, it would embarrass him." He began to scribble on the pad, frowning with concentration.

The phone rang intermittently, and I dealt with it.

I thought of the statement Alan had issued that July when he took himself out of consideration for vice president. Again he had been on Carter's list. A decision of such magnitude had not been easy; all the tangibles and intangibles of a lifetime had been weighed in that choice.

His letter to Carter had said that, while he had the highest respect for the office, he simply did not want "to relinquish my present work as a senator, with all the independence and substantive opportunities that role offers, for the alternatives provided by the vice-presidency." He added:

> I really look upon myself as a 'Senate Man.' My life, my hopes, and my ambitions lie in the Senate and this is where I hope to remain and serve our country for as long as the people of California and I feel that I am serving wisely and well.
>
> The most important thing I can do in my life, I believe, is to continue to contribute to the restoration of the strength and vitality of Congress so that it, and particularly the Senate, may fulfill its Constitutional role in the separation—and hence the limitation—of power in our government.
>
> Along with the Bill of Rights, our system of checks and balances is the principal guarantor of our individual freedoms.

Now, in the morning sunlight I asked, "Wouldn't you even consider it for a moment?"

"No," he said. "In the Senate I'm my own man, serving at the pleasure of twenty million bosses, not just one. That's the way I like it. As secretary of state, I could be out, anytime! In the Senate, if I get to be whip, I can probably accomplish a great deal more. At least I think so and hope so. . . ."

"Oh, come on. Kissinger made things happen. You could too."

"It *would* be fun, flying 'round to all the different countries," he said, and grinned.

"Well, isn't it wonderful that you have the chance!"

"Yes."

"How do you think it all happened?" I asked, reverting to my question list.

"'Aim high,'" he said, with a lighthearted, half-mocking air. He had told me that when he was in the eighth grade at the Los Altos grammar school, his teacher wrote on the blackboard, "Aim high." He'd added, "I looked at that all year."

He read his notes aloud, then called Roy back. They discussed wordings and tactics. The rumor—which Roy was certain was true—was already provoking press inquiries. Alan would make a simple press statement. "Please work on it and call me back soon. I'll be leaving."

I looked at my watch and groaned.

"You can't catch up with me," he said, laughing.

Roy called again. Murray Flander, Alan's press secretary, and Peg Cuthbertson, his assistant, were also on the line. The four went over the statement word by word and made further changes. When it was settled, Alan thanked them warmly. Then he jumped up and threw the crumpled scraps of yellow paper into the wastebasket, his scattered files into his briefcase. He showered and dressed in three minutes. Then he gave me the yellow page of his scribbled draft to keep. Before I could ask even one question, we heard a car racing up the hill to take him to the airport.

As he strode out the door with his heavy bags, I said, "Good luck!"

He smiled, looking both eager and wistful. "We'll need it!"

"Get elected whip!"

"I'll try!"

Then he was gone.

The next night he telephoned from Washington. Someone he trusted had seen four lists for secretary of state. Alan was on all four and on Carter's final remaining list.

Reportedly Mondale had hit the roof, saying, "We need him in the Senate!"

Alan's chuckle came over the wire. "You'd have been amused at [Alan's California staff chief] Lu Haas's parting shot as he saw me off from Los Angeles: 'That's a great outfit you have on! Green pants, blue shirt, sneakers, business jacket. When did you shave last? Well, there goes the next secretary of state!'"

★ ★ ★ ★ ★ ★ ★ ★ ★
Early Years
★ ★ ★ ★ ★ ★ ★ ★ ★

The year was 1929. Alan, a slender, brown-eyed boy of fourteen, waited at the Palo Alto station to welcome a new president. Herbert Hoover, recently sworn in, was returning to his hometown for a triumphant celebration.

The afternoon sunlight poured down on the tree-lined streets and new store buildings of the little university town, shimmered on the grove of oaks and eucalyptus at Stanford across the Camino Real, and glowed on the excited crowd waiting beside the old yellow Victorian station.

A whistle blew and a moment later the train pulled in, jerked to a series of false stops, and came to a halt, letting off an obscuring cloud of white steam.

President Hoover, his rubicund face beaming with delight, appeared at the top of the steps of the last car. The crowd roared. Alan, who had properly gauged the action of the train, dashed to the foot of the steps, smiling, to welcome the president. A policeman raced to grab him by his neck and the seat of his pants, lifted him up, and dumped him down unceremoniously outside the circle of welcoming city fathers.

The incident of the delighted president and the boy with a million freckles was shown on newsreels across the country. Alan had begun to show his knack for being in the way of things happening.

*   *   *

He was born in Palo Alto on June 19, 1914. Soon afterward the family moved to a home in the country, the Red Barn, an old, brown-shingled farmhouse on a hilltop at Los Altos, a ranching community

5

in the foothills a few miles from Palo Alto. Adobe Creek and the Southern Pacific railroad meandered through the town.

The Red Barn had thirteen acres of orchards and a panoramic view of the mountains, with the folded deep-blue coast range as a backdrop. The Santa Clara Valley spread out below, stretching away, hazy in the distance, with the soft green scalloping of apricot and prune orchards covering the plain to the blue of San Francisco Bay and Mount Hamilton.

Alan's memories began there. His first is of standing up in his brass crib by himself and seeing Mother's surprised face at a window. His second is of refusing to kiss Father goodnight, an early clash between two very strong-willed people.

He remembers his childhood on a farm as happy. Sometimes on rainy days he pasted comic strips into scrapbooks Mother made him. His first ambition was to be a cartoonist. He spent endless hours copying cartoons and drawing his own. The funny papers with their funny people and their funny problems gave him a small manageable world.

There were evening prayers on the sleeping porch and Sunday night services around the fireplace. Sometimes Alan sang war songs like "Tenting Tonight" and "Over There" by himself. "You all stared at me once when I forgot the words," he said recently. "It set back my public speaking about twenty years."

Frances Ketman, our occasional nurse during Mother's illnesses and travels, helped him with his collection of stamps, studying the places they came from. He used to ride round and round the veranda on his tricycle pretending he was visiting all the different countries.

Father loved bringing home treasures he found in houses he bought and sold. Once he came home triumphantly with a flag and a tall white flagpole, which he erected on top of our hill at the Red Barn. Alan was charged with the responsibility of putting the flag up and down.

"Always get it down before sunset," Father told Alan sternly, "and *never* let it touch the ground!"

Big as the flag was and small as Alan was, that was his first responsibility and his first athletic challenge — until he hit on the expedient of using a wheelbarrow. Seeing Alan racing past the fig trees and the veranda with the big wheelbarrow, trundling the flag, just before the rim of the sun sank below the hills, became a suspenseful part of the evening's entertainment — which Alan enjoyed more than anyone.

The sound of the squeaky wheel rapidly cutting the gravel failed to drown out Father's shout of, "Put the wheelbarrow away-ay-ay!"

Alan vaguely remembers the First World War — trenches in the adjacent hills and fields at Camp Fremont, the roar of dynamite blasts set off by the soldiers and sometimes mistaken by his anxious family for bombs or battle sounds.

Father threw himself into the war effort. In Palo Alto in September 1918, he was awarded a bronze plaque:

> To William MacGregor Cranston
> For his distinguished service to his
> community and his country as Chairman
> of the Palo Alto War Work Council.

Mother proudly hung the plaque in the living room on the paneled wall of the staircase that wound up behind the stone chimney.

One day in 1919 five-year-old Alan carried in the morning newspaper and ice-cold bottles of milk. He saw huge black headlines and heard Father's grieved exclamation, "Teddy Roosevelt's dead!" It was Alan's first memory of the impact of a political figure.

Poring over the paper at breakfast, Mother said to Father, "I wonder if Alan might ever be president."

"Oh no," he said.

"Oh, why not?" Mother asked.

"No, no chance!" he said very firmly.

Alan resented that. He remembered it always, and perhaps it influenced him to get into politics to prove what could be done.

Both Father and Mother's families were of Scottish descent and had political tie-ins. In 1849 Mother's grandfather, Hiram Harlow Dixon, a state senator in Vermont, introduced the Homestead Act, which became a law. Father's uncle, James Bolt, from the Shetland Isles, served in the British House of Commons. All four of Alan's grandparents came to California in the 1800s.

His grandfather, Robert Dickie Cranston, came to San Francisco from Ontario, Canada, in 1870 as an early passenger on the first transcontinental railroad. Alan still has his grandfather's pearl-handled dagger and a derringer pistol. He built many Victorian houses still standing. Occasionally today some San Francisco constituent will tell Alan he has found a card of R. D. Cranston's hidden in a newel post.

During a difficult boyhood in San Francisco because of poor economic conditions, Father worked hard, read a great deal, and dreamed dreams. Like his father before him, he had energy and drive. He met Mother at Stanford. He graduated with a B.A., majoring in law, and married her in Sacramento, the state capital, in 1903.

When Alan was elected state controller a half century later, his office in the corner of the capitol building was just a stone's throw away from the spot where the wedding had been held. The house at 1201 L Street is gone, but old photographs of it show a diagonal sidewalk running between the two points like a magic carpet. The house faced what later became the Senator Hotel.

The great San Francisco earthquake and fire in 1906 destroyed Father's real estate office at 20 Montgomery Street. He and Mother lost everything but their personal belongings. They moved to Palo Alto and started over again on a farm. Father sold real estate from the seat of a bicycle. Tragedy struck them again when their first child William, born in 1907, died of a rare gland infection.

After these setbacks, Alan came as a joy to them. He inherited Father's joyous, optimistic nature, Mother's cool judgment, the sense of humor common to both of them, and — from neither of them — a set of iron nerves. He was small, slender, and wiry, with large, dark, glowing eyes that missed very little.

In 1922 we moved to a house that lay below our hill on the outskirts of Los Altos, bounded by Adobe Creek and the railroad tracks beyond an old prune orchard. The house was a gabled rectangle, gray-shingled, white-trimmed, with a green roof — a long, welcoming, friendly, English house, set far back on the land in a grove of century-old oaks on the bank of the creek. An ancient ranch house by the creek and a little shed in the field went back to much earlier times, almost certainly to the days of the Mexican land grant.

Alan began to assert himself. He was unwilling to fit himself passively into the genteel and conventional new life that Father had dreamed of for the family. Alan was single-mindedly determined to make the place a center for his friends' enjoyment. Its wide flat lawn — a velvety expanse of greenness (the pride of Tanaka, the gardener) — became their meadow, their village green, the scene of their perpetual football games and track meets. (Their score cards are still in his files.) The ancient shed in the field became their Desperate Deeds

Club; the pool by the waterfall, their fishing hole. They reveled in the orchard and woods.

On rainy days they were in transports of joy when they sent golf balls down the long upstairs hall, caromed them from door to door, and heard them go bounce, bounce, bounce down the stairs, and roll out to a score on the living room rug. ("It's best to know where they are," said Mother resignedly.)

Once Alan and his good friend Junior Dutton told me in utmost confidence that they were putting fireworks (called torpedos) on the railway tracks bordering our prune orchard. They worked scientifically with timetables and used bigger and bigger torpedos. They also transferred signal flares from the path of the Southern Pacific daily commute train to the path of the silent, electric interurban streetcar. The flares exploded with terrifying bangs, frightening the passengers who thought the car was being shot up.

I thought of a plan for stopping them and telephoned Alan from the Palo Alto station.

"This is the office of the president of the Southern Pacific," I told him, disguising my voice in a husky bass.

Alan said, "Oh," in a shocked voice, muttering an aside to Junior.

"This is Mr. Shoup's secretary," I added. "Have you been putting torpedos on the railroad tracks?"

"Yes," Alan answered somewhat inaudibly.

"You'll have to stop it," I croaked. "You might kill a lot of people. If you don't stop it, we'll put you in jail. Will you stop?"

"Yes," he said firmly, and they did, despite their wild elation at getting a call from the president's office. Perhaps I should add that they never derailed any trains or streetcars.

Except for his love of people and animals, sports and comics, and his jokes and his pranks, you could never tell very much about what was going on behind the freckles and the large, dark eyes.

I was baffled enough to write a composition about him when he was ten.

"He makes himself an unendurable nuisance. He has an insatiable curiosity. But when he believes anyone to be meddling in his own affairs, he has a talent amounting to genius for misunderstanding or ignoring objectionable questions. . . ."

I marvelled at his reading habits. Alan had a systematic approach to books. He collected the Frank W. Burgess *Bedtime Books* in their entirety; read several other complete series. When he first encountered *Treasure Island*, he read it three times through without stopping. Later he read every Shakespearean play and every Shaw play, including the prefaces.

His school life was happily busy and its friendships were lasting. Through many years, he had a childhood sweetheart, Hope Austen.

His earliest ventures into school politics were not wildly successful. He was rather shy. He was even defeated for the office of keeper of the benches.

As a high school sophomore he went out for football, but he was still small and light and not very good. In his junior year he emerged as a track star. Track gave him his first self-confidence and released him from his uncertainties about himself. I saw Alan compete in the Santa Clara Valley High School championships in 1932, in one of his glory days. He was the star of the meet, easily winning the 100 and the 440 and anchoring the Mountain View relay to victory. An admiring freshman followed him everywhere, carrying his warm-up togs from starting line to finish line, helping him take them off and put them on.

In his senior year at Mountain View High School, he was elected president of the Boys' League, the boys' student body. He edited the school annual and also wrote a humorous column called "School Daze" for the school paper, the *Mountain Eagle*, that was printed in the town's weekly newspaper, the Mountain View *Register-Leader* as an economy measure during the depression.

At seventeen he began his first diary, written in a weird microscopic scribble, for reasons of security, we can assume. The front page said, "KEEP OUT! Yes, You." The diaries, which he kept for a few years, were filled with aspirations and strivings:

> I typed (an article on the 1932 Olympic Games in Los Angeles) and took it over to the Mountain View *Register Leader* office. "Pop" Smith barely glanced at it and said, "Yes, I'll be glad to take it." He told me to come around Friday, the day the paper comes out and he'll pay me then. I s'pose I'll get about a dollar for it. WHOOPEE!!! AT LAST I'VE SOLD SOMETHING! Am I happy.

Later:

> I want to make a real dent in the world.

CHAPTER 2

★ ★ ★ ★ ★ ★ ★ ★ ★ ★ ★ ★ ★ ★ ★ ★

European and Mexican Summers

★ ★ ★ ★ ★ ★ ★ ★ ★ ★ ★ ★ ★ ★ ★ ★

The September he left for college, Alan wrote in his diary: "I had a lump in my throat as I went out the driveway for the last time for some time to come." As he drove off to Pomona, perhaps he knew that it was the end of a graceful era—for others as well as for him. He was never again to spend more than a few weeks at a time at Villa Warec (as Father had whimsically named it, for William, Alan, Ruth Eleanor, and Carol).

That spring he became the star of Pomona's freshman track team. During holidays he hitchhiked and hoboed for the experience. Once he rode the freights to New Orleans and sent a postcard reminiscent of Huck Finn: "I'm sitting on the banks of a levee by the Mississippi cooking breakfast with some other tramps. I have only 11¢ left."

In January 1934 in his sophomore year, Alan transferred to Stanford. He plunged into campus activities and wrote regularly for the *Stanford Daily*. He joined Sigma Nu.

He achieved considerable notoriety when he ran the campaign of one of the candidates for Queen of the Masque Ball. He became Helen Ramming's press agent and hired a plane to write her name in the skies. The students' previous record for raising money in queen contests to benefit the Stanford Convalescent Home was $285. Alan raised $391. Helen , known as "Bedroom Eyes," was a non-sorority girl. Alan's publicity alarmed the sororities, who banded together, raised $860 for their candidate, and defeated Helen.

Alan was criticized for writing a coed's name all over the skies. In a

11

letter to the *Stanford Daily*, he defended the skywriting by saying he had made the fundraising drive more successful. He insisted, "The end justifies the means."

Recently he remarked, "I've now become convinced that means *are* ends and shape the ends. You see that constantly in politics and diplomacy. If you use improper means, you louse up the ends before you get there."

Track continued to absorb him. In 1935, in his junior year, he became a member of the fastest mile relay team in America. His best time in his regular event, the 440, was 48 seconds. His best time as a sprinter, in which he would specialize much later, was 09.9 seconds in the 100-yard dash. He won his block S twice.

He had always dreamed of the 1936 Olympic Games in Berlin. Bob Atkinson, a teammate, remembers: "If Alan had concentrated and avoided feminine distractions, he would have become a world-class quarter-miler. With 47.5 seconds he could have won the IC4A [intercollegiate championship]. The world record then was 46.4, held by Stanford's Ben Eastman."

Ben Eastman, who had been the world's greatest quarter-miler while Alan was in high school, was Alan's idol. At Stanford Alan ran against Ben three times and managed to beat him twice, but Ben was beyond his prime while Alan was approaching his. A new competitor for Alan that spring was Archie Williams, a superb black runner, who appeared on the University of California team. For a while Archie and Alan ran neck-and-neck. Alan beat him once, early in the season. But Williams made the Olympic team and was the Olympic champion that year in the quarter mile. Alan concedes that he hadn't taken it as seriously as he should. Somehow he had failed in his mental discipline. He made up his mind this would never happen again.

"Track taught me a great deal about victory, defeat, and discipline," he was to say later. "You have to look at anything you spend time on as important in terms of discipline. *How* you do it is important. Applying discipline to one thing, you learn how to apply it to your next undertaking. How to achieve, not fail."

Looking back on those years, Alan remembers certain influences that shaped his life. Books, especially those of Mark Twain and Charles Dickens, led him toward newspaper work. Richard Halliburton's travel adventures, *A Royal Road to Romance*, and Vincent

Sheean's experiences as a foreign correspondent, *Personal History*, and similar books fired Alan's ambitions. He majored in English, and studied Spanish, German, and French.

Father's friendship with Lincoln Steffens, the journalist, editor, and muckraker, and with the famous crusading editor of the San Francisco *Call-Bulletin*, Fremont Older, further whetted Alan's interest. Father's stories about Older's role in San Francisco's graft prosecutions after the 1906 earthquake and his subsequent fight to free the imprisoned labor leaders, Mooney and Billings, opened up a new world to Alan.

On January 15, 1935, Alan described in his diary a Sunday luncheon when Fremont and Cora Older were guests at Villa Warec:

> We were discussing Roosevelt's administration, saying what he'd done wrong. Father [who was a Republican] was doing most of the criticizing, when wise old Mr. Older, smart and alert as ever, and he's now 78 or 79, said 'You're saying what you wouldn't have done, which is very easy. But suppose you, instead of Roosevelt, had been elected President in 1932. What *would* you have done!"

> Father thought for a few minutes, then said, "Well, first of all I'd disenfranchise all civil office holders and their dependents." And Mr. Older snapped back with the perfect answer, the cleverest thing I've heard in many a day, "If you *could* do that, you wouldn't have to."

> We were discussing Germany. Mr. Older said, "Hitler is a tyrant." "*Why* is he a tyrant?" I asked to draw him out, "He's doing what he thinks right for Germany."

> Mr. Older turned his big head, his whole body towards me, and said, "Why— *he kills people!*"

At Sunday luncheons at the Olders' ranch in nearby Saratoga, Alan met fascinating figures from the newspaper world, as well as an extraordinary assemblage of authors, political figures, and other notables— even an occasional ex-convict the Olders were trying to help.

When Older died suddenly of heart failure in 1935, Father lost his best friend, and Alan wrote in his diary:

> . . . I consider him one of the greatest of all Californians. . . .
> Annie Laurie [a *Call-Bulletin* columnist] brought tears to my eyes with one of her typical heart-tearing articles in the *Examiner* this morning on Fremont Older.

In his cramped and slanted writing, Alan copied her article in its entirety into his diary:

. . . You never knew or cared whether a man was rich or poor, clever or dull. No, you didn't even care whether he was good or bad; not if you liked him, and you liked so many people, Fremont. Some of us of smaller vision found fault with you for that. I wonder, will it count for you or against you when you make your reckoning up there beyond the stars. . . .

Alan had found a model for the kind of man he later sought to become. He himself wrote:

How I loved those Sundays. They are no more. But I can't believe that Fremont Older is completely gone; he couldn't be here one minute, so alive, so active, so alert, so kindly; and gone the next, completely lost. It just can't be.

Cora Older, Fremont's widow, a writer and historian, later started Alan on his newspaper career by introducing him to leading newsmen in New York.

A very different sort of influence on Alan was his friendship with Milton K. "Pop" Smith, the big, slow-moving, square-jawed fearless editor of the Mountain View *Register-Leader*, who printed Alan's columns. An extreme conservative, "Pop" loved his paper and his work and fired his editorial guns at will.

Alan got along well with "Pop" and was influenced by his views on a free press and his love of news work. Their friendship helped teach Alan how to maintain warm relationships with those who hold totally different views on politics.

In the Great Depression of the 1930s, Father suffered terrible losses, and Alan watched him set out to rebuild his financial base for the third time, almost from scratch. But what mainly impressed Alan at the time was watching President Franklin Roosevelt seek to improve people's lives through his policies and programs. Alan's interest in politics deepened.

During Alan's sophomore year at Stanford in 1934, he explored Europe with a classmate, Vincent Meyer. In Paris they heard the news that Chancellor Dollfuss of Austria had been assassinated. They caught the next train for Vienna, where they used credentials from the tiny Mountain View *Register-Leader* to work their way into the courtroom where the murderers were being tried while even the correspondent from the famous London *Daily Mail* was left fuming in the corridor outside.

"Pop" Smith proudly noted over Alan's story: "We have a particular delight in presenting this splendid account of the world-famed, history-making trial, by one of our own boys. . . ."

Alan reported the trial in detail and concluded his article with this paragraph:

> It is later. Vin and I are having our first meal of the day: steaks and beer on a little balcony overhanging the gay Ring Strasse, main street of Vienna. We look at our watches, 4:35. Little Planetta and tiny Holzweber [the convicted assassins] are dying now in "Poor Sinners' Court.

It was the best piece he had written.

Soon after the trial, Germany's President von Hindenburg died. Hitler merged the presidency with the chancellorship and assumed the title "der Führer." Curious as to what was happening in Germany, Alan decided to spend several weeks there. Traveling by canoe, bicycle, and afoot, and knowing the language, he asked countless Germans in all walks of life their opinion of Hitler and the Nazi regime. Almost everyone he met praised Hitler, proudly pointed to the cut in unemployment, and spoke of Germany's new unity and of great hopes for the Third Reich.

One biting cold night in Munich, he stood in the lamplight on a street outside the Brown House for over an hour with a jovial, enthusiastic crowd waiting for a glimpse of its idol. Finally Hitler emerged. The crowd roared and raised a forest of arms in the Nazi salute. Hitler bowed his head and sternly returned the gesture. He climbed into the front seat of a low open car. Alan, who had pushed to within five or six feet of the stationary car and Hitler, stared at him in utter fascination. The Führer stood for a moment, slowly turning, saluting again. Then he sat down and was whisked away. Hitler's serious demeanor enthralled the crowd. People ran halfway down the block in rapturous pursuit.

The demonstration convinced Alan that the great majority of Germans backed their leader. He wrote in the *Register-Leader*: "The charge at home that Hitler is nothing more nor less than a fool is not worth considering."

Yet signs of repression were everywhere. When Alan entered a store in Munich he startled the shopkeeper who was bent over an American newspaper. She had mistaken his brown leather jacket for the uniform of a Nazi officer. Non-German papers were *verboten*.

Walking down a street in Sackingen with a portly German acquaintance, Alan remarked, "I saw Hitler one night in Munich." The remark often made him a hero in German eyes. Many stated that they
would pass up a gallon of beer for the privilege.

"Well, I don't want to see him!" growled his companion. Alan looked
at him in surprise. "That dirty rat — Heil Hitler," (this to another passer-
by). "That loud mouth — Heil Hitler," (another acquaintance) "—
has the whole world down on our ears. Shouts about uniting all the
Germans in Europe under one flag. No wonder our diplomats — ha!
ha! diplomats — stand alone at foreign conferences. If that damned
Hitler stays in power another year there just won't be any Germany;
we'll starve — Heil Hitler!"

And so this weird dialog continued all the way to their destination.
"Pop" Smith published Alan's article with the caption:

> From the pen of a clear-eyed, level-headed, unprejudiced American college
> student, we have a picture of the little man who is holding 60,000,000 Germans in
> the hollow of his hand — for a time.

Alan returned to Stanford. So far his experiences as a reporter had
been encouraging. Now he was to have one that was instructive in a
different way, and which held possibilities for disaster.

In 1935, at the end of Alan's junior year, he and another Stanford
friend, Johnny Atkinson, who shared many future adventures, drove
to Mexico City on the Pan American highway the week it opened.
They drove down in John's secondhand Ford, enrolled in courses at
the University of Mexico, and found lodgings in an old Mexican
boardinghouse where three gigantic meals were served for 54¢ a day!

As he had done in Hitler's Germany, Alan talked to hundreds of
people in all walks of life and wrote columns about Mexican history,
politics, and conditions for the *Register-Leader*.

During those first few weeks at the university, the subject that dominated most people's conversation was the situation in the state of
Tabasco, on the southern edge of the Gulf of Mexico. A ruthless dictator, Tomas Garrido Canibal, had ruled Tabasco for ten years, mur-
dering those who crossed him.

A group of University of Mexico students had gone down to campaign against his puppet candidates. The day after they arrived,

Canibal himself handled one of the three Thompson submachine guns that were turned on the students as they walked through the streets. Five were killed outright, and six were badly wounded. All Mexico City was aroused.

The day the dead and wounded students were brought home, Alan and Johnny with virtually the entire university student body went out to the airport. Five thousand angry, grief-stricken Mexicans, mostly students, were there to meet the plane. By using his press credentials, Alan got Johnny and himself past the guards and right up to the plane, where they met Arthur Constantine, the Hearst newspapers' veteran correspondent. Seeing their interest, Constantine directed them to an unofficial headquarters in an office building thronged with an excited mob of students. A punitive expedition to Tabasco was being organized. An official asked, "Do you want to go to Tabasco?" Alan exclaimed, "Yes, we sure do!" It was all arranged. To the other students going, Alan was a great capture, for they wanted the American public to gain a fair account of their journey.

Alan told Constantine that he was going, and the Hearst correspondent arranged for Alan to wire him whenever anything happened— a break into big-time reporting, Alan felt.

Two days later, on July 19, Alan and Johnny marched to the station through the streets of Mexico City with the students' punitive expedition, eighty-four strong. They boarded a little train set on rails barely three feet wide, which would take them to Vera Cruz to board a ship for Villahermosa, the capital of Tabasco. There the students would campaign against Garrido—peacefully, they hoped. But this time they came armed, because they would be in danger of being fired on at any moment. Alan and Johnny planned to rush to the American consul as soon as they arrived, with the news that two young and raw American journalists had arrived in town.

But the day they left Mexico City, Constantine wired the Hearst papers in the United States that Alan and Johnny had *joined* the revolution. He failed to mention their newspaper alliance. Johnny had passed himself off as a reporter for the *Pasadena Star*. Fortunately for their peace of mind, the boys did not know then that the *San Francisco Examiner* had come out imaginatively with a front page article headed **"THE STANFORD INSURRECTION!"** This, to Alan's subsequent outrage, quoted him as exclaiming as he and John boarded the train, "We stand with the University of Mexico, even though we're only summer school students. Down with Dictator Garrido Canibal! *What a lark!*"

Of the passengers on the train to Vera Cruz, about twenty-five were students, and some sixty were job-seekers, adventurers, and soldiers of fortune. The man sitting next to Alan on the hard wooden bench introduced himself as a comrade-in-arms of Pancho Villa in the 1910 revolution.

Flickering kerosene lamps hung from the crude wooden roof overhead, casting strange shadows on the men sprawled about Alan as the little train rattled on through dense, black jungle and over deep gorges and high mountains. He saw that his companions were armed with every known weapon from long razor blades to deadly German Luger automatics. None of the soldier-students had been allowed on the train unarmed. He learned that the car behind them was stacked with dynamite and hand grenades.

He strolled into it and was promptly surrounded by Mexicans. They pulled long, curved machetes from their trousers, showed pistols attached to their belts, and asked him what state he was from. Where was his gun?

He showed them his fountain pen and told them, "I can do more good with that than with any gun."

About midnight Alan fell asleep. At 1:00 A.M. a shot rang out. Everyone dived to the floor. Garrido attacks north of Tabasco were not unexpected. Their fears were false. A sleepy revolutionist had been merely inspecting his gun.

A fellow who had come aboard the train dead drunk and fallen asleep in a corner woke too. He tried to find out why he was on the train. Where in hell was it taking him? No one had the heart to tell him. He wandered from one group to another, mumbling questions and staring wide-eyed at the pistol butts bulging beneath the coats.

Finally someone told him he was going to Tabasco to fight Garrido and his twelve thousand Red Shirts. He sat in his corner again, a helpless look on his face, while the rest of the group gibed at him.

Alan described his fellow passengers in a column:

> They are going to an almost certain death; yet they're as playful and carefree as the members of the Stanford track team with which I've traveled. It's pitiful that so many of them must inevitably die; but it's men like them, who are willing to

sacrifice everything they have, to better their people, who keep this world turning; and as long as this world keeps on turning out men such as these, it can't help but keep on improving.

Someday, when wars are forever outlawed, such men as these will be able to accomplish things in other ways. Today they must fight. I'm not blind; probably twenty-five or thirty of the students along are idealists; but many of the rest, among whom are some of the toughest *hombres* I've ever seen, are merely job-seekers, hoping for a fine position if they survive the tearing down of the Garrido government; while the others are just adventurers and soldiers of fortune, who follow wars around the earth, or, in this case, revolution all over Mexico.

Alan slept again briefly, one leg twisted around a support so he wouldn't fall off the twelve-inch bench. His other foot served as a Mexican's pillow. His neck and head rested on a dusty pair of hob-nailed boots. He awoke to resounding shouts of *"Viva!"* His companions were standing in the aisles greeting a heavily built soldier in khaki pants, shirt, and broad-brimmed army hat, who strode through the train shaking hands right and left with the revolutionaries.

A student said, "It's General Chavez on leave from the regular army. He's come to command us."

"Tough, looks like the best leader yet," said Johnny.

"Yes," Alan said, "but look at the guy over there! I want to talk to him."

Alan learned that the little dark man seated before him on a box of dynamite precariously balanced on the narrow bench had been a revolutionist against the Cuban dictator Machado. He had been captured and, in the hope of wringing a few secrets from him, Machado's men had pulled out all of his nails. They cut off two of his fingers and all of his toes. His family had all been killed. He escaped to the United States, then went to Mexico. Machado had put a price of $5,000 on his head.

Sworn enemy of all cruel governments, he had joined the Tabasco crusade. His specialty was high explosives. He sat on a box of bombs he had made which he asserted were powerful enough to destroy a ten-story building. He took one out to show Alan and carelessly waved it around. Nervously Alan asked if the whole car would blow to kingdom come if he should drop it. For an answer the Cuban hurled the bomb to the floor! An observer nearby jumped a mile. The action was much too quick for Alan's already overworked nerves to make him move.

The Cuban showed Alan one of fifteen smaller bombs he planned to carry in his hat when they landed at Tabasco. He also showed Alan his shoes. Where five human toes should have been, he had stuffed fuses, cotton, and acid to ignite the bombs.

A companion said, "Those two little shoes can blow Garrido to bits. If Garrido puts my friend in prison, he can blow the prison up and perhaps escape."

The Cuban asked Alan, "Will you walk up the streets in Tabasco with me when we land?"

Alan thought of the hatful of bombs and glanced at the shoes resting between his own. He realized that this man cared little whether he lived or died. Now or tomorrow, it was all the same to him. Even though Alan was accompanying this expedition, he wanted to live a while yet. What if he should get clapped into prison with those awful shoes? Walk up the street with him?

Hurriedly, he said, "No, I'm afraid not!"

The train wound down a precipitous mountain and chugged into Vera Cruz in the early morning. They were to board a chartered steamer later that day to sail down the coast and up a broad river to Villahermosa.

Sunday, Monday, Tuesday, they did not sail. *Mañana* was all they heard in Vera Cruz, a town of torpid heat, pretty girls, flies that swarmed everywhere, buzzards that roosted on every building, coconut trees, ashcans, and horrible smells that met the two wherever they went. They joined others swimming in the warm, shark-infested gulf, cautiously going in only up to their necks.

Word reached them that a troop of Garrido's Red Shirts had dug a trench upriver toward Villahermosa and had mounted several small cannons and machine guns along the banks. Had the boat sailed on time, Alan, Johnny, and their companions would have been blown up. Five hours after the boat would have arrived there, a band of revolting agrarians, tired of the Garrido regime, surprised the Red Shirts and disarmed them.

On Tuesday news swept through the town that federal troops had overthrown Garrido. Cardenas had appointed a new governor. The revolutionaries were jubilant. The purpose of their expedition achieved, they drifted apart. Alan and Johnny caught a train back to Mexico City that night.

A pile of letters awaited them full of clippings of their "revolutionary" activities. Constantine's story of the "Stanford uprising" angered and horrified Alan. Fortunately, Father and Mother were in Europe, so letters from meddling friends would not have had time to reach them.

Despite the cost he cabled to reassure them:

SAFE IN SCHOOL. DON'T BELIEVE ANYTHING YOU HEAR TO CON—TRARY. COVERED AN INCIPIENT REVOLUTION A FEW DAYS AGO FOR INTERNATIONAL PRESS.

Having received Alan's cable, Father wrote to me from Austria on July 29.

> I will breathe more freely when Alan shows up safely at Warec. Much of his charm lies in his spirit, but it only takes one slip to cause him and us a disaster.

Father spoke more truly than he knew. Constantine had, of course, neglected to identify Alan as a press correspondent when he portrayed him in the Hearst papers as a revolutionary. Constantine's version of the Mexican episode cropped up many years later in Alan's political life, when extremist opponents labeled him a Red. At a press conference in 1958 in Alan's first campaign for public office, Carl Greenberg, ironically a correspondent for a Hearst newspaper, the *Los Angeles Examiner,* suddenly asked him, "What were you doing in that Mexican revolution in 1935?"

In his senior year, Alan made a new friend on the Stanford track squad: Lars Skattebol, a blond Nordic so fair that Alan called him "the albino." A self-styled revolutionary and socialist, Lars planned to become a writer and social reformer. Alan had never met anyone like him. Ideas flew out of Lars like chaff from a threshing machine, interspersed with wit, literary allusions, and spellbinding references to his allegedly seamy past.

"Your friends and your folks are totally parasitical!" he challenged Alan. "I'm a proletarian genius who's going to shake up the world!"

Lars filled shoe boxes with penciled notes from his vast reading and taught Alan the habit. Lars joyfully plagiarized in conversation, scorning other students for not recognizing the most famous sources. Eloquently he expressed the new ideas emerging out of the Depression.

"He keeps me thinking!" Alan wrote in his diary. They matched wits. Lars egged him on in family arguments about Franklin Roosevelt. Lars interested Alan in the League of Nations' fight over Italy's invasion of Ethiopia. They collaborated on articles for the *Register-Leader*. They complemented each other: Alan was disciplined; Lars indeed did have flashes of genius. They vowed to form "a Combine to lick the world," to travel and write, and first to find newspaper jobs overseas, and later to become publishers and statesmen.

Shortly after the formation of the Combine, Alan met a striking brunette, Dorothea Merrill, a Stanford pre-law student. To Lars's disgust, Alan took time from the Combine to date the slender, dark-haired girl. His track times suffered also. In April, Alan and Dorothea became briefly engaged. His plans for Europe and the summer seemed even more exciting because both Dorothea and Lars planned to meet him there.

★ ★ ★ ★ ★ ★ ★ ★ ★ ★ ★ ★ ★ ★ ★ ★ ★ ★ ★ ★

CHAPTER 3

Foreign Correspondent
June–October 1936

★ ★ ★ ★ ★ ★ ★ ★ ★ ★ ★ ★ ★ ★ ★ ★ ★ ★ ★ ★

Fresh out of Stanford and armed with letters of introduction, Alan set out for New York, hoping for a career in journalism. Determination and a measure of luck would, in a remarkably short time, carry him to London, Rome, and Ethiopia, a country whose plight was to capture his concern.

"I'm seeing newspaper people right and left," he wrote me in late June from New York, after visits to Chicago, Boston, and Philadelphia. The Depression was worsening, and at first no one could help him become accredited overseas. But a few days later he wrote, "Lady Luck has certainly smiled or rather had hysterics over your kid brother."

His first break had come when a letter from Mrs. Fremont Older brought him a thirty-second meeting with William A. Curley, the editor of the *New York Evening Journal*, then the biggest evening paper in America. Curley invited Alan back the next day to meet Amster Spiro, the city editor.

When Alan emerged from the elevator the following day, he heard the man guarding the editorial offices screaming at someone, "I don't give a goddamn if you have an appointment with Curley. He's busy and won't see anybody. That's all. Ya can't see him! That's all!"

The visitor left with a sour look, and Alan asked the guard confidentially, "Where's the washroom?"

"Second door to the right."

Having thus passed the reception desk, Alan leaned against the wall outside Curley's office, borrowed a cigarette from a passing reporter, and loitered.

Curley suddenly burst out with a big rush, saw him and said, "Oh, hello, c'mon in and meet Spiro . . ."

Spiro, a big, husky fellow looking like an unshaven Al Capone, was in an especially jovial mood. Alan poked a scrapbook of his *Register-Leader* columns at him, and Spiro read the leads of a number of articles. "That's the key to anybody's writing," he said. In five minutes they were pals, and Alan was sitting on the edge of his desk.

Spiro was the archetype of the editors of the roaring twenties. Hardboiled, imaginative, and strong, Spiro thought up news stories when no real front page news was happening. Reportedly, one summer he'd hired two haywagons to hook wheels on the Brooklyn Bridge, thus creating a monumental traffic jam that enabled the *Journal* to scoop the city. Spiro had built up the story of the Dionne quintuplets.

Before Alan sailed on the *Bremen* a few days later, Spiro gave him credentials as a *Journal* correspondent and promised serious attention to Alan's proposed vagabond column. ("Boy! If I could be a columnist so soon!") * Through Spiro he also got credentials from the editor of the *Boston Transcript*.

"Then Lady Luck had hysterics again," his letter continued. He called on a King Features executive in New York (who was unable to help him) at the very same hour that Bill Hillman, chief of Hearst's International News Service in Europe, happened by. Alan showed Hillman his scrapbook, they had a long talk, and Hillman invited Alan to see him in London.

There, Hillman offered him odd jobs at ungodly hours with no pay. Soon Alan graduated to a real job, working for $5 a day at the headquarters of International News Service (INS) on Fleet Street. INS later merged with United Press into today's United Press International (UPI).

"What luck!" Alan wrote. "It's the most fascinating work on earth." All INS's European news stories were filed through the Fleet Street office. "Imagine my having a foreign job so soon! Most people don't get such news posts till they're aged or cynical or both." Aged he was definitely not, and cynical he never would be.

The first story he filed concerned the ominous preparations for war and its destructiveness, a theme that was to weave through his political concerns for years to come. His many human interest stories bore such headlines as:

---

*Unless otherwise noted, quotations are from Alan's letters to his family.

SOLDIER SEEKS BLIND GIRL WHO AIDED HIM
LOVERS HAVE TROUBLE GETTING MARRIED
'ONE HOSS SHAY' IS CONFISCATED BY COPS
ENGLISH COUNTRYSIDE FRIGHTENED BY 'THING'

Immediately more luck fell into his lap. The INS office cleared stories telegraphed directly from the 1936 Olympic Games in Berlin. Since Alan knew more about track, and especially the American team, than any other foreign correspondent, he was able to be of use. Through Archie Williams, the black Olympic quarter-miler who had edged Alan out in competition in California, he met Jesse Owens, the hero of the 1936 Olympics and one of the biggest news personalities of that year. They became friends and roamed around London, where Alan helped fend off reporters. He met many people drawn to the famous black athlete, who had won three events and a relay, running Hitler's supermen into the very cinders of the Berlin stadium.

Jesse confided to him his plans to turn professional, make some money, and then return to college and prepare himself for a possible political career. He hoped to use his fame to better relations between blacks and whites. With Jesse's permission, Alan sent the story to his friend Amster Spiro. But he soon learned that a story filed was not necessarily a story in print. Spiro, who tended to pursue a dozen ideas at once, failed to reply. Parts of the story were used, but without any credit to Alan.*

Alan enjoyed the stories Hillman assigned him. He was even able to charm as formidable a subject as John L. Lewis, president of the United Mine Workers and a leading labor figure in the United States, who came to London on a mysterious and hurried four-day visit. He refused to tell the press why. Alan trailed Lewis around the city.

Daily Alan would meet the bushy-browed Lewis, reputedly as bearish as he looked, in his hotel lobby. The labor leader would say he had nothing to say. They'd chat and then he'd go out. Alan would pretend to say good-bye but would grab a cab right behind him and trail him wherever he went. If Lewis knew, he didn't let on. Alan's meeting him in the lobby got to be a standing joke between them.

Finally, through Dorothea Merrill, he learned that Mrs. Lewis and

---

*Owens was subsequently acclaimed "Champion of the Century" (1960). He has had a successful life, using his talents to promote race relations.

Frances Perkins, Franklin Roosevelt's secretary of labor, were close friends. Alan wrote home, "That knowledge started me on a chain of investigation that eventually disclosed that Perkins made a secret visit to London from Monday to Wednesday, undoubtedly to see Lewis. That gave me the story, and we beat all the other papers and news sources on it. For the first couple of days it seemed like a hopeless chase, so I'm surely glad I finally got the story." It also delighted Hillman.

The day Lewis left, Alan went to the station to see if he might break down and say something newsworthy. He didn't, but he was startled to see Alan still at his heels. Cordially he urged Alan to look him up when he returned to the United States.

Dorothea had come to London to see Alan in the midst of his pursuit of Lewis. He couldn't see her much. They quarreled. Unable to compromise their differing ideas and ambitions, they decided to try a test estrangement or moratorium on their engagement. Dorothea headed for Yale Law School.

"It's perfectly amicable," Alan wrote to Father and Mother, who were in Paris. "I think we love and understand each other more than before. We just realize some of the difficulties in our way. . . . But I claim it's further proof that my emotions don't becloud my reason." He concluded, "Take care of Dottie."

*   *   *

Every reporter longs for a big scoop. Alan got his chance that summer. Through Dorothea's father, a timber financier, he received a tip that the French franc was about to be devalued, perhaps by August 15. The manipulation of the franc was a big international subject in 1936, so Alan tried to sell the story to INS. They were skeptical. Alan was sure of the reliability of his sources. He wired Spiro in New York but the *Journal* did not take it up either. August 15 came and went without the crisis Alan had predicted. Alan agonized, fearing what Spiro would think. But a few weeks later the franc was indeed devalued, and Alan received a wire from New York: "YOU WERE RIGHT — SPIRO."

Spiro followed with a letter expressing "admiration for your achievement on the French money story," and assuring Alan that there was a job for him on the *Journal* when he got back. Alan's big scoop never saw print, but he had earned the respect of an important newsman. The incident established a long relationship.

Alan was settling easily into the ways of a foreign correspondent. He wrote Father that there was little routine or discipline in the newspaper office, as Father had supposed and hoped. Alan wrote that he and his fellow correspondents sat around and talked a good bit of the time, but when they were called upon, they "had to work at terrific speed and make no errors. That's the kind of work I like."

"I certainly have my hand on the pulse of the world here," he wrote. "Everything that happens comes in here by phone or cable. Last night I took down General Van Wiegand's story from Madrid over the phone on the dictaphone and put in calls to Rome, Paris, and Berlin for Hillman. That's covering territory, isn't it?"

He delighted in exploring London. "I'm having all kinds of adventures," he wrote. He visited a Fascist headquarters and found "a bunch of damn fools trotting around in black shirts and red sleeves, saluting each other and calling their big shot 'leader'." An unemployed communist he met in Hyde Park took him on a tour of London's seamier side — flophouses, soldiers' and sailors' homes, notorious dives, even a pickpockets' hangout.

"The people in some of the cellar holes were exactly as rough and ragged as Dickens's characters."

He wrote to Spiro: "You can feel things are tense as soon as you get over here. . . . There are countless places war could break out. Europe was never so combustible, though people are going to be careful with their matches. No one *wants* war. . . ."

After Alan had worked for INS about seven weeks, Bill Hillman reminded him that his position was only temporary, that he had been a replacement for vacationing regulars.

"They're all back now," said Hillman.

"Yes," Alan admitted glumly.

"So I guess we won't be able to keep you busy around here any more."

Alan pulled a long face.

"But you have what we want, after a few rough spots are worn off," Hillman said with a broad grin. "If you'll go down to Italy and learn the language fluently in three months, I'll give you a darn good job in the Rome INS office under Gervasi!"

Overjoyed at the offer of a job with Frank Gervasi, a first-rate American journalist, Alan was ready to leave at once.

Father and Mother, now in London, were anxious about Alan's going deep into Fascist territory. They knew that under Benito

Mussolini's dictatorship, censorship and spying were rife and that people were jailed without warning or due process. Alan wasn't sure of a job, and war was threatening. They expressed their many concerns in farewell letters as they left for home. Father wrote: "Beware of pick-pockets! Money belt! Look out for Italian girls!" But Mother, after expressing her fears, was confident that Alan's Scottish shrewdness and deep sense of right and wrong would serve him well.

★ ★ ★ ★ ★ ★ ★ ★ ★ ★ ★ ★ ★ ★
With INS in Rome
★ ★ ★ ★ ★ ★ ★ ★ ★ ★ ★ ★ ★ ★

"I studied Italian until my eyes rebelled," Alan wrote of his twenty-six-hour train journey to Rome in third class. He plunged into *Italian in Three Months* on the journey and started memorizing a dictionary word by word.

"Gad, I've got a lot to do: write the column, learn the language in the shortest possible time, write articles for the *Boston Transcript*, write forty-one letters," he wrote to me.

He viewed the ancient city with delight. "Rome is swell and I love the whole idea of the place, the people, the old ruins, the Colosseum, the Tiber. At present I live in a heckuva dump, a cold room on the fourth floor of a *pensione* facing a piazza. The meals are lousy and the elevator's locked most of the time. But from a balcony here last night, I had a swell view of the comic opera side of Fascism." Several thousand people had gathered in the square below to listen to Mussolini. Bands played and troops of uniformed blackshirts marched around and then stood at attention while Il Duce spoke. Mussolini himself, however, was missing: the address was one he had given a year before, announcing the Ethiopian war, and was being rebroadcast over special loudspeakers via victrola and radio.

Alan's introduction to Roman life was eased considerably by Frank Gervasi, chief of INS, a man of bronzed, rugged good looks. He was only twenty-eight. He and his young wife, Kay, took Alan in, fed him pancakes, introduced him to friends. Gervasi had a strong personality that could explode now and then, as Alan saw when he came close to throwing a typewriter out of a window after a speech by Mussolini.

Having fallen under the spell of Alan's letters, his good friend and fellow adventurer in Mexico, Johnny Atkinson, soon joined him in Via Dei Serpenti and eventually got a job with United Press.

As a newsman, though, Alan was pretty much on his own since the INS post was contingent upon his learning enough Italian to handle the job. But he was not one to sit around and wait for things to happen. In December, on his return from a trip to Florence, Bologna, Genoa, and other Italian cities, Alan was almost broke. Gervasi was short-handed and expecting the arrival of Wallis Simpson. So Alan declared himself ready for duty, though he had been in Italy only eight weeks. A few days later a call came through to Gervasi from Hillman saying, "Put Cranston on the staff immediately!"

The pay was $12.50 a week. "That's about $120 a month for what it'll buy in Rome compared to California," he wrote me jubilantly.

Gervasi assigned him to the midnight-to-nine shift. Alone in the office, Alan had to answer the telephone. He found that communicating with Italians in the flesh—when he could see their expressive gestures and faces—was one thing, but trying to comprehend a Neapolitan accent, for example, over a 1936 Italian telephone could be terrifying. "Occasionally I didn't even report anything to Gervasi after a phone call because I hadn't understood a word and didn't know what on earth had happened—what the story was." Later he wrote:

> The telephone still has me intimidated by sight and sound. I'm scared stiff it's going to bring me some excited Italian with a phony dialect—but hot news— at any moment. My informer will probably be so excited I won't know what he's talking about. Besides trying to get details, I'm ordered to get his name and number. Then hang up and on our *two* office phones make *four* simultaneous calls: first call the guy back immediately to verify and keep him busy and his line occupied so he can't call rivals with news. Also—first call London; tell them we have the report and are checking on it. First call Berlin; tell them the same thing. First call Gervasi, so he can try to check.

Alan's apprehensions were heightened because Pope Pius XI was ailing, and his death was expected at any moment. INS had orders from New York to spare no expense trying to scoop Associated Press and United Press on this story when it broke. "MUST CAPITALIZE ON DEATH OF HIS EMINENCE!" cabled New York. AP had been scooping INS frequently on the Pope's ups and downs—they had a Vatican telephone operator on their payroll, eavesdropping on medical conversations between the Pope's doctor and specialists the world over.

Once a tipster sidled into the INS office claiming he had "a beega secret." Gervasi paid for it, and the old man showed him a scrap of paper purloined from the Vatican drugstore. Alan deciphered it. It was the Pope's urinalysis! Alan fervently hoped the Pope would not die when he was on duty.

Alan survived those night watches, reading from end to end the twenty volumes of the *Catholic Encyclopedia,* the only books in the office.

Lee Falk, the creator of *Mandrake the Magician*, and *The Phantom*, came through Rome on a tour for King Features, which carried his comic strips and Alan met him. Lee was to remain a friend throughout his career. A suave, dark, green-eyed man with a small mustache and a sardonic, Mephistophelian face, he was to Alan the prototype of the dashing Mandrake. Here was not only a live cartoonist, but a live comic-strip hero as well.

Lee Falk recalls Alan humorously then as "a tall young guy with holes in his shoes, who was always hungry, frantically trying to learn Italian, sitting there in the Hearst office, dying when the phone rang, petrified that some news break would come!"

Gervasi went to Berlin and London for a week and left Alan in charge of the Rome bureau. He also left in the files a story with a "hold" on it, not to be released until a certain impending date. Gervasi had just interviewed the toughest Fascist of them all, Roberto Farinacci. The story is told that during the Ethiopian war, Farinacci was fishing with hand grenades, blowing fish out of the water. A grenade blew his hand off and his gloved steel hand remained as a mark of that episode. Farinacci was Mussolini's minister of the interior. He had told Gervasi that, due to the alliance with Hitler, Mussolini was about to initiate an anti-Semitic policy.

Late one afternoon, Alan was in the office when Russ Simontown, an editor of the *New York Daily News* who was on vacation, dropped in to talk shop and have a drink. Alan was delighted to meet this new Amster Spiro type, a man in his mid-forties, tough, heavyset, not very tall. They sat around and exchanged anecdotes for a while. Alan had to leave the office for three to four minutes. When he came back, Simontown was reading the file with the "hold" story about Farinacci. He dropped it, saying nothing. Alan also said nothing.

Simontown hastily ended his visit and took off. Alan suddenly got suspicious. He raced into the Western Union office downstairs, and there was Simontown, trying in English to persuade the Italian girl to

send a telegram for him. He was talking about Farinacci. Alan listened, making sure he was really stealing the story. Then he dropped
a hand on the editor's shoulder. Simontown looked around. "Oops,
you caught me!"

"Come on back. Let's go up to the office and talk about it."

"Okay. This stupid girl won't understand what I want to do. But I'll
get this story out of here, no matter what you say!"

"Come up and we'll talk about it."

"That's a red-hot story," said Simontown, when they were back in
the office. "The 'hold' doesn't bind me. If I send it to New York, it'll
pay for my whole vacation. So I'm going to send it. There's nothing
you can do about it!"

"You'll wipe me out!"

"It's a cutthroat business," said the editor, enjoying his drink. Alan
tried to argue that he was going to ruin Gervasi as well as himself, but
decided that the only thing to do was to get Simontown drunk to prevent him from sending the story. He ordered more drinks and called
Johnny Atkinson with an invitation to join them, adding a few words
in Italian to alert him.

There followed a night of stalling tactics that would have done justice to the Marx Brothers. Johnny abstained totally. Alan pretended to
match Simontown drink for drink until the Western Union office
closed. Drunk but adamant, Simontown swayed off to his hotel to telephone, accompanied by Johnny and a still relatively sober Alan. But
Simontown had even less luck over the hotel phone than he'd had with
the Western Union girl. Alan ordered more drinks. Barely ambula-
tory, Simontown tried to leave the hotel for Western Union headquarters. Alan and Johnny stymied him in the revolving door. Alan
got in with him, Johnny pushed hard, and they landed back in the
lobby. They went through this merry-go-round three or four times,
laughing uproariously. Then Alan persuaded the concierge to lock the
door, to keep Simontown inside the hotel for his own safety.

"It's just a rule," Alan said. "Mussolini makes 'em lock the doors at
eleven. The concierge'll go to prison if he lets us out." He and John
had somehow managed to give Simontown the befuddled impression
they were as eager as he to get out of the hotel.

From time to time, guests would show up, pound on the door, and
demand admission. The concierge would unlock the revolving door.
Simontown would rush into it, Alan at his elbow. Johnny, following in

the next compartment, would give a sudden push and round the door would whirl, depositing startled guests, a staggering Simontown, and a delighted Alan, back in the lobby — sometimes all landing in a heap.

Simontown decided this was no way to escape and went on a prowl around the hotel. Alan and Johnny followed him about for most of the night while he tried to open windows and doors that Alan and Johnny managed to hold shut. They kept on drinking steadily, but eventually the bar closed, and Simontown sobered up enough to realize what was being perpetrated. Using his former tactic, Alan lured him up to his room again for a talk. Simontown finally collapsed on his bed, angry but spent. His guardians took turns standing watch. Simontown awoke the next morning in a fury. He threatened to sue Alan for kidnapping.

"I was only visiting you and protecting you," Alan told him. "I wasn't transporting you anywhere. Besides," he added, laughing, "Italian laws don't mind kidnapping. It's a national policy, actually!"

Johnny got moralistic and lectured the prisoner about stealing Gervasi's story.

"For God's sake, Cranston, get this animal out of here!" Simontown said. "If there's one thing I can't stand it's moralizing!" Johnny ordered breakfast, and Simontown calmed down. Suddenly he looked at Alan. "You've outwitted me on this and outmaneuvered me. I don't want to send the story any more. If you'll stop this business of holding me in this damn room, I'll call it quits. I won't send it!"

Alan stuck out his hand and said, "I'll trust you, and that's it!" They shook hands, said a friendly good-bye, and walked out of the room arm in arm, while Johnny, tagging along, stared in amazement. "Hell, we couldn't have kept him in that hotel all week till Gervasi got back," Alan explained after they had parted from Simontown downstairs at the revolving door.

Gervasi's story was saved. Simontown didn't send it, and he and Alan became friends, seeing each other now and then in later years when Alan returned to New York.

The usual problem correspondents faced in Mussolini's Italy was getting stories out, not keeping them in. The government imposed a rigid system of self-censorship. Reporters could send what they wished. If the Fascists didn't like it, out went the reporter.

The Fascists controlled the Italian press and all official sources of information.

Furthermore, many Italians whom Alan encountered seemed to

exist in a sort of cynical accommodation with Mussolini's regime. Alan was eating in a Roman club once with an Italian who told him, "I have no problems with fascism." Alan asked him how he could feel so secure. The man reached up to his lapel and rubbed like a good luck charm the Fascist party button he was wearing.

Unlike the Germans, the Italians had a sense of humor about their dictator. Alan went out with a girlfriend of the minister of propaganda and information. She was a fountain of anti-Mussolini and anti-Fascist jokes. Alan's favorite was a definition of fascism. "Everything not forbidden is compulsory."

He had developed a sympathy with the Italians' efforts to catch up with the rest of the world. As Alan wrote to Amster Spiro:

> I'm busy looking at fascism. I'd read dozens of books and came here with prejudices, but some are fading away as I see causes as well as manifestations. It's a phenomenon of flat-broke countries. . . . I think the majority of Italians feel Mussolini has done them more good than harm, and therefore support him. Rome has been on the march ever since the march on Rome, all but the Fascist-educated hate the war-ism, as they hate the regimentation and spying, and loss of liberty. But they feel these are part of the only means Italy has to get anything from an ungenerous and foolish world. And they are willing to make sacrifices if Il Duce thinks it's necessary. But I do thank God that America is a rich country.

He wrote to me:

> Saw the most heartbreaking thing of my life yesterday, soldiers coming back from Ethiopia. Gad, what wrecks they were. With horror, I watched human captives marched through the Arch of Constantine in an elaborate restaging of the way imperial conquests were celebrated during the first Roman empire.

Mussolini had crushed Italian democracy. Watching the effect of Fascism on his acquaintances, Alan saw the general uneasiness of people about expressing themselves, their fear of being watched and reported on. Later, that was what he remembered most. *"They were so afraid!"*

In January of 1937, Spiro asked Alan to send him a few columns on his observations of life in Fascist countries. The prospective column, something Alan had wanted to do from the very beginning, fired Alan's enthusiasm — a chance to travel and write. He told Spiro he'd like to take "a canoe trip down the Danube, through several Fascist and semi-Fascist countries from Germany through Austria, Hungary,

Yugoslavia, Bulgaria, and Rumania, to the Black Sea. I don't know a damn thing about canoeing, but that would add to the excitement!" He put in sixteen hours a day on the columns, and on March 1 mailed eight to the *Journal*'s city editor.

"Now it's up to you and fate," he wrote Spiro.

Five months passed with no word. Alan wrote again, inquiring, and mentioned that a good opportunity might come up in the fall: "Gervasi's planning a two-month vacation to the United States. He'll leave me in charge of INS if higher-ups don't recall that I'm only twenty-three."

Spiro still failed to reply.

Not only did Spiro not answer his letters, but New York vetoed his request for a raise. He regretfully wrote Gervasi a formal letter of resignation in September citing exactly what expenses absorbed his $12.50 a week.

ROOM	(I get this cheap rate by sharing one room with a friend)	$10
FOOD	(This is at lowest possible estimate, 2 meals per day at 40¢ for each)	24
BUSES	(Necessary since I am forced to live far from office, to attend daily press conferences, etc.)	3
BATHS	(They cost 25¢ each)	2
LAUNDRY	(At rate of $1.25 per week)	5
	TOTAL FOR MONTH'S LIVING EXPENSES	$44

Alan decided it would take too long to get where he wanted in news work. He was too young for rapid advancement, and he lacked the connections he could have developed if he'd launched his career in America rather than in Europe. More importantly, he wanted more freedom and independence, and he was moving toward a different goal: he didn't like what he saw transpiring in the world, and he didn't want simply to report on it. He yearned to engage in the action. He began to think about a career in politics and government.

Frank Gervasi wrote to me later, "Alan was the only reliable, loyal assistant of the three I had in the Rome Bureau of INS during those years. He was a tall, quiet, lean fellow with a good mind and a quick smile. I recall his love of California. One of his characteristics was a final reserve, a reticence, a sort of privacy no one dared trespass."

Gervasi did not let Alan sever his ties with INS entirely. He used his influence to pull some wires in the Italian government. After two months of waiting, he obtained permission for Alan to visit Ethiopia — making him the first foreign correspondent to visit the Italian Empire in East Africa since the conquest.

Alan resigned from INS in Rome and sailed from Naples for East Africa on March 7, 1938. Just after he left, a wire arrived from Austria offering him a job as head of INS in Vienna at a salary of $80 per week! But Alan was off to an even more adventurous region, a country he had known about only through books and newspapers.

★ ★ ★ ★ ★ ★ ★ ★ ★ ★ ★ ★ ★ ★ ★
African Adventure
★ ★ ★ ★ ★ ★ ★ ★ ★ ★ ★ ★ ★ ★ ★

"I got permission to go to Africa!" Alan wrote to his Stanford friend and collaborator, Lars Skattebol. "I'll be the first non-German and non-Italian correspondent to cover the building up of the last wrested-from-barbarism empire! INS will buy my articles. The Combine's getting momentum!" Two years before, Alan and Lars had followed with dismay the accounts of the Italian invasion of Ethiopia and the failure of the League of Nations to act.

He had learned much about self-control from Gervasi. "He's got himself as well organized as Edison's most ingenious invention; he can concentrate as thoroughly on any subject as Newton's apple could in falling dead down; he can absorb knowledge like the proverbial sponge; turn sleep on and off like a light. I wonder if a guy can wean himself without destroying energy? Think of the time a fellow wastes normally — a third of his life he's dead!"

He wrote Lars again "from Mid Red Sea aboard S.S. *Tevere:* I landed at Port Said with a bunch of Italians and kept exclaiming inwardly, 'You're in AFRICA!' — bazaars, Egyptians, veiled Arabian women, many apparently beautiful, ships in the Suez. I bought a sun helmet. Imagine me in one of those!"

Characteristically he looked ahead. "I'll hope to find you in Rome when I get back, to help clean up on magazine articles and a book. Of course I have no way of knowing when you ever will come, after your interminable series of delays."

He left the ship at the Red Sea port of Massawa in Eritrea, the door of the new Italian empire. He likened the port to the gold-rush boom town of San Francisco in 1849, "ships choking the harbor, men working day and night, movement never stopping. There never was such a field for newspaper articles!"

He wrote to Gervasi jubilantly, "The government is breaking its neck to give me a favorable impression of their progress in empire building. They met me at the dock, put a car and soldier-chauffeur at my disposal, and put me up in the best hotel in Massawa; drove me up to the capital, Asmara, threw some poor devil out in the street so I'd have a good room; gave me an immediate audience with the governor. . . .

"If you should happen to need any help when Hitler comes down, I suspect Johnny Atkinson's practically flat broke. . . ."

Alan's next letter reflected his angry frustration over the censorship. "I never ran into such a helluva time in my life till I started trying to get these four articles off, after a couple of days of thinking they were only kidding. The ink spot in article no. 4 is the remains of my only remark military. I referred to the battle of 1895 as a 'fearful' defeat. The dictionary said that meant 'tremenda' so they were sore as hell. If they're that way about the last century, you can imagine what they are about this one. You probably thought I'd had sunstroke when you read my last lead. I've sent twelve articles, all red-penciled."

He translated his articles into Italian himself to save time and petty wrangling. He wrote to me, still from Asmara, that his trip to Addis Ababa was stalled by the authorities. "It was fun leading the life of Reilly again for a few days. But now the walls and halls of this ultra-modern hotel in the heart of Africa, with modern conveniences till you feel like a robot, are beginning to seem like a prison, and the precision of the dining room, though I eat there at government expense, drives me out to workers' restaurants."

Having to work under such constraints and interference in Germany and Italy, as well as in Ethiopia, left in Alan an abiding concern for the rights of a free press. Years later he would remember that as a correspondent he would not have had access to unofficial information had he not been able to honor the anonymity of his sources. In 1973, in the midst of Watergate and Richard Nixon's anti-press moves, Alan introduced in the Senate a bill to guarantee newsmen the right to keep the identity of their informants confidential.

Reaching Addis Ababa at last, he wrote to Lars: "I came up here in a Caproni bomber. Near Makalle we were above jagged mountains when the motor suddenly went dead—I was looking down at the cliffs through the bomber's observation hole. The wind caught us and buffeted us, and suddenly I saw sky instead of land! And then came the miracle of an airfield looming up beneath us. We made a forced landing in country conquered three years ago, that had till then hardly even seen the shadow of a plane! Nice baptism to the air for me!

"Had another forced landing when the plane overshot a tiny landing field in a high wind near Gambela."

Alan's letters reveal the sort of whirlwind life he led in Ethiopia, driving and flying thousands of miles. The flying was done in Caproni bombers, the driving in special government cars, and sleeping and eating either free, in the best hotels, in journalists' houses, or in governors' palaces. "I've met every big shot, and just interviewed the Duke of Aosta, the first interview he's granted since becoming Viceroy last December."

Alan had no illusions, however, as to why he was treated so royally. "Fortunately I realize it's not I but what I might do—not a young squirt but INS and its eight hundred papers that's important. There's so much yet to be done in the world, I can't see how any human with a long view can ever get swellheaded."

The war was supposed to be over when Alan arrived but actually was still in the mop-up stage. "I heard shooting every night I was there. Once a bullet was fired into the jeep I was in—just went whistling by from the bushes." Another time he flew to an outpost somewhere over near the Sudan. While he was there, native headhunters brought in a tribesman's head they had cut off a few hours before. They had stuck it on a spear. In a dance ceremony they offered the head to the Italian leader of the outpost, to show their loyalty. They claimed the victim was anti-Italian.

A week later when the supply plane came to pick Alan up, it flew in a little too low and ripped into some trees, tearing its canvas bottom. The pilot was afraid to take off again, because the wind would have stripped off the canvas and blown the covering off the plane. So a native tailor in a loincloth sat for two days in the shade of the airplane, sewing it back together before they took off.

By June Alan had sent over fifty articles.

One day in Addis Ababa, Lieutenant Bertoletti, the irksome escort and censor assigned to him, offered to arrange an interview with the Ethiopian puppet leader, Ras Hailu, a former ambassador to France and one of the richest princes of the realm. They drove to a beautiful palace where the handsome, erect, grey-haired native leader entertained them with tea and told Alan about his life.

In the early '20s when Selassie was crowned King of Kings, he went to Europe to visit other crowned heads. Instead of taking his friends with him, the emperor took his worst enemies, so they couldn't take the country away from him in his absence. Among the enemies included in the entourage was Ras Hailu.

While in Italy, Hailu secretly established contact with Mussolini, who had designs on East Africa and Ethiopia even then. Some years later, Selassie's agents intercepted messages between Mussolini and Ras Hailu. "They threw me into prison," Hailu told Alan bitterly. "And they captured a nephew of mine and sawed him in half in a public square, to show what happened to traitors!"

Mussolini had always claimed the war started when Ethiopians attacked Italians at a water hole. Yet here was actual evidence that Mussolini had been involved in a plot to take over the country years before.

Alan knew he would have trouble getting the story past censor Bertoletti, so he decided to back into it indirectly. The Italians were always attempting to prove that the Ethiopians were barbarians and needed the Italian guiding hand. First Alan covered the business of sawing a man in half in the public square, as an example of Selassie's brutality. Then he explained how it happened — because of Hailu's relationship with Mussolini and Italy's ambitions in Ethiopia.

Bertoletti let the story go through. He failed to realize the significance of the second part. It was widely printed in the *London Daily Standard* and other British and American newspapers, including the *New York Evening Journal.*

Selassie sued the *Standard* for libel, saying he had not had any man sawed in half.

INS, which had distributed the story, was dragged into the lawsuit. Gervasi wired Alan urgently for documentation. **"IMPORTANTEST UNFAIL!"**

Alan told Bertoletti that he wanted to go back to the Ras and get more documentation on the atrocity. The censor was delighted to assist. They went back to the palace and had tea with the Ras again.

Then discrepancies began to develop. Hailu had been careless with his details. It had not been Hailu's nephew but his son, and he had lost a leg, not one-half of his body.

"Why did you tell me it was your nephew if it was your son?" Alan asked testily.

"I have so many sons, daughters, nephews," replied the Ras languidly. "More than the hair on my head. How can I remember who is son and who is nephew?"

Alan went all out to document the case, but ran into all sorts of snags and barriers. The Italians were reluctant to have him delve too deeply into their pre-1935 activities in Ethiopia, especially Hailu's relationship with Mussolini. Alan learned some facts from talking with Greeks, Armenians, and others who had resided in the country for years. Ras Hailu had indeed conspired with Italians in a plot against Selassie. The plan failed and Selassie jailed Hailu. One of Hailu's nephews was also imprisoned. That much was clear. What happened next was murky. One version had it that the nephew's ankles were bound in steel shackles which were too tight and caused one leg to become infected. A western doctor amputated his leg to save his life. Another version had it that the nephew had been beheaded—not sawed in half.

Pierre Van Paassen wrote later in *The Days of Our Years* that in the early '30s he had seen a naked man imprisoned in a pen where Selassie kept him like an animal, a collar around his neck, chained at ground level to a post, wallowing in his excrement, a pitiful creature who had lost all semblance to a human being. This seemingly crazed captive stared up at Van Paassen with utterly mad eyes.

"Why is that man in this condition?" the journalist exclaimed. "Who is he? What did he do?"

"That is Ras Hailu," said the guard. "He was discovered conspiring with Mussolini against the King of Kings!"

The missionary doctor, who had shown the wretched prisoner to Van Paassen, further related that Hailu's brother, a powerful ras in Tigré, had come to intercede on his brother's behalf and threatened to take up arms.

Selassie had the man tied between two oak boards and sawn in twain, according to Van Paassen.

Though it was well known that Draconian punishments had been meted out in Selassie's Ethiopia, the facts couldn't be sorted out in the case. The former emperor won his libel suit in London—where lèse majesté may have been another factor. That cost the *Standard* about 3,000 pounds and INS 15,000 pounds.

Gervasi had written Alan telling him to, "Keep your chin up, kid. You are now in the process of learning how to take it."

On his twenty-fourth birthday, June 19, 1938, Alan received

Gervasi's letter and replied, "Thanks much for the kind words that came with your letter. And don't worry. I can take anything this world can offer."

His money was running low and the heavy rains of summer were setting in. In July, after four months in Africa, he made plans to leave for Rome. Even considering the restrictions he'd had to face, he had become a confident and self-reliant journalist.

In Rome Alan met his replacement in the INS office, Cecil Brown, a young, wandering journalist, later a famous newscaster. One of the great journalism stories of World War II had to do with him. At the start of the war, two British battleships were sunk off Malaysia. Cecil Brown was on the H.M.S. *Repulse,* when it went down, was rescued and wrote a great story. The next day another correspondent who had been on the H.M.S. *Prince of Wales* also filed a superb story. Willie Gallagher, a reporter posted in Singapore for the *London Daily Express,* received an angry wire from his editor in frugal cablese:

CECIL BROWN SUNK *REPULSE,* BEAUTIFUL STORY. SO-AND-SO SUNK *PRINCE OF WALES,* BEAUTIFUL STORY. WHY YOU UNSUNK?

After leaving Rome, Alan met Lars Skattebol in London. They lived in the apartment of the writer, R. H. Tawney, and wrote a book on anti-Semitism in Italy. The English publisher, Victor Gollancz, though interested, did not accept the manuscript.

The sense of inevitable war was growing stronger. In London during Chamberlain's empty "Peace in Our Time" negotiations with Hitler, Alan watched anxiously, sure then that there would be no peace from appeasement. "Please come home if war is coming," our parents wrote him anxiously after the fatal compromises made at Munich. After three months in London, he wired them: "RETURNING HOME."

Alan arrived in New York on a snowy day in late November. He wrote Mother and Father, filling eight typewritten pages with excited news and plans and ideas. He had seen Spiro and spent the weekend with him, was setting up lectures, and had sold a series of articles to the *Toronto Star,* Canada's biggest paper, which would syndicate them throughout that country. He concluded his letter:

It's certainly wonderful to hear American spoken everywhere, this seems like the promised land right now. [Walter] Winchell had a swell maxim in his column night before last: "Those who kick about government should try countries where the government kicks the people." That sums up how I feel now, after escape from the dark continents across the water. *Now the thing is to make sure we never do get a government that would want to kick the people.*

He determined to devote himself to that end. His experiences during the last two and a half years, combined with his growing up during the Depression, had helped lead him toward politics. As he recalls now, "Seeing dictatorship in Germany and Italy at its worst, I became frustrated just writing about the awful things I saw. A strong supporter of the League of Nations, I had watched that body further weakened during my years in Europe. I believed that the conquest of Ethiopia was the start of World War II. This led to my belief in the need for an effective world body, to my interest in the United Nations and the World Federalists, and to my deep interest in foreign policy and peace."

★ ★

Introduction to Capitol Hill

★ ★

"I'll get home for Christmas, no matter what," Alan wrote home on November 30, 1938.

"Come soon, but get a job!" Father replied.

Alan hoped to help alert the American people that they were facing war against Hitler — and to find a job to sustain himself in the process.

The first thing he had done when he reached New York was to contact Amster Spiro. Alan found him not at the *Journal* but on the corner of Twenty-Second Street and Second Avenue in a toy factory! He was in partnership with Ely Culbertson, the bridge wizard, producing the game, "Autobridge," was planning countless other like enterprises, and also had a printing shop.

When he last saw him Spiro was reputedly one of the best news editors in New York. Now he was sitting with an equally messed-up desk and madhouse office. But the desk was now overrun with fancy printed papers, gaudy boxes, paper dolls, dice, and every conceivable kind of game.

Alan tried out on him his latest ideas for publishing books. "You could reap the satisfactions of the newspaper business without its curses by going into publishing paperback books," Alan told Spiro, mindful of his own unpublished book. "In England, Gollancz markets first-rate books in such bulk they can be sold for fifteen cents. Not dime novels. Serious books, good novels, biographies, topical books. As topical as mine on Italian anti-Semitism. They could have a liberal twist."

Immediately he had Spiro's rapt attention. Alan added another lure: "Think of the social value of giving America high-grade progressive reading at dirt cheap costs."

Spiro's enthusiasm led him to fire off cables, call in printers, and stir up a cyclone of inquiries exploring the more practical matters of printing costs, financial backing, distribution, and sales.

But nothing could be set up so quickly. While this idea hung fire, Alan managed to sell a few articles but had no real job or regular income. Sometimes he stayed with friends and sometimes in flophouses. Once an old man in a flophouse asked him, "This your first night here?"

"Yep, and my last," Alan told him.

"That's what *I* said twenty-eight years ago!" said the old man caustically.

Alan was down to his last nickel. "I was about to spend it on a subway ride to try and get a job. I looked at it and — incredible luck — it was a rare V-nickel without 'cents.' I sold it for about three dollars, and that kept me going for a little while."

That Christmas eve he came home to Villa Warec. He came up the driveway lined with cypresses and oleanders and saw again the green circle of lawn, the friendly house, the oaks, the encircling creek, the blue view of Black Mountain. His old friends came and went. He heard the sound of their cars on the gravel, the slam of the big front door, and excited Japanese voices — dear Tanaka and his wife Mina, back for this special occasion. He enjoyed the smell of roasted turkey on the blue and brown platter from Quimper; the tang of homemade cranberry jelly in a cut-glass bowl — all the old sights and sounds and smells, all the talk, all the love and the warmth. For a little while it was all as it had always been. And then the holidays were over and gone, and Alan was anxious to leave for Los Angeles.

"Try to have more than ten dollars in your pocket next time you come home again," Father said to him wryly. Before Alan left, Father gave a lunch for him at the Bohemian Club, where Alan talked of his travels. Father was not unproud of his young itinerant son.

Alan drove his long-time friend, Mrs. Fremont Older, the widow of San Francisco's crusading editor, to Governor Culbert Olson's inauguration in Sacramento. In the ornate gold and crimson Assembly Chamber, Olson kept his promise that his first deed as governor would be to pardon Tom Mooney, the accused bomber of the 1916 Preparedness Day Parade. Mrs. Older spoke to the governor about her husband's long fight to free Mooney, and Alan met Olson — the first of many governors he was to know.

Then Alan drove Mrs. Older to Los Angeles where she helped him meet a number of well-known writers. At a party Alan met Tom Mooney, just out of prison, and witnessed his first encounter with ice cubes. Twenty years earlier, when Mooney had gone to prison, icemen delivered ice in great chunks. Now he was fondling the ice cubes with amazement.

Pope Pius XI died while Alan was in Los Angeles. The local press published many of the articles about the attendant ceremonies that Alan had written long before; they appeared as if they had been written that very day in Rome.

The most significant event of his southern stay was a blind date with a girl named Geneva McMath. They spent their first evening together at a meeting of the Silver Shirts, an American fascist organization. After his experiences in Hitler's Germany and Mussolini's Italy, Alan was keeping a wary eye on would-be emulators of the dictators in the United States. He wrote to Geneva when he returned to New York.

Unfortunately Spiro was better at newspaper work than he was at business. He went off on a tangent and produced sets of paperback books. One had to buy the whole set. Individual sales might have worked, as the paperback industry has since proved.

Spiro was also trying to start a newspaper in Brooklyn. Alan worked on that venture. They got out one edition but never had enough money to do more.

It was then that Alan got the idea of doing a paperback edition of *Mein Kampf.* Adolf Hitler's amazingly frank blueprint for world conquest was selling in America in a carefully expurgated edition that did not fully reveal Hitler's real purpose. Alan wanted to get out an unauthorized version that would divulge the actual Hitler plan for world conquest.

He sold the idea to Spiro, who became very excited about it. Armed with books about Hitler, Alan went to Spiro's house in Connecticut for the weekend. Arriving late, he went to sleep on a spare bed in the room of his thirteen-year-old son, Dick. In the morning Dick woke up and was horrified to discover a stranger in his room and books about Hitler all over the place. Alan had brought several different versions of *Mein Kampf:* the Hitler-authorized version, another version he had bought in England, an original German language version he'd picked up in Berlin, along with two or three other books about Hitler and the Brownshirts.

In about eight days, Alan put together the first unexpurgated edition to be published in the United States. It contained supplemental notes, not at the bottom of the page or off to the rear but right in the middle of a paragraph or a page, pointing out a lie, a distortion, and warning America what Hitler was up to. The original book ran something like 300,000 words. To make it readable, Alan cut it down to about 70,000 — *Reader's Digest* style — without omitting anything significant or changing any thrust. He dictated for about eighteen hours a day to a battery of secretaries, one after another.

One of the secretaries was Jewish. She didn't know what sort of a terrible thing she'd become mixed up in. Here she was in a New York loft with some sort of wildman who was dictating a new *Mein Kampf* to her! She sneaked out and phoned B'nai B'rith's Anti-Defamation League, and soon a young man named Ben Epstein came sleuthing. He ended up pitching in to help with some of the research, putting the Anti-Defamation League's research facilities at Alan's disposal.

His edition of *Mein Kampf* was published with amazing speed — as a tabloid, splashed with black and red printing and pictures. Suddenly it appeared all over the country on newsstands and in book and magazine stores. Fritz Kuhn's American Nazis threw stink bombs at newsstands selling it in Yorkville and St. Louis. Hitler's agents sued for violation of copyright. The courts ruled against Alan and Spiro. The book was ordered off the stands.

Alan's friend Lee Falk recalls:

> When I came to California in 1964 to help Alan in his campaign against Pierre Salinger, no one knew about all this. I began to prod him to talk about it, when I was sitting in on an interview. He had been sued by Hitler, this twenty-four-year-old appalled by Nazi Germany, coming back to the United States and finding a launderized version of *Mein Kampf*. And bringing out a revised one for ten cents — his own anti-Nazi version. During the ten days it was on sale, half a million copies were sold. Of course, he was violating Hitler's copyright. Copies have become a collector's item. Alan recently had to pay $50 for one. No other American has ever been sued by Hitler!
>
> Of course, no other American provoked a lawsuit by both Hitler and Emperor Haile Selassie, either!

Had this venture succeeded, Alan planned to bring out a second book — this one intended to get at Mussolini. Il Duce was riding high with Americans then. He had "made the trains run on time," and he had negotiated a concordat with the Vatican, the first between the

Italian government and the Pope. But when he was young, Mussolini had written a flamboyant novel called *The Cardinal's Mistress* and had run it in his socialist weekly in Milan to build up that paper's circulation. Alan thought it would be great to republish the book in America—again in tabloid form and again for ten cents—convinced that the combination of author and title would insure huge sales and that the consequences would do Mussolini no good and damage his standing with American Catholics. But Alan and Amster Spiro decided they didn't need another copyright suit.

In New York, while still working—mostly unpaid—on the incipient *Brooklyn Express,* Alan found a temporary job with the Seven Arts Syndicate to sustain him.

Almost daily a ship arrived from Europe filled with Jewish refugees from the Hitler terror. Headlines shouting, **"800 JEWS LAND IN NEW YORK!"** or **"1200 JEWISH REFUGEES ARRIVE!"** led the American Jewish community to fear a rise of anti-Semitism.

For a short time, whenever a ship came in, Alan was there to meet it. He uncovered a number of heart-rending human interest stories that he called to the attention of other reporters. He also wrote them up for the Jewish press.

Alan remembers a beautiful girl named Felicita, her husband, and the twelve-year-old orphan boy they'd taken under their wing. All three lacked proper papers and weren't going to be allowed to leave the ship; they were to be shipped back to Nazi Germany to a concentration camp and death. Alan stirred up interest in them among the reporters, and their story made all the papers that day. Sailing time was in twenty-four hours, and Alan spent that time trying to get them off the ship. He phoned Walter Winchell at the Stork Club around midnight. Winchell said, "It's fascinating, but I've gotta go shave." Alan finally involved some Manhattan attorneys who looked very hard-boiled, but inside had very soft hearts. "I'll never forget sitting with them as one dictated a writ of *habeas corpus;* then we all rushed to a judge they knew, and lo and behold, it was issued. We got beautiful Felicita and her husband and the little boy off the ship—and saved their lives!"

This work led to Alan's first job in Washington. Read Lewis, head of the Common Council for American Unity, hired him at a modest salary to do some lobbying on Capitol Hill against discriminatory legislation affecting aliens and the foreign born. Lewis's organization was an outgrowth of World War I's Creel Committee, headed by George Creel, President Woodrow Wilson's propaganda chief. It put out information to foreign language newspapers and radio stations and interpreted America to the newcomers and helped them with naturalization and immigration problems.

Lewis was a tall, lean, hard-working bachelor. His organization was pretty much a one-man show. Alan wrote the newsletters and articles for their magazine *Common Ground* and recalls agonizing meetings, with Lewis going over every word, crossing out, inserting, and revising. But it was helpful. Lewis was deliberate and cautious compared with the plunge-ahead tactics of Hillman, Gervasi, and Spiro.

Alan first went down to Washington on Lincoln's birthday in 1940. "That was the first day I ever saw Congress," he wrote. "I sat in the House gallery, enthralled. It was love at first sight." His task was to deal with a bill authored by Congressman John J. Dempsey that would have made subject to deportation anyone who "believes in, advocates, teaches, or advises" certain measures, including the overthrow of the government. A very long bill. The idea of deporting someone just for "believing in" something was the problem.

Alan asked Congressman Dempsey, later the governor of New Mexico, "How do you prove someone's belief? You're not going to deport them for that!"

"The bill doesn't call for deporting someone just on belief," he said.

"Well," Alan answered, "the way I read it, it does." Then he got Dempsey to read the bill, pointing out how the word "believe" carried on down into the body of the bill.

"Well, I didn't really mean that," he said and dropped the bill.

Alan says now, "I was entranced to discover how easy it was for someone to show up and affect what happens in Congress — how a great deal could be achieved very swiftly."

It was at this time that Alan met California's Senator Hiram Johnson. As governor during the reform period from 1911 to 1917, Johnson had broken the power of the railroads, written the initiative and referendum into California's constitution, and achieved other reforms that have kept political machines out of California ever since. He had been senator for all but three years of Alan's life. He was one of those senators who kept the United States out of the League of Nations. Alan met him in an old hideaway Capitol office, looking out toward the Washington and Lincoln monuments — by coincidence, it is now the majority whip's office, which Alan occupies today. His most vivid memory is how very old the senator was, yet interesting to talk to and pleasant. They discussed immigration legislation. Alan was trying to meet every senator and House member who'd have any impact on legislation in that field.

That year Alan registered as a Democrat. During the previous presidential election he had been in Rome.

When he was in New York, Alan still lurked around Spiro's *Brooklyn Express* office. He wrote to me describing the view from the twenty-fourth floor as he looked across the edge of Brooklyn beyond the East River to the twinkling skyline of lower Manhattan. The murky bay, splashed with ships, was dimly there. Over beyond the tall 'scrapers, the *Queen Mary* and the *Mauritania* were steaming up, reportedly for a dash to Australia. And he could imagine British men-of-war standing by out to sea, waiting to convoy them past the German warships lurking just beyond.

After that he added, "That paragraph is the *Express*-and-Spiro influence. I have to stimulate the hobgoblin corners of my mind, after a day spent wrestling with hard-and-cold facts at the Common Council office."

Social work seemed to him, in his words, "screwy." He liked it because it was new, and he was learning. But the people in it weren't tough, like reporters and editors. He enjoyed his encounters with the legislators in Washington, who were just as rough as newspapermen — only more so! "I still hope to get into politics someday, and this social stuff is perfect training for that, along with news work," he wrote.

"Those Congressional louses are going to adjourn shortly," he added. "They *should* recess, so they could get together quickly, if anyone tries to usurp too much power. But they'll adjourn, because that way they get train fare home!"

During 1940 Alan wrote a play with Lee Falk, "The Big Story," based on Alan's newspaper experiences. Producer Gilbert Miller bought it and tried it out in New Jersey. *Variety* predicted it would be a Broadway hit. It never reached New York, but Alan was cheered soon after when *The American Mercury* bought his article "Crown Prince to the Dictator: Count Galleazzo Ciano." Ciano was Mussolini's son-in-law.

Meanwhile he was falling in love by mail with Geneva McMath. At his suggestion she came to New York for three months to do some writing. They had a picture taken on the boardwalk at the New York World's Fair that shows them strolling along through the crowds, holding hands, and looking lost to the world.

Tall, slender Geneva had wavy auburn hair, cornflower blue eyes, high cheekbones, and angular eyebrows in a skeptical, sophisticated face. She looked a little bit like Garbo. Alan admired her quick, critical mind and offbeat sense of humor. Her paradoxical nature intrigued him: He found her sensitive but bold, informed yet not studious, serious but playful, indolent yet harddriving.

Soon after Geneva returned to California, Alan wrote to Father and Mother, telling them he and Geneva were engaged. Their wedding plans were complicated by uncertainties about the draft.

"Our fate was in that fishbowl when Henry L. Stimson reached in and drew the first number," Alan recalls. "If the number was low, I'd enlist right then. Not wait to be drafted. If it was high, we'd get married and continue my work and my interventionist activities.

"That morning I had a toothache and waited for the dentist to arrive at 9:00 A.M. The tooth hurt like hell. I read the *New York Times* while I was waiting, going through the 10,000 numbers in the order they'd been drawn, searching for my own draft number. I finally found it up in the 8000s, a high number. That meant we'd get married right away."

Alan's wedding plans caught my husband and me in the east, unable to return to California. Mother wrote me in some detail:

> Alan flew to Los Altos for two days, then drove us down to Los Angeles. The wedding was at 8:15 in the evening in the Wee Kirk of the Heather in Glendale, a lovely little church, beautifully decorated with flowers. Scottish, of course.
>
> Johnny Atkinson, Alan's best man, drove us to the reception. Geneva wore a coat of military or soldier's blue, over a dress of the same colour, and looked stunning.

Alan and Geneva spent their wedding night at the Miramar Hotel in Santa Monica, then dashed south to Palm Springs. They quickly drove north to Los Altos to return the family car. They flew south to Los Angeles and went by train to New Orleans, where they took the boat to New York. Then they entrained to Washington. "My first experience with Alan's strenuous scheduling!" says Geneva.

Their first real home was a little walk-up apartment on the back of

Capitol Hill. In a few months they moved to 120 C Street, North East. "When I first went to the Senate, I could look out the window of my office in the new Senate Office Building, and see 120 C Street, right across the street, and the window of the place where we had lived. Strangely—just as Father and Mother were married in a home right across the street from my future office in the capitol in Sacramento."

Alan's work in Common Council's fight against discriminatory legislation was about to end. The war was spreading. He was a strong interventionist. I baited him by quoting Ann Lindbergh's *The Wave of the Future*, and he responded:

> I'm against neutrality, or rather the idea of neutrality. I think it is non-existent in this world of warring ideas and material forces. I favor aid to Britain now, including naval aid. If we permit England to go down, we will fight Hitler later anyway, with less chance then, of defending ourselves without terrific loss. And I think a Hitler victory will mean the virtual end of democracy—or any hope of progress for many years. If we had refused to aid England from the very first, democracy here might have survived a Hitler victory. But to quit on them now would bring a moral letdown here. In South America and in Canada that would be ruinous. . . . More important than world trade, or rubber, is the spirit of freedom and respect for other men that characterizes America as against Germany, Italy, Russia. I don't think that spirit could withstand the propaganda onslaught of a successful Germany. . . .
>
> Re the Lindbergh book, I can't see the Nazis as the scum on "the wave of the future." There is nothing new in their program. Using weapons created by men, more or less free, they are going straight back to the Roman pattern—with the weapons insuring that, if victorious, they should retain power far longer than the Caesars. Is it a "wave of the future" that smashes Yugoslavia and goes back to the twelfth century to find ancestors for a modern Italian king to rule the vanquished land? The whole story of man living socially—apart from man's march in science—has been one of progressive freedom, with temporary setbacks. If this is the "wave of the future" we have been wrong—all of us—for some two thousand years.
>
> Can you believe the Nazis don't have designs on us?. . .

On the side, Alan worked with a boyhood chum, now a newsman, Tom Crane, on a project they dreamed up—a plan to organize American volunteers to work on merchant ships carrying war supplies to Europe through dangerous areas infested with Nazi submarines. This would help relieve the severe shortage of men on British and American vessels.

Alan and Tom—both of whom intended to volunteer to sail on the first ship—hoped Americans would show other nations they recognized the urgency of immediate all-out aid to the Allies and perhaps expedite repeal of the Neutrality Act. This would counteract the isolationist line of the America-Firsters and U.S. Communists and their sympathizers.

Alan enlisted the interest of David K. Niles in the White House, Senator Tom Connally, chairman of the Senate Foreign Relations Committee, the Maritime Commission, and others in powerful places, but the project never quite came off. The end of neutrality and the attack on Pearl Harbor drew near.

William MacGregor Cranston, our father. He was born in Yountville, Napa County, California, in 1879 and grew up in San Francisco.

Carol Dixon Cranston, our mother. She was the daughter of a physician in Sacramento.

William and Carol Cranston, before they were married, on Governor's Lane at Stanford.

The Cranston home on Copper Street in Palo Alto, where Alan was born.

Alan at six; with the Marmon.

Alan and Eleanor.

Alan at seven.

Alan at ten.

SCHOOL YEARS:

Grammar school graduation portrait.

Mountain View High School graduation.

Stanford graduation.

Villa Warec, Los Altos.

Fremont Older, the crusading San Francisco editor.

Alan as correspondent in Rome.

Alan and Geneva McMath in New York in 1940; just engaged.

Alan worked with Eleanor Roosevelt hoping to prevent the setting up of relocation camps for Japanese-Americans in 1942.

Grenville Clark, international lawyer; influential in the World Federalist movement.

Campaigning: Pat Brown and Clair Engle with Alan in 1958.

Sworn in as State Controller, 1959.

Animal Farm, Sacramento. The Cranston family: Geneva, Kim, Robin and Alan.

★ ★ ★ ★ ★ ★ ★ ★ ★ ★ ★ ★ ★ ★ ★ ★ ★

CHAPTER 7

Working in the Wartime Government

★ ★ ★ ★ ★ ★ ★ ★ ★ ★ ★ ★ ★ ★ ★ ★ ★

A nation of nations . . .

— Walt Whitman

December 7, 1941, found Alan in the New York penthouse of a Columbia University law professor, drafting a bill for the supervision of deportable aliens. The phone rang with the news of the bombing of Pearl Harbor.

They rushed to the radio and listened to the reports coming in, interspersed with jazz and a football game.

A plane droned over the Hudson. For the first time in America, Alan — like many New Yorkers that day — wondered if it might drop a bomb. The ultimate fight between tyranny and democracy was joined at last. Democracy could end here. He caught his breath and felt an odd mixture of excitement and sorrow.

Later that Sunday night he went down to Grand Central Station to watch a trainload of soldiers and sailors leaving for a destination unknown. They were happy, grinning, confident, kissing their girls and families goodbye. "They looked strong, ready for everything!" he wrote home. "But I remembered the sight of Italy's battered soldiers returning from the war in Ethiopia, and my heart went out to them."

Around midnight on Monday he returned to Washington, a darkened city. Steel-helmeted guards stood or paced outside government buildings.

The Capitol dome was blacked out. It had been a great attraction beyond their window every night until midnight, white and bright under the search lights.

"At least our rent should drop!" he told Geneva jokingly, for she was shaken and depressed.

Alan thought of enlisting, but in view of his young marriage and the luck of the draw in the draft that had determined his wedding date with Geneva, he decided to see first what work he could find that was directly connected with the war effort. His boss, Read Lewis, recommended him to Archibald MacLeish, head of the U.S. Office of Facts and Figures. OFF had been set up by President Franklin D. Roosevelt to deal with the informational matters of the war and activities such as Lend-Lease and Aid-to-the-Allies. Now, after Pearl Harbor, it was immediately expanded. MacLeish appointed Alan to set up and head its foreign language division. Thus Alan was to work in the government bringing the knowledge he'd gained in the Common Council — the successor to the old Creel Committee, the informational arm of the government in World War I — to its new arm in World War II.

Alan took an instant liking to MacLeish, an impressive man, America's unofficial poet laureate. Elated and hopeful, he went to work on the first Monday in January, 1942. It was the kind of job he had dreamed about.

"If Alan hadn't had a receding hairline," Geneva wrote me then, "and therefore looked older than twenty-seven, he would never have been given that important job! He's so delighted with his new work. The list of his new acquaintances and associates is very impressive, and his responsibility is growing as the work develops. At a game of 'Who Am I?' the other night, people were not stumped by 'an important government official, whose last name begins with c.' It was A. C. obviously. Frankly I'm very relieved that his work is confined to office hours, rather than being strewn through the day, till about 3:00 A.M. It's a much more regular schedule now."

She hoped this could be the beginning of a more peaceful, well-ordered life. He was earning a decent salary at last.

"Can't we live more like other people now?" she asked.

"How do other people live?" Alan asked with a grin.

"More peacefully and more lightly."

"In the middle of a war?"

His sympathy for her and for all those affected by the war was often at odds those days. He tried to include her in his activities, driving around Washington with her on weekends, enjoying its views and

monuments, which they both loved. Often they had dinner at
O'Donnell's and The Steak House with his new associates in OFF,
Bradford Smith, the novelist, Charles Olson, the poet, among others.

Geneva took Alan's place at the Common Council, handling its
legislative work. Then she landed a short-term job, successfully lobbying for the repeal of the Chinese Exclusion Act. "Between us, we're
earning more than a Congressman!" Alan wrote home.

From his desk in the Office of Facts and Figures in the Library of
Congress Annex on Capitol Hill, Alan looked out on the old green
copper dome and Corinthian columns of the Library of Congress. His
desk sat in one corner of a huge room like the city room of a newspaper, adjoining the small, cramped private offices of MacLeish and
a few others.

He drafted his talented friend Lee Falk as associate chief of the
foreign language division at a salary of a dollar a year, and an equally
talented friend of Amster Spiro, David Karr, who had worked with
Alan on the *Brooklyn Express,* as his press chief. Lee brought sophisti-
cation, loyalty, and his delightful humor, another form of perception.
Karr, only twenty-three, a brown-haired, brown-eyed man with three
dimples, had remarkably good connections with the White House and
elsewhere, as well as limitless ambition and audacity, and was a total
pragmatist. The three friends worked together night and day, pooling
their ideas for the war effort. "Between us," Karr recalled, "we moved
men and mountains."*

OFF began as a small, compact, hard-hitting group of a few hundred people creating support for the war effort and advising the White
House on the informational aspects. Within a few months, however,
OFF and several other organizations were combined to form the Office
of War Information (OWI). Elmer Davis, the wry, tough, talented
newsman, perhaps the most famous radio commentator of them all,
became its head. The more dreamy and idealistic MacLeish became
an assistant secretary of state.

OWI had a remarkable crew: great writers, historians, and colorful, rambunctious newspapermen, radiomen, and editors from

---

*" 'An engagingly immodest man, Karr [President of Fairbanks Whitney] claims he has an IQ
of 189, or roughly fifty points above what is usually considered the threshold of genius.' David
Karr in the President's Chair." *Fortune,* June 1961.

national and ethnic magazines. Alan delighted in the exciting city-room atmosphere. The air crackled with ideas and there was great freedom to carry them out.

Once he attended a meeting where William B. Lewis, a top C.B.S. executive turned OWI deputy leader, a dark-haired, ambitious man, described plans for a big radio series to be entitled, "This Is War!" It was to be aired soon, driving home to the American people what the war was about.

Someone exclaimed, "It's too good! Too sophisticated. It'll go over the heads of the American people. They won't like it."

Bill Lewis responded cheerfully and confidently, "Even if it's good they'll like it!"

They had many frenzied days at OWI. Alan's work was to explain the draft, price controls, gas rationing, and such matters — along with war aims — in thirty-seven languages through press, radio, organizations, and other outlets.

The first big issue was that of concentration camps for the Japanese-Americans, mostly Californians. MacLeish was opposed to the concept of internment. As a Californian, Alan was drafted to work with MacLeish and Eleanor Roosevelt to try to persuade the president against the camps. However, the views of General DeWitt, head of the Fourth Army, California Attorney General Earl Warren, and others, prevailed.

Later Alan visited two Japanese relocation centers, California's Tule Lake and Wyoming's Heart Mountain, each housing between 10,000 and 15,000 Japanese. At Tule Lake he didn't know any of the Japanese and spent his time with Caucasian officials. The director of the camp said conversationally, "We really don't know what goes on down there in the village, in their houses."

At Heart Mountain, Alan found out. The first day he arrived he told the press chief he was going down in the village to see some friends, and when he didn't return for lunch, dinner, or the night's diversions (ping-pong), they began to be alarmed, thinking maybe he'd been kidnapped for ransom or murdered. He spent the next three days in the cold, snow-covered camp, hurrying through the howling wind to the mess halls, visiting with Tanaka (our former gardener) and Mina, Fujimiya and Kiku, old friends from Villa Warec, and many other old friends from Los Altos grammar school and Mountain

View high school. The barracks were so simple that, after the first few, the army was able to put up each one in fifty-nine minutes flat; they were long buildings divided into crowded one-room apartments.

Alan found Fujimiya and Kiku as jolly as ever, and wrote home that Fujimiya took great delight in kidding Tanaka about how he took a former cook's job in order to keep warm and "swears all his customers are getting ulcers. He kicks about many things, but in such a kidding manner that you can't tell whether he really means it." Outside his house Fujimiya went about in a sort of coonskin hat that made him look precisely like Chiang Kai-shek, and many called him that.

Tanaka was the same as he was at Villa Warec, though a bit grayer. He had made some beautiful chairs and tables for their house out of crude and scarce lumber.

The crowning ambition of all the Issei (Japanese-born) was to return to California or wherever they came from — anywhere except Japan. Alan really didn't learn terribly much more from them than from the Caucasians; but among the Nisei (American-born), old classmates like Henry Hamasaki, the Furuichi clan, and friends they introduced him to, really cut loose and told him how they felt after they'd eaten several meals together, talked over old times, walked around in the biting weather, played poker together in wanton violation of camp rules, and danced at the football rally.

Their primary ambition was to regain the American citizenship they felt they had been robbed of, and to get "outside." They felt they'd proved their love of democracy and their Americanism, and every day they were wondering more and more if America was going to prove its democracy.

They felt they proved their loyalty when they helped the authorities round up a few Kibei and Issei, and when they accepted relocation without grumbling. But more and more they wondered if they should have done the latter, for they felt their loyalty and cooperativeness had not been sufficiently stressed by the government; more and more they worried about the racial basis upon which they were ousted. They said the argument that they had to be removed in case of paratroop attack was false, because the Chinese remained in California and few Californians, they said, "can tell one from another."

The argument that they were removed for their own good, to save them from possible vigilante murders and beatings and mass ousters, didn't go. They said they'd rather be killed due to incidental failings of individual citizens of a democracy, than be deprived of their liberties by the real government of a democracy.

Morale took a nosedive at Heart Mountain shortly before Alan's arrival, when the army suddenly put a barbed wire fence around the camp, separating the barracks from the snow-covered wastelands. It was explained that the fence was to keep out cows that would be grazing there next spring. But the inmates suspected it was to aid the soldiers in guarding the camp, and it gave the whole camp claustrophobia.

An incongruous sight was that of American soldiers—Nisei—spending their furloughs in the centers visiting their relatives.

Perhaps one of the most pathetic things Alan saw was an extremely intelligent and progressive-minded mother who was still managing—with considerable difficulty and great dexterity—to conceal from her alert four-year-old son that they were in what most of the inmates considered a racial concentration camp.

Tanaka told him the story about a little girl who, several days after the long, long train trip and the arrival in camp, and the setting up of housekeeping, said "Mama, I don't like Japan. Let's go back to America."

Alan felt he really got to know the Americans of Japanese background better in his four days among them than in his twelve years of school with them. He hoped that some of the ideas he brought back with him would help them.* But when he returned to Washington, he was unable to do anything that would significantly ease their plight.

Also in 1942, Elmer Davis dispatched Alan to Los Angeles when the bloody Zoot Suit Riots erupted between sailors who were pursuing the prettiest girls in the Hispanic community and angry Mexican-American youths. Alan investigated, then helped set up programs to alleviate the tension, working closely with Monsignor Timothy O'Dwyer, a remarkable Catholic social leader, and with Hollywood celebrities like Walter Wanger, Constance Bennett, and Anthony Quinn.

Los Angeles newspapers had alleged that to join East side gangs, Mexican-American girls had to indulge in orgies and sex rites with all

---

*Alan is currently trying to help Japanese-Americans receive compensation for property they lost when they were taken to the camps.

the male members. To counteract this charge, the girls made a startling proposal. They suggested that Alan help them organize a march to city hall to see Mayor Fletcher Bowron. There they would all demand physical examinations to prove they were virgins.

"There might be something better to do," Alan told the girls. "Let me think it over." (He wrote to Geneva, "Can you imagine what pious Mayor Bowron would have done!") He thought about it for a day, then suggested, "Why don't you organize a blood donors' drive in your community? The acceptance of your blood will indicate you are pure and not diseased. And you'll be making a patriotic effort in support of the armed forces. Not a combative one." The girls cheered. They organized their drive, but then the Red Cross told the girls, "We can't accept Mexican blood. Anglos don't want it."

Everyone was outraged. Alan reached the highest levels of the Red Cross in Washington and persuaded them to drop that rule. The Mexican-American girls held a successful, highly publicized blood drive. This contributed immensely to cooling off the Zoot suit tensions. Alan recognized the urgent need to avoid hysteria against German-Americans, Japanese-Americans, Italian-Americans, and Mexican-Americans. He organized a staff of about twenty to work with America's many different nationality groups. Henry Rutz dealt with the German-Americans; Ignacio Lopez, then Sparky Saldana, with the Spanish-speaking Americans; and Joe Facci, a Dante-like character in appearance and a refugee from the Mussolini regime, handled the work for the Italian-American community.

There were incredible problems within every single nationality group. When America entered the war aliens from Italy and Germany were officially labeled "enemies." They couldn't travel freely and couldn't take certain jobs. Loyal native-born and naturalized Americans of these ancestries, as well as the aliens, resented these restrictions. As the Rome-Berlin axis began to falter and Italians became unhappy with their alliance with the Nazis, Facci came up with an idea designed to impose greater strains on the alliance and to solve the problems of these Italian-Americans. He proposed that Roosevelt issue a proclamation ending the enemy alien certification for Italians living in America. He convinced Alan, who took on the task of selling the idea. He sold it in OWI all the way to the top, to Elmer Davis. Then he sold it all the way to the top in the Department of Justice to

Attorney General Francis Biddle. Then, with David Niles's help in the White House he sold it to President Roosevelt, and to Secretary of State Cordell Hull.

Accordingly, in his Columbus Day speech in 1943, Roosevelt announced that Italians were no longer enemy aliens. Restrictions on them were lifted. Leaflets were dropped all over Italy announcing that Americans now considered them friends.

Bruno Foa, director of the Bureau of Latin American Research, wrote Alan: "Congratulations on the superb piece of work which you initiated and put through. It was certainly an enormous step forward in the grand strategy of political warfare."

Count Carlo Sforza, Italy's first postwar foreign minister, declared then that this act establishing that we were "friends not enemies" saved the lives of countless American soldiers—and Italians, too— when the Allies landed in Italy to drive out the Nazis.

Randolfo Pacciardi, the leader of refugee anti-Fascist Italians in America during the war, and postwar minister of defense, arranged for Alan to be decorated by the Italian government with the Star of Solidarity in 1946.

On one of the darkest days of the war, Hitler announced that the town of Lidice in Czechoslovakia had been ruthlessly and totally obliterated in retaliation for the nearby assassination of Heydrich, the Nazi *gauleiter*. All the men and boys were killed, all the women transported away. The Nazis leveled the whole town, razed it, wiped it off the face of the earth—a lesson for those who dared to attack Nazi leaders. Shocked OWI leaders met to discuss how to respond to this atrocity. In the course of the meeting, an idea came to Alan.

"Let's show the Nazis they *can't* wipe Lidice off the face of the earth," he suggested. "Let's name an American town 'Lidice'!"

Elmer Davis accepted the idea immediately and told Alan to implement it. Alan sent David Karr out to Illinois to persuade his friend, Mayor Kelly, to select a community in the suburbs and rename it Lidice. In June 1942, Stern Gardens, Illinois, became Lidice, Illinois.

"The event was celebrated with great fanfare," Alan recalls. Wendell Willkie made the principal address. An eternal flame was lighted. Edna St. Vincent Millay memorialized Lidice, Illinois, in a poem. The radio networks covered the story live. Other countries christened their own Lidices. Later *Pic* magazine called the event, "the most effective and moving propaganda stunt of the war."

All that year, events proceeded fortuitously for Alan, as the country slowly cranked itself up for the war effort. But 1943 brought changes — as though the tide that he had taken at its flood had gone, leaving treacherous, ominous shallows.

One of Alan's most difficult and delicate undertakings was to try to unite the different national groups in victory councils to support the war. Meetings were held with leaders of the Italian-American, German-American, all the different Slavic-American factions, and others, many of whom detested each other because of their different ideologies. Nazis, Fascists, Communists, Trotskyites, Socialists, Social Democrats, Conservatives — all were there, in every community. The Italian-Americans and the German-Americans were the most difficult nationalist groups of all because of their deep internal divisions. Some violence was inevitable.

CHAPTER

★ ★ ★ ★ ★ ★ ★ ★ ★ ★ ★ ★ ★ ★ ★

Eruptions at OWI

★ ★ ★ ★ ★ ★ ★ ★ ★ ★ ★ ★ ★ ★ ★

On January 11, 1943, at about ten in the evening, Carlo Tresca, a sixty-eight-year-old anti-Fascist editor, was murdered on a sidewalk in downtown Manhattan. He had just left the offices of his newspaper *Il Martello* (The Hammer) with a friend to keep a date with his wife at a nearby restaurant.

Lee Falk, at Alan's suggestion, had met with Tresca six days before. They had spent the evening discussing plans to set up an Italian-American Victory Council to unite the community behind the war effort. Tresca was one of a dozen New York leaders who could ensure its success.

Following that meeting, Lee had mailed letters to a dozen prominent Italian-Americans inviting them to a meeting to discuss the creation of an Italian-American Victory Council in New York. Lee indicated that various labor, political, and fraternal groups had urged that the organization be broadly conceived so as to represent all Americans of Italian descent. "OWI is acting in a liaison capacity only, the purpose being to promote unity for the war effort, both for the armed forces and on the production front," Lee wrote.

The Tresca murder split the Italian-American community more widely than ever, with as many theories, charges and counter-charges surfacing as there were political factions. Anti-Fascists declared that pro-Fascists had committed the crime. Mussolini's onetime supporters in the community hotly denied it. Socialists accused Communists. Communists accused Nazis. An early rumor suggested that a jealous husband was the real murderer.

Ten days after the murder, the *New York Sun* reported Lee Falk's visit. With this revelation, all the hatreds and animosities in the

65

Italian-American community between the Fascists, Communists, Socialists and others boiled over again. They had found their scapegoat in OWI.

Alan wrote home on January 18, seeking to break the news gently to Mother and Father, who were not exactly comforted to read: "I've been mixed up, as little as possible, but every day I'm afraid it may become too much, in a classic murder mystery."

Luigi Antonini, a rigid doctrinaire liberal, president of the Italian-American Labor Council, charged that OWI officials had urged Tresca to accept participation in the Victory Council, attributing to Tresca the view that Communists should be welcomed as participants. No charge was made that Communists had either been invited or had attended. Antonini further asserted that Tresca had opposed Communist participation in the anti-Fascist Mazzini Society, and deduced from that that Tresca would likewise oppose Communist participation in the Victory Council. Therefore, the OWI was in some way responsible for the murder. He charged that Communists had killed Tresca because of his opposition to their involvement in the Mazzini Society, and implied that they had an added motive because of his opposition to their inclusion in the Victory Council.

Alan stated publicly that OWI did not choose the organizations to be represented on the Victory Council. That was left to the leaders themselves. OWI acted in a liaison capacity only. Elmer Davis was prompted by one confusing article to write a letter of complaint to the *New York Times*:

> I should like to indicate mild pain over the *Time*'s front page story on the 22nd about the OWI and the Tresca murder. While the story does not precisely say so, it would lead the careless reader to infer that if Alan Cranston did not pull the trigger, he was certainly the master mind in the back room.
>
> My denial was duly published, but three sticks on page 17 hardly outweigh the impression created by a story well displayed out in front.

Antonini proceeded to retract his charges. An aide to Sulzberger of the *Times,* E.L. James, thereupon wrote to Davis saying:

> Mr. Antonini now tells a tale different from that which he told at the start. It is a little tough knowing when Antonini is telling the truth, but if his statement today is correct, then I think we ought to express to you our regrets that we were imposed upon in our story of January 27, to which you called our attention.

The OWI aspect of the case subsided. The murderer was never found.

The Tresca case showed the explosive mixture Alan had to work with as head of the Foreign Language Division of OWI and the difficulties and perils of his fight against Fascism.

There was an ironic footnote. The Socialists believed that Fascism was already defeated. They concentrated on beating down the Communists. So when Alan was misquoted as saying that Tresca favored working with Communists to win the war, they were outraged. They went after Alan hammer and tongs.

Elmer Davis and Alan came to suspect that a file clerk in OWI, a Socialist, was sneaking confidential OWI information out to other Socialists. They decided to set a trap. "Why don't you try baiting him with something," Davis suggested to Alan. "See if he makes efforts to get it outside."

"Any suggestions?" Alan asked.

"How about a memo from me to you saying, 'Now that the Antonini and Tresca affair has blown over, I believe we'd better get rid of Lee Falk!'?"

Lee failed to see any humor in this and protested violently, "What if we don't stop it, and it shows up on the front page of the *New York Times?*" he howled.

So Davis told Alan to think up another memo, strong enough to tempt the suspected clerk, yet harmless in case their quarry sneaked it out without being caught.

Alan pondered, then sent a memo to Davis, prominently red-penciled, "SECRET AND CONFIDENTIAL!" This read: "We have a report that the Communists, led by one Donini, and the Fascists, represented by Generoso Pope, are so outraged by the Socialist efforts to hang the Tresca murder on them, that they are ganging up against the Socialists."

The carbons were sent to central files, and a watch was set. The suspect gleefully pounced on the copies, scribbled hasty notes, went to a phone, started to report to an outside ally, and was in turn pounced upon. He quietly departed from OWI.

*   *   *

The next eruption at OWI was the Cox case.

The great battle of the Atlantic was at its height.

"We lost another ship," Lee Falk told Alan grimly one morning, drawing a chair up to Alan's desk in OWI's crowded city room.

Alan laid down his pen, slouched back in his swivel chair and said, "The FCC [Federal Communications Commission] believes that foreign-language radio announcers are tipping off enemy submarines. I've been in touch with the FBI, and with Wild Bill Donovan's outfit [OSS, forerunner of the CIA]. They suspect that some of these people work for the Nazis and Fascists."

For several years, according to the FCC and FBI, Nazi and Fascist agents had infiltrated German and Italian radio stations in America. After Pearl Harbor, some were interned or convicted of espionage. Others fled to continue broadcasting from Tokyo, Berlin, and Rome.

Those who were more subtle managed to stay on the air but showed where their sympathies were. They would announce, for example, that German General Rommel had advanced against the Allies in North Africa and then play the "Victory March" from *Aida*. Or they'd quote President Roosevelt and then play, "I'll be Glad When You're Dead, You Rascal You!"

"I'm sure the Navy would like to shut down all the foreign language stations," Alan said to Lee Falk, "but of course they can't. First Amendment."

Lee frowned. "So what do we do?"

Alan suggested, "I think you should go out to the National Broadcasters' Association convention in Cleveland next week and lobby for self-regulation of the industry. Convince them it's their patriotic duty to clean house. And that all hell may break loose if they don't."

Lee nodded thoughtfully, then gave Alan a mock but affectionate salute.

In Cleveland, the Foreign Language Broadcasters Wartime Control Committee was set up to preserve foreign language radio as a means of reaching millions of citizens in their native tongues and to protect a business running into millions of dollars and employing thousands of people. At the committee's request, Lee Falk agreed to act as liaison with government agencies.

The Broadcasters' Committee issued a Code of Wartime Practices stating that the media was to be "a positive force." No person would be employed whose past record indicated he would not faithfully co-operate with the war effort.

Procedures were set up. Lee outlined them for Alan:

Station personnel will submit fingerprints and personal history statements to OWI. In our liaison capacity, we'll transmit these to the FBI with requests for pertinent information. We'll make reports directly to station managers, acting solely in an advisory capacity. The station managers will make the final decisions on retention or dismissal of individual broadcasters.

At this time, Congressman Edward Eugene Cox of Georgia, who had been angrily pursuing an investigation against his enemy, the Federal Communications Commission (FCC) for weeks, charged the FCC with "over-all ineptitude," particularly in the foreign monitoring it was doing for the armed services. He accused the FCC of "Gestapo tactics" against the personnel of private radio stations.

Months earlier the FCC had given the Department of Justice evidence that Cox had accepted $2,500 from Radio Station WALB in Albany, Georgia. Cox, if tried and found guilty, would face a maximum $10,000 fine and two years in prison under Section 113 of the Criminal Code, which forbids congressmen to be paid for services rendered in matters to which the government is a party.

Cox now charged that OWI, in the person of Lee Falk, had forced the dismissal of unpopular radio personnel and had been guilty of "sinister conspiracies" to ruin private enterprise.

The fact was that shortly after the Broadcasters' Committee set up its clearance procedure, OWI chief Elmer Davis sought the advice of Attorney General Biddle, the FCC, and the Office of Censorship to determine what their respective spheres of action should be. The attorney general felt that this vital work should be continued and ruled that the Office of Censorship had complete power to remove personnel from the air. Since then, OWI suggestions about individual broadcasters had been made to the Office of Censorship or to the Department of Justice. No suggestions were made directly to the industry.

For a time, the press played up the Cox charges against the FCC and OWI. Then slowly the tide turned. It was revealed that the actions taken against broadcasters aiding the enemy were far less drastic than the Cox Committee itself felt should have been undertaken even before Pearl Harbor. Cox had castigated the FCC for failing to ban all Japanese-language broadcasts in Hawaii before December 7, 1941.

The New York *Herald Tribune* accused Cox's committee of "about as disreputable a piece of shyster propaganda as could be imagined."

In an unusual move, the *Washington Post*, published a public letter on its front page to Speaker Sam Rayburn from its editor and publisher, Eugene Meyer, denouncing Cox and urging Rayburn to investigate and discipline his committee. "In the opinion of no qualified and dispassionate observer has this investigation proved anything but a mockery of basic American traditions of fair play," declared Meyer. "It has been a star chamber; it has been black with bias; it has sought to terrorize those who exposed the chairman's own corrupt practices."

Cox soon dropped his investigation of the FCC and OWI.

One day as the furor was subsiding, Alan visited Elmer Davis in his large modern office in the building later occupied by HEW. After they had discussed Alan's current projects and the Cox case, Alan got up to go.

Davis smiled at him warmly, and said in his gravelly Kansas voice, "You keep us in constant turmoil. You've probably got the most difficult, controversial job around here. But you're helping us win the war, you know. Bound to have some sort of excitement all the time." He took a few steps toward his laden desk with a sigh. "Don't take it to heart," he added kindly, "will you?"

Alan looked at him, admiring his toughness and humanity and his relaxed air of firmness about his work. "I hate to see the bureaucracy closing in on us," Alan volunteered.

"All the red tape," muttered Davis. "But you're doing a great job." He seemed reluctant to have Alan leave.

Alan recognized his momentary desire for some respite and company and said, "I decided something last night. There are only three ways I would ever want to work in government again—one is in the House or Senate—in Congress—where you can be *independent*; or second, on a high level like the Cabinet, above all the red tape; or third, at a relatively low level like mine, in a brand-new agency—only in its first year of existence when you can do so much before the bureaucracy and Congress close in on you!"

"Well, you can have them all," said Davis caustically. "I don't ever want to work for the government again in any role. And I sure as hell don't have any political ambitions."

"That's probably fortunate for me," said Alan. "Otherwise you might not tolerate all these eruptions!"

"I'll stick to commentating," said Davis, showing distaste for the cumbersome word. He looked out the window a moment. "The trouble here is that we're dealing with all the most tempestuous domestic aspects of the war. All the nationality groups. All the conflicting ambitions, all the loves and hates. Every foreign war, conflict, civil clash anywhere on earth — between the Slovaks and Slovenes, the Serbs and the Croats echoes and erupts here in the good old United States. So, Alan, it's up to you to just reconcile all their differences. Get 'em all behind the war."

Alan nodded and smiled. "Despite all their own separate war aims, their clashing agendas. Thank you for making it all less difficult."

For a moment the two men studied each other thoughtfully. Then Davis put up two fingers briefly in the victory salute, strolled back to his desk, and bent his head to his work.

Alan turned and went out, walking with a springier step, greatly encouraged.

Alan was in constant combat, meanwhile, with Adolph A. Berle, Jr., his *bête noire* at the State Department. Berle was one of FDR's original brain-trusters and was now an assistant secretary of state. Alan wrote to Father and Mother, suggesting they read the current *New Yorker* wherein Berle was "torn to shreds in a profile. Elmer Davis has practically instructed me to declare open warfare on the man."

Father replied, "As Berle is in a more influential position than you and able to do you serious damage, you probably should use all the skill you can muster in an effort to get along with him. I had a similar enemy once and, looking backward, realize that he did me incalculable harm whereas I never even had an opportunity to reciprocate."

Two weeks later Alan wrote: "The scrap with Berle proceeds apace. You're absolutely right that he's a big customer to chew off, but I have no other choice but to try to inflict a few bites. If you read Drew Pearson's column for the next few days, you may see him cuffing Berle about a bit. I spent a good portion of the afternoon with Drew."

The essence of the dispute between Alan and Berle lay in their clashing views of the appropriate role of America's nationality groups in the war. As Alan saw it, Berle wanted to use them to restore a world that was gone forever — the old order — and hoped the war would perpetuate the monarchies of Europe and Asia. He appeared to flirt with Archduke Otto of Austria, who dreamed of restoring the Hapsburg dynasty, and with King Zog of Albania. He preferred Laval and Petain to de Gaulle and the Free French.

The task assigned to Alan by OWI was to unite the nationality groups behind the war, and his method — exemplified by his Victory Council approach — was to organize them to help defeat the enemy, not to struggle for post-war power in their various lands of origin. Alan did do all he could to strengthen the hands of those who were working for democracy in their motherlands — exiled leaders like Italy's Pacciardi and Sforza.

Arguments were constant over which faction or force or government to support, and Alan and Berle each did their utmost to enlist the support of the White House. The difference of opinion was so fundamental that Alan felt he couldn't do a good job if he didn't oppose Berle. Davis agreed and told him not only to stand his ground but to advance wherever possible.

This was Alan's first experience with the territorial imperative that lies under so much bureaucratic infighting in all governments everywhere. Berle's domain was foreign policy, and he felt Alan was invading it; while Alan's domain included the activities of the refugees and the nationality groups inside America. While resisting Berle's domestic interventions, Alan in turn — to strengthen his own efforts at home — found reasons to interfere abroad. This, together with their philosophical differences, made collision inevitable.

Except in Italy, where Alan's refugee friends took over, and in France, where those he admired from afar assumed power, neither Alan nor Berle saw the sort of order emerge in the postwar world that they had yearned for. Each in his own way worked for alternatives to the harsh Communist regimes that fell into place in eastern and central Europe after V-E Day. And while they had differing views on the nature of those alternatives, powers far greater than those at the command of either were to determine the sweep of events.

One of Alan's old OWI associates, David Karr, whom I interviewed two years ago, provided another insight stemming from those years: Alan's achievements at that time gave him a sense of his own potential, being able to participate in the decision-making process when he was so young. He had an additional advantage in having been there at the beginning, when Washington was still a tiny town: the leading grocery story, McGruder's, would close in April and move to Newport for the summer when Congress went home. Under his eyes, that town became the capital of the free world. "We had participated in decisions involving millions of dollars and lives," David Karr concluded. "Thus Alan didn't flinch from moving into the state controllership in California. We had coped with problems all over the earth. We were not in awe of the decision-makers or big names. Having known Eleanor Roosevelt, we had none of the hang-ups of working with women in high places. We had seen all the mighty of the world, who had fallen, come to us, as refugees, leaving behind their families, their palaces, their country places, their governments, and their power structures."

The time was at last approaching when Alan's draft number would be reached. Though Elmer Davis urged him to request deferment, Alan declined. Mother and Father were distressed, feeling that he was taking unnecessary risks. "We were very glad indeed to receive your letter," Father wrote, "but, naturally, do not share your enthusiasm about having a soldier in the family." Their concern was aggravated when Alan revealed that he had decided to enlist as a private, rather than to seek officer status. Father urged him to reconsider. Alan held firm.

CHAPTER

★ ★ ★ ★ ★ ★ ★ ★ ★ ★ ★ ★ ★ ★ ★ ★ ★ ★ ★

War, Peace, and the World Federalists

★ ★ ★ ★ ★ ★ ★ ★ ★ ★ ★ ★ ★ ★ ★ ★ ★ ★ ★

> Power gave him no pleasure; he
> had no distorted psychology to
> feed. The result was a relaxed
> man.
>
> —from Louis Fischer's
> biography of Ghandi

In 1944 Alan refused a government deferment and enlisted in the army. He took infantry and basic training at Camp Croft, South Carolina, and got into beautiful shape. Though at twenty-nine he was among the elders, he could run faster than anyone there.

He was astounded that although the men were headed straight for active combat and were being taught facts crucial for their survival — how to read a compass at night, how to find their way, how to handle all sorts of weapons — sitting in the hot sun of South Carolina, a lot of them would immediately fall asleep rather than listen.

Alan wrote a column for the camp newspaper, "On the Ground," and gave lectures during the orientation period. Most of the men in the group were assigned to an infantry battalion and were sent directly overseas, but Alan was pulled out of the group for reassignment.

While waiting for the new assignment, Alan was a lifeguard at the Women's Army Corps swimming pool. Nobody ever asked if he could swim (he can) — he was just told to lifeguard!

There was a lot of KP. He peeled potatoes for hundreds of people. And he flew over the camp in a glider — an exciting, but dangerous experience.

He was finally transferred to the 23d Infantry Division in Fort Leonard Wood in the Ozarks. Geneva had joined him at Camp Croft, and they drove to Missouri together. They lived for about six weeks in a town beside the camp, sharing a little two-bedroom house with about sixteen other people. The bathtub was rented to someone who slept in it. One refrigerator and one stove were used by all the families. Alan and Geneva shared a cot on an open screened porch.

Once when they were driving their aging car around the Ozark hills, Geneva asked Alan what he would like to be doing in twenty years. He replied he'd like to be governor of California, which was about as presumptuous as a young private with no political roots could get! Yet only fourteen years later he was in the controller's office, right across the hall from the governor's office. Meanwhile, though, Alan had become much more interested in the Senate and the opportunity it held to deal with national and worldwide issues, like justice, equal opportunity, taxes, war, and peace.

At last Alan's permanent assignment came: He was transferred out of infantry and into the Army Service Forces to work with *Army Talk* and give lectures at camps around the country on why we were fighting the Axis. It was basically similar to his work at OWI. A famous group worked at *Army Talk,* Herb Block among them. Ted Waller from Menlo School also showed up, after having been a paratrooper. They have stayed in touch all their lives.

Although only earning a private's pay of $21 a month, Alan and Geneva lived in an apartment that was a bit better than ever before. Geneva had a well-paid job helping Orson Welles write a column for the *New York Post.*

Concerned that the Senate might again keep us out of whatever international body was created after the war, Alan started to write a book, *The Killing of the Peace.* Roosevelt and Churchill were beginning to plan the United Nations, and Alan hoped the story of the Senate's great struggle over the League of Nations after World War I would undermine the tactics and strategies of isolationists trying to keep the United States out of World War II's peace-keeping organization. He wrote wherever and whenever possible. A few pages were actually written late at night inside the Pentagon — under the photo of Henry L. Stimson, secretary of war, whose role in the League struggle was questioned in the book. Alan suppressed vague and uneasy concerns that his book could be grounds for a court-martial.

After about one-tenth of the writing was complete, Alan sold it to Viking, received an advance, and was able to hire a research assistant. The book was written swiftly, but Viking had set a condition: the book had to come out before the U.N. Charter was agreed upon and came to the Senate. Less than four months later, the book was still unfinished, and about twenty-four hours remained before the deadline. The manuscript was due the next morning. Alan came home from work at 5:30 and stayed up all night, writing away like mad. Much to his astonishment, what he had written that night reads just as smoothly as the earlier parts, which had been tediously rewritten — partly because he was in the swing and the style had already been established. He went to the YMCA for physical exercise in the morning and delivered the manuscript on his way to work.

The *New York Times* rated *The Killing of the Peace* as one of the ten best books of 1945, saying it was written with "white heat in it and a sure, strong purpose." Viking reissued it as a paperback in the 1960s. Alan could little have dreamed that in 1979 he would hand the book to the president at a White House breakfast. President Carter, just returned from a summit meeting in Russia, said, "It will be my most important text in the coming struggle over SALT."

The war ended with Alan still in his original army job, though he had gone through the ranks: private, private first class, corporal, and buck sergeant.

In the aftermath of the war, there was a need for an organization to promote good relations, trade, and cultural exchanges with Italy. Spearheading the idea primarily were Italian-Americans and people in the government's foreign-economic administration. Learning of Alan's part in the exemption of Italian-Americans from "enemy alien" status, they asked him to form this organization and to head it. He was released from the army on September 7, 1945.

Between his discharge and this new job, Geneva and Alan spent one wonderful week at Provincetown up on Cape Cod. Then they drove back to Washington, to establish the Council for American-Italian Affairs. Among those on the board of directors was Allen Dulles, a leading figure in World War II intelligence work who was soon to be head of the CIA.

After about a year, when the task of getting new relations between the United States and Italy off to a good start seemed to have been largely accomplished, Alan resigned and returned west. He hoped eventually to get into politics, but first he wanted to make some money and to reestablish himself in California.

But before Alan left the East, *The Killing of the Peace* had led him into another experience which was to have far-reaching consequences.

In October 1945 Alan and Geneva drove up to New Hampshire through the beautiful clear golds and reds of New England's fall to attend what later became celebrated as "the Dublin Conference." Just out of the army, Alan was in a curious and skeptical mood about the meeting. Coming soon after the peace that followed Hiroshima and Nagasaki, its extraordinary purpose was to consider the implications of war and peace in the wake of the nuclear bomb and whether, in this unprecedented circumstance, the new United Nations would be adequate to the challenge.

The invitations had been issued by former Supreme Court Justice Owen D. Roberts, head of the Pearl Harbor inquiry; former Governor Robert Bass of New Hampshire; Thomas H. Mahony, prominent lay Catholic leader and Boston attorney; and the session's remarkable instigator, Grenville Clark. Probably because his book, *The Killing of the Peace,* had come to Clark's attention, Alan was invited.

Who was Clark? Heir to a banking and railroad fortune, partner of Elihu Root, Jr., in an international Wall Street law firm, member of Harvard's seven-man governing board, the Harvard Corporation, and advisor to four presidents on matters of foreign policy and national defense—he was now a man in his sixties, of great vigor and style, tall, strong framed, with a powerful, craggy face. With his kind, shrewd eyes and jutting jaw, he looked to Alan the soul of bulldog determination.

Alan at first felt a bit skeptical about him precisely because of Clark's imposing background: the older man's Wall Street connection (Alan, though far from suspicious by nature, was still a young westerner) and Clark's close association with Henry L. Stimson and old Elihu Root. They were hardly the heroes of Alan's book, though he generally admired Stimson. But at Dublin Alan soon began to feel that Clark was absolutely straightforward and certainly one of the most compelling, creative thinkers he had ever met. However, vague doubts lingered.

Invited to the conference were forty-eight people, including Beardsley Ruml, author of the pay-as-you-go plan of federal taxation (1943) and soon-to-be chairman of the Federal Reserve Bank of New York;

Clarence Streit, author of *Union Now*; Thomas K. Finletter, later secretary of the air force; Robert D. Smythe, physicist, one of the creators of the bomb; Louis Fischer and Edgar Ansel Mowrer, writers; New Hampshire's Republican Senator Styles Bridges; and noted editors, educators, businessmen, and lawyers.

As Norman Cousins later described it at a New York meeting, Clark "sprinkled in with the salt a little bit of the pepper of youth, the younger people felt to be among the future leaders of the country." Among these were Cord Meyer, Jr., a writer and future top CIA official; Charles Bolte, head of the American Veterans Committee; Marshall Field, Jr.; and Kingman Brewster, a youthful lieutenant in uniform, later president of Yale and U.S. ambassador to the Court of St. James. Norman Cousins persists in the belief that another slim, uniformed lieutenant, John F. Kennedy, still on active duty, came for a few hours one afternoon. Cousins was of course a rather young man himself but already editor of the *Saturday Review*. "Of those people Clark selected as future leaders," Cousins said in 1968, "Alan Cranston is now the one in a position to perhaps provide the greatest leadership—in the Senate."

The conference was held in Dublin, near Clark's old red brick farmhouse in the New Hampshire hills, deliberately away from a big city. The participants would stay together, think together, live together a whole week, isolated; it was not easy to go off for a day or an evening and then come back. If you went to the trouble of getting there, you stayed.

Grenville Clark made the opening presentation. He expressed the fear that the United States and Soviet Russia would not retain their wartime alliance and would engage in a struggle for power, including a nuclear arms race. He strongly felt a holocaust could be prevented only through organizing a world government with "limited but adequate" powers.

"Listening to Grenny Clark that day in Dublin was an unforgettable experience," Cousins wrote. "When he spoke about the need for world law, he was not merely trying to prevent world war; he was speaking to a condition necessary for human progress."*

*Unless otherwise noted, quotations in this chapter are from *Memoirs of a Man*, a book composed of a number of tributes to Grenville Clark, including Alan's, collected by his daughter Mary Clark Dimond. The book was edited by Norman Cousins and J. Garry Clifford and published by W. W. Norton and Co., Inc., in 1975.

Clark's leadership resulted in a document which became the basis for the world law movement in the United States and elsewhere. He was also the inspiration for young men like Cord Meyer, Jr., Kingman Brewster, and Alan to "labor diligently in the world law movement."

A heated debate sprang up between those who wanted to extend the rule of law only in the Atlantic world, through a federal union of the western democracies, and those, led by Clark, who wanted to strive for world law. "I cannot stand discrimination. I have always fought against it in this country," Clark exclaimed. "I cannot promote it internationally. Our organization must be universal."

At the climax of the Dublin debate Alan quoted George Washington, "It is too probable that no plan we propose will be adopted. Perhaps another dreadful conflict is to be sustained. But if, to please the people, we offer that which we ourselves disapprove, how can we afterward defend our work? Let us raise a standard to which the wise and honest can repair. The event is in the hand of God."*

"When you quoted Washington at that point, for that purpose," Clark told Alan afterward, "you caught my fancy." Clark had Alan appointed chairman of the Dublin Conference Committee to further the views agreed upon there and to work closely with him toward the goal of limited, well-defined, enforceable world laws to insure disarmament, under adequate safeguards, and maintain peace.

As they worked together, Alan's original doubts about Clark were soon replaced by appreciation and admiration, and then by affection. Alan felt closer to him than he had any older man except Father. He and Geneva became frequent weekend visitors at Grenny and Fanny's rambling farmhouse. They stayed in the simple guest house, talked by comfortable fires, walked in Fanny's garden, and enjoyed the view of looming Mount Monadnock to the south. The house on its wooded slopes with its white trim, fieldstone wall, high chimneys, many fireplaces, book-lined rooms, and Audubon prints, had been in the family a hundred and fifty years and was the picture of traditional stability.

Alan was impressed not only with Clark's ideas, but also his actions. He had had an important hand in preparing America for World War I by persuading Theodore Roosevelt, a close friend, to accept the

---

*Spoken at a turning point in the Constitutional Convention, when Washington's opponents thought the creation of a more perfect union, a federal union, an impractical dream.

Plattsburg Camp Idea — to have volunteers train to become officers in their spare time. When war came, sixty thousand were ready.

To prepare for World War II, Clark was primarily responsible for writing the draft law — the Selective Service Act — and helping to ram it through Congress. He was responsible for Franklin Roosevelt's appointment of Henry L. Stimson and Frank Knox, Republicans, as secretaries of war and of the navy, respectively, thus gaining bipartisan support for the war effort.

Clark's policy was always to decline appointments. With some difficulty, Stimson had persuaded Clark to become his aide in the War Department. On the day of the Normandy landing, he walked into Stimson's office and handed in his resignation. "We've won," he said. "My job's over. I've helped us get ready for two wars, but we can't have a third. Now I'm going to devote the rest of my life to peace."

"Go home and prevent World War III!" the secretary of war told him.

Now, in his efforts for peace, Clark enlisted the help of private citizens like Alan in furthering the cause of world law. In line with his belief that government officials were too enmeshed in present problems to plan for the future with vision, he said, "The strength of a nation rests on the vigor and integrity of its individual citizens." Alan soon realized that as chairman of the Dublin Conference Committee, his major task was to carry Clark's ideas about world law to influential people all around the world.

Thus, he flew off to London for the first session of the United Nations, to converse with Paul Henri Spaak, a young Andrei Gromyko, and other world leaders. Before going, Alan conferred with President Harry S. Truman. Typically, thoughtfully, and at his own expense, Clark sent Geneva to London too.

At Lake Success, Alan explored the Dublin plan with the American delegation to the United Nations Assembly. In his spare time there, he also teamed up with a group of prominent Californians, including San Francisco's Mayor Roger Lapham and California's former Attorney General Robert Kenny to try to bring the U.N. to San Francisco — to the Presidio. However, John D. Rockefeller, Jr., offered free land in New York and a generous loan, an offer the U.N. could not refuse.

Meanwhile, Alan helped write three speeches on world law that were delivered to the Assembly with great fire and eloquence by

General Carlos P. Romulo, one of the founders of the Philippine Republic and its ambassador to the U.N.

Romulo expressed this theme:

> We of the small nations should be willing to give up the fiction of equality in a U.N. that has no teeth for a vote equal to the role of each of our nations in the world in a U.N. with the power to keep the peace.
> Unless we empower it with the rule of law, the U.N. will become a hollow shell, and the peace of the world an empty dream.

To convey Clark's views to Asia, Alan flew to New Delhi and visited Nehru and other Indian leaders. He went on to Tokyo to talk with the Japanese Diet. When he returned to America, Alan chaired a Clark-inspired conference in Princeton, similar to the one in Dublin. Here Albert Einstein was a participant. Alan noticed the great theoretical physicist was raising his hand to vote aye, and then again to vote no, on every issue.

"Why?" Alan asked him during a break.

"The people on both sides are so nice," he explained, smiling apologetically, "I can't vote against any of them!"

Alan's work for the world law movement was reinforced by Clark's masterwork, *World Peace Through World Law,* written with Louis Sohn, which addressed itself to the practical problems involved in transforming the United Nations into an instrument of enforceable limited world law. In it Clark presented a world constitution built upon the foundation of the U.N. Charter. This constitution was designed to protect the peoples of the world from war by limiting the powers of governments, just as the U.S. Constitution limits the powers of government in order to protect American citizens from abuses that could lead to tyranny. The book won the American Bar Association's Gold Medal in 1959 for a major contribution to world literature on the subject of law and peace. Translated into twelve languages, including Russian and Chinese, this blueprint for a world without war was distributed to leaders around the world by Clark's emissaries.

Alan was delighted to discover that this lofty and serious thinker possessed delightful humor. After Pope John XXIII issued his *Pacem in Terris* Encyclical, a woman friend remarked to Clark at a dinner party that she suspected he had influenced Pope John's thinking. He responded with a twinkle, "He was a pope and I am a Unitarian, but we were thick as thieves."

"Clark was a man who worked behind the scenes and achieved remarkable things," Alan said recently. "He knew how to use the levers of power, even spiritual power, to effect his aims. One reason I thought we might achieve world law was that Clark was devoting his energies to it. I observed his achievements at first hand, and I knew his long record of incredible accomplishments despite impossible obstacles."

Sometimes when Alan has had his own moments of doubt about our ability to surmount the vast, intricate problems of our time, he has renewed his strength by reflecting on the standards set by Clark and on his supreme ability to achieve.

Because he had his own responsibilities and his own ideas, Alan eventually began with some difficulty to extricate himself from Clark's fascinating but powerful influence. He wanted to get into public service, but first he would have to create his financial base.

*   *   *

In early 1947, Alan returned with Geneva to Los Altos, California to go into the real estate business with Father and eventually into politics. Their son Robin was born that November.

Alan focused on low-cost housing (one pioneering project was integrated), and the staid family business, static for years, became a swirl of furious activity and social purpose, somewhat to the discomfiture of Father and his secretary of thirty years. Alan provided housing for his family by building a home on a country lane in Los Altos, using his "own bare hands" and the help of his boyhood friend, Ralph Raymond, and of Mel Hawley, soon-to-be county sheriff.

The following year Alan was urged to run for Congress, but he resisted, feeling he couldn't win in that district. He had not established himself well enough in California. In his own words, "I always felt, and learned more and more as I watched others, that timing is the key element in politics. You've got to know when to run, and when not to run. It was wise not to run in 1948, because I would have been defeated, and off to a poor start."

The United World Federalists, an organization dedicated to world law, was founded in 1947.* Headed by Cord Meyer, Jr., its board included leaders as disparate as Clark, Einstein, Cousins, William O. Douglas, Douglas Fairbanks, Jr., Raymond Gram Swing, and W. T. Holliday, president of Standard Oil of Ohio, all joining together for the dynamic purpose of heading off an atomic arms race. Grenville Clark was its moving spirit and elder statesman.

Alan was soon drawn into its activities: speaking, forming UWF chapters in Los Altos, Palo Alto, and elsewhere, and heading a mushrooming California branch. Community leaders flocked to his call.

Fascinated with the political possibilities of the movement, he worked to put through the state legislature a resolution calling for a national convention to amend the U.S. Constitution. In effect the amendment would authorize the United States to enter into a world body capable of enacting, interpreting, and enforcing world law adequate to preserve the peace. "My first lobbying effort at the state level—fascinating!" he recalls. "I did it mainly by getting to know the two powers-that-be and working with the sort of people you'd think wouldn't be interested."

These two were Tommy Maloney, speaker of the Assembly, or majority leader (he later lost his Assembly seat to future Congressman Phil Burton), and Harold B. ("Butch") Powers, president pro tem of the Senate, later lieutenant governor. Both were Republicans. "To persuade Powers to the wisdom of our efforts," Alan recalls, "Geneva and Rob, then an infant, and I drove all the way up to Eagleville, way up in northern California, and spent a couple of hours talking to him at his ranch house. He was so impressed by my coming all that way that he became a staunch ally, as did Maloney."

At first the resolution breezed through the Assembly with an aura of Mother's Day about it. Then right-wing opposition arose in the person of superpatriot Myron P. Fagin, head of the Cinema Education Guild in Los Angeles, an associate of the notorious racist and rabble-rouser, Gerald L. K. Smith. Fagin stumped the state claiming that the World Federalists were trying to give away America, and that Milton Mayer, "a prominent leader of the United World Federalists," had cried out at a public meeting, "Let's haul down the American flag, stamp on it, and spit on it!"

---

*The name of the United World Federalists resulted from the merger of several groups and demonstrated its members' symbolic willingness to submerge their differences. Later it was renamed World Federalists U.S.A.

Mayer was not even a member of the United World Federalists, much less a leader. A professor at the University of Chicago when Robert Maynard Hutchins was its president, Mayer was vaguely opposed to the movement for being too visionary. At a public meeting, he had been asked to comment on the proposed, highly theoretical and sweeping World Constitution drafted by Hutchins, Stringfellow Barr, the president of St. John's College, and other leading intellectuals. Professor Mayer struck a comic pose and exclaimed, "What? Haul down the American flag, stamp on it, and spit on it?"

This ironic query was far harder to lay to rest than a factual statement could have been.

Despite the battles caused by the now-famous quotation — battles Alan's respectable followers and legislative adherents found somewhat horrendous — Alan enjoyed his new political experience. He had been through the hellfire and brimstone at OWI, and he considered Fagin ridiculous. Alan mobilized support for the world law resolution in some decidedly unexpected quarters.

He enlisted the support of Paul Smith, the editor of the *San Francisco Chronicle*, and persuaded him to urge Artie Samish to help. Samish was an all-powerful lobbyist in Sacramento, a notorious figure in 1948. Upon an earlier occasion, before the war, when Alan was working with Common Council, he sat beside Samish on a plane flying from Burbank to Sacramento. Alan appealed to him to help kill legislation unfair to minorities. The bill was killed.

Smith phoned Samish, "Artie, will you help us get a world government resolution through the legislature?"

"What's world government?" asked Samish.

But he agreed to help. And the World Federalists won.

Describing his experiences with the world law resolution in the California legislature, Alan wrote to Clark: "Some of the legislative leaders have become firm and understanding federalists. Most of them had not previously encountered the idea.

"Never, to my knowledge, has such a perfect device been found for building nationwide strength behind an organized effort for organized peace."

UWF's membership rolls in California increased by the thousands. An attractive young moderate Republican assemblyman, Robert Kirkwood, became a member as did a popular motion picture actor, Ronald Reagan.

A decade later, Kirkwood was Alan's opponent in the race for state controller. His UWF membership, and Reagan's, helped keep UWF from ever becoming an issue in Alan's campaigns for public office.

In early 1949, Alan was asked to succeed Cord Meyer, Jr., as national president of UWF. If he accepted, he would have to move to New York. It was one of the toughest decisions Alan ever faced.

CHAPTER 10

★★★★★★★★★★★★★★★★★★★★
The Pendulum Swings: New York-California
★★★★★★★★★★★★★★★★★★★★

Alan had just begun to make some money but hadn't been able to store away enough to turn to world government with a blithe spirit. Also he was just beginning to make some headway in politics. Finally, he felt California was naturally the perfect place to live and raise a family. In addition, Father, Mother, and I plus many lifelong friends lived nearby.

On the other hand, world government as a goal, and UWF as an instrument seemed important enough to consider changing his plans for a while. Geneva felt the same way. It might be beneficial personally, if all went well; but if UWF's financial troubles increased, or if the tide turned against world government, or if any one of a long and dreary list of possibilities occurred, it could turn out to be something of a personal calamity. Upshur Evans, a UWF leader who was urging Alan to accept, put it candidly, "Only an ass would take the job, and he must face the fact that it could ruin his career."

About the same time, Father advised Alan on the decision: "The situation is not too promising. However, you have ability, special skill in this kind of work, enormous energy, and a wife who will be of assistance." He went on to urge Alan not to follow any impulse to forego a salary but to insist on being paid at least as much as his predecessor.

Despite Father's worries, after several telephone discussions with Grenville Clark, Alan decided to seek the presidency of UWF and was

87

unanimously elected. By prearrangement, he cabled Father and Mother in Florence, "ALOFT" (family cablese for "arrived safely"). Father replied, "Congratulations! We are so glad for you, although it means having you move away."

Assuming the presidency of UWF, Alan quit the family business, which was then sold to Father's longtime friend, Edward Ames, and in turn to James Hawley. Alan, Geneva, and Robin moved to New York, to an apartment in Gramercy Park. By strange coincidence, in that city of almost eight million people, Lee Falk decided on the same day to move into an apartment in the same building. He and Alan bumped into each other in the foyer.

For the next three years Alan collaborated with Clark, traveling about the country and abroad, speaking, lobbying, and working with the State Department, the U.N. delegation then headed by Warren Austin, and on Capitol Hill.

"California's world law resolution became the pattern for a nation-wide effort," Alan recalls. "More than twenty states passed the resolution before its high watermark was reached and right-wing opposition rose to crush it." Alan spoke in almost every state, addressing committees in the Virginia legislature among others and developed his ability for public speaking.

His old friend Ted Waller, from Menlo School and army days, was UWF's Washington lobbyist. They put together a world law resolution sponsored by the very conservative Republican Congressman Walter Judd of Minnesota, and a moderate southern Democrat, Brooks Hays of Arkansas, which won the support of 112 members of the House and about 30 senators. However, it was never brought to a vote.

"That was the first time I ever saw Richard Nixon," Alan recalls.

We heard he might be willing to go along in Congress, but we could never catch up to him. We were running out of time. He was important, a conservative figure.

One day I saw him at a hearing of the House Un-American Activities Committee. I sent a note up to him. My card said, "Alan Cranston, President of the United World Federalists. May I see you for a moment?" He picked up this note, looked at it, making a very ugly face, crumpled it up, and threw it away.

We had already been upset with Nixon over the rough campaign to defeat Jerry Voorhis, a great man who had been a teacher of Geneva's at Pomona. I had worked with Jerry while he was in the House on the world law resolution and on Italian-American legislation, where he was very helpful. So we didn't start with the warmest of feelings toward Nixon when he arrived in Congress.

Then in 1950 Nixon took on Helen Douglas, another very good friend of mine. Before she first ran for office, she consulted me on the idea of running for the House. We had a long visit in the Hay Adams Hotel in Washington, while I was in the army. I urged her to run and gave her some thoughts on doing so. She served two terms in the House. Then Nixon beat her [when they ran for Downey's seat], and he moved into the Senate seat I have now. The same seat!

In 1952 at the end of three terms, Alan quit the presidency of UWF to be succeeded by Norman Cousins. During the last year, Alan had been based in California but traveled constantly. Their second son, Kim, was born there in 1951, so both children are native great-grand-sons of the Golden State.

Before leaving UWF, Alan had a long discussion with Ted Waller about what they were going to do with their lives. Ted had done a great job of lobbying. Both men were thinking about running for the Senate. Waller suggested they consider each going to a small state like Nevada or Montana, where they might succeed more swiftly. But Alan was determined to go back to California, where his roots and his family were and where he could also gain the additional strength that coming from one of the largest states could give him in the Senate.

"I'm glad I felt that way then," he recently observed. "California is home. The smaller states aren't directly affected by as many issues, and their constituencies are less diverse. Just about every issue that exists in the country exists in California, with Californians on both sides of every one of those issues. A few years ago we figured out that coal was the only issue that didn't have a California impact. Now, with the energy crisis, there are proposals to burn coal in California — so nothing is left out! But I manage to find a way to work on the issues that I consider most important."

Alan and Waller also considered becoming partners in a lobbying operation for good causes — and for enough business interests so they could afford to represent the good causes. They were convinced that from outside they could work miracles together inside Congress and the Executive Branch. But Alan decided he would rather try to be in the Senate with a vote than outside lobbying. Ted Waller went his own way to achieve success in the book-publishing world and today is executive vice president of the Grolier Society in New York.

Alan found a prime candidate to succeed Ted as Washington representative in the person of an aspiring radio news reporter covering the capitol. He offered him the job for $10,000 a year. The young reporter thought it over, and then declined. His name was Walter Cronkite.

Though no longer UWF president, Alan maintained a close relationship with Clark through letters, notes, and interminable phone calls. Sadly, there were fewer of these after Alan was elected to state office. In 1968 when Alan was elected to the Senate, he hung a framed photograph of Grenville Clark on the wall by his desk beside his pictures of Father and Mother. Even now, years after Clark's death, Alan often pauses in the midst of a complicated situation to ask, "What would Grenny do? How would he approach this?"

On May 22, 1975, following the Mayaguez incident and the U.S. bombing of Cambodia, Alan and a bipartisan group of senators organized a "great debate" on U.S. foreign and defense policies. Alan closed his speech with a sentence Grenville Clark would thoroughly approve: "Our long-range security lies in the reduction of world tensions, the de-escalation and reversal of the arms race and, ultimately, the establishment throughout the world of order and justice under law."

*   *   *

When Alan returned to California, he was thirty-seven. The movement for world peace and justice had absorbed seven years of his life. Adding three more years given to OWI and the army, a whole decade had been consumed by matters of war and peace.

He had been an interventionist, an advocate, and an enlisted man. He had suffered deeply over war's horrors and tragedies. To him war was the most destructive aspect of the human experience.

At last he was sure of his own goal: the Senate. That was where decisions were made and work was done, for good or ill, that affected the whole country, even the world. He began to dare to hope such a career could be achieved. As with Father, financial necessity had often determined his course. Depression and war had slowed him. But he was beginning to make money, and Father was able to give him a bit of help. Now he was impatient—champing at the bit—to throw himself into politics.

The state Democratic party was a shambles in 1952. In the June primary, conservative Republican Senator William F. Knowland had won both the Republican and Democratic party nominations. Cross-filing had left the Democrats with no senatorial candidate at all. But

Adlai E. Stevenson was campaigning for the presidency, and his eloquence and excitement offered hope of a party revival. Alan threw himself full tilt into the campaign.

He greatly admired Stevenson's intelligence and idealism and was deeply impressed with the Illinois governor's record. They had formed a slight friendship during Alan's years in OWI, when they had served together on an interagency committee.

Eventually the County Central Committee put Alan in charge of organizing precinct work in Santa Clara. Apparently, a precinct-by-precinct structure had never before been put together in the county. With friends, he formed a Stevenson-Sparkman Club in Los Altos, the first Democratic club in the history of the town. Other clubs sprang up in the county, mostly instigated by Alan. Soon he put together the Santa Clara County Council of clubs and was elected its president.

Tired of war and the turmoil of postwar problems, the country opted for likable Ike, a national hero, in November. But the following year, the clubs Alan helped form became part of the foundation for the Democratic club movement in California with all that foreshadowed for him and the state.

Meanwhile he worked with Father in the real estate business, concentrating on management of the family properties in Los Altos, Palo Alto, and San Bruno. After Father's death in 1953, Villa Warec was sold, but on the condition that the buyer would develop the land creatively, preserving the trees and the wild atmosphere along the creek.

When the town of Los Altos was threatened by the advent of nearby shopping centers, Alan led a successful effort to bring in sewers, develop a parking plaza, and convert the town itself into a shopping center. It was a brilliant proposal — but it involved a number of conflicting interests. "That was a terrible, painstaking job," Alan recalls. "It was like my lobbying at the U.N. or the state legislature or Congress — getting every property owner, absentee or present, to go along. We needed a two-thirds majority."

The plan was adopted, supported by bond issues. Alan had envisioned what creating and preserving a lovely downtown area where people could park to shop would mean to the community as a whole. Today Los Altos is one of the few communities in California whose business center is markedly more successful than it was before the competition of big shopping centers came along.

Alan's ability to attend to small as well as large matters was perhaps best summed up by former Santa Clara County newspaper publisher Joe Houghteling, who is known for his dry and acerbic wit. He introduced Alan at a political meeting in the 1950s as "a man who attends to everything — from Los Altos sewers to world government!"

★ ★ ★ ★ ★ ★ ★ ★ ★ ★ ★ ★ ★ ★ ★

CHAPTER 11

The Cutting Edge in California Politics: The CDC

★ ★ ★ ★ ★ ★ ★ ★ ★ ★ ★ ★ ★ ★ ★

Asilomar, Pacific Grove, California, January 1953. There by the sea, in a fog-shrouded cypress forest on the Monterey Peninsula, they gathered in the rambling wooden buildings of the old conference center to survey the wreckage of the party in the wake of the election — the tough, entrenched old pros, the political scientists, and a surprising number of newcomers — angry, idealistic volunteers from the Stevenson-Sparkman clubs.

"What's Wrong — and What's Right — with the Democratic Party in California?" was the theme of the conference called by state Senator George Miller, Jr., the party chairman.

"One of the reasons for Asilomar," Alan recalls "was that almost nothing we could do would make things worse. And anything we did might cause things to get a little better — which they did!" It was a chance for him to put long-held beliefs into practice.

What had caused the Democrats' nationwide downfall, the delegates at Asilomar demanded. Why had the party suffered defeat after defeat in California? Why had Republican Senator Knowland — who had filed for both party nominations — proceeded to win both? This had occurred under a reform device called cross-filing, which allowed candidates to file for and win the nominations of both parties. The consensus of the conference was that, as Alan stated in a speech, "Our problems are primarily due to lack of Democratic discipline and to absence of sound organizational structure."

93

At Asilomar Alan first emerged as a leader in the party by coming up with some new suggestions about clubs and councils and primary endorsements. Delegates from clubs and official party organs in northern California met in Stockton in May 1953 to plan machinery to make local primary endorsements in the north.

"The delegates at Stockton, however," wrote Francis Carney,* "had little opportunity to do much planning, as Cranston met them with a blueprint of his own for a coordinated organization. Cranston's proposal met little opposition and was unanimously approved by the delegates."

They also enthusiastically adopted a resolution calling for extension of the principle to the whole state through the creation of a California Democratic Council (CDC). On November 29 over five hundred delegates from the various clubs in the state met at the old California Hotel in Fresno to organize a California Democratic Council. Simultaneously, a rival organization had been established, at least on paper. Called "Dime-A-Day for Democracy" and headed by Elizabeth Snyder and Del Smith of Los Angeles, it too was inviting delegates to join up.

Alan and Miller persuaded Snyder and Smith to bring Dime-A-Day to Fresno and participate in the convention. CDC delegates buzzed with alarm, but Alan was unperturbed. "Controversy makes a good convention," he said.

In an atmosphere hushed and tense with excitement, Alan came onto the stage in the crowded, smoke-filled ballroom of the old hotel. Laying his familiar yellow legal pad with his scrawled hand-printed speech before him, his dark eyes glancing about the crowd, he leaned forward, his long slender fingers on the lectern, smiled, and in an easy but strong voice that held an undercurrent of excitement spoke to the founding convention:

> We are gathered here to do all within our power to end the stranglehold Republicans have held for too long upon politics in California.
> We failed to carry California for Stevenson last fall.
> We have had only one Democratic governor in the twentieth century. The state legislature for longer than anyone can remember has been controlled by the Republicans—and/or Artie Samish. Today we have two Republican senators.
> There is only one Democrat in partisan statewide office—Attorney General

---

*All quotations from Carney come from *The Rise of the Democratic Clubs in California,* Case Studies in Practical Politics, by Francis Carney, Holt, Rinehart and Winston, 1958.

Edmund G. ["Pat"] Brown. Altogether, there are 162 elective, partisan offices. Republicans hold 111. In nonpartisan office we find an even more overwhelming majority of Republicans — all of this is in a state in which there are almost a *million* more registered Democrats than registered Republicans — approximately three million to two million.

A primary objective of those who have sought to blueprint the CDC has been a structure that would give all Democrats who wish it a full and fair voice in party affairs — and *thus in the affairs of their government.*

His point was not lost on delegates wavering between a broad mass-membership CDC and the more professional and elitist Dime-A-Day. Slowing his voice to emphasize his words, he continued:

The CDC would give the party an effective arm in the primaries. It should end the Republican habit of winning Democratic primaries.

Republican candidates, he charged, were often selected by elite party leaders in collusion with men with special interests. Alan cited the "Nixon fund" that had launched Nixon on his career.* The primary purpose of the CDC, he said, "would be to conduct a pre-primary convention every two years to endorse the best possible Democratic candidates for partisan office — and to build party unity behind them.

Here in California the opposition is threatened from within by the inevitable coming struggle for power between two incredibly ambitious men — Nixon and Knowland. . . .

Our country is challenged . . . to seize the initiative from communism by developing policies capable of meeting human needs and aspirations — physical and spiritual — by democratic methods . . . to resist those who would embrace totalitarianism in the name of combating it and . . . to achieve secure and lasting peace.

After full debate but no real disagreement over CDC's real purposes, the delegates enthusiastically adopted a constitution and elected officers. Alan was unanimously elected president (and was reelected each year until he resigned in December 1957). Though Alan's personality was low-keyed and relaxed, he had become a surprisingly effective platform speaker, displaying a knack with words and exuding

---

*In 1953, during the period of Earl Warren's leadership, the Republicans developed a volunteer organization, the California Republican Assembly, which made preprimary endorsements. Republican funds and energy were concentrated on one carefully picked candidate. Democratic resources were dissipated among many contenders.

assurance and optimism. While lacking glamorous triumphs in elections or party politics, he had a surprising hold on the affection and loyalty of the men and women in the party ranks.

Joseph Wyatt, Jr., a Pasadena attorney and a leader in the Young Democrats—one of the founders of Dime-A-Day—was elected secretary. He also became CDC's parliamentarian. A curly-haired, blue-eyed, popular man of serious purpose but immense drollery and wit, he later succeeded Alan as CDC president.

On the first weekend in February 1954, over a thousand delegates met in Fresno to make the first statewide preprimary endorsements of the California Democratic Party. They greeted with a roar Alan's announcement: "We are here to nominate a Democratic candidate for United States Senator and a slate of delegates for the administration of this state!"

Great rows broke out over who would be nominated for what offices. Presiding over the convention with a strong gavel, Alan reveled in the free-for-all of the idealistic, dynamic, brawling CDC. "A chancy forum," a *Los Angeles Times* reporter described it.

Tension concentrated on the endorsement of candidates for the United States Senate. Two years earlier, Republican Thomas Kuchel had been appointed to the Senate when Nixon resigned to become vice-president. Since Kuchel had not been elected to the seat, Democratic hopes ran high.

People had urged Alan to run for statewide office that year. But he felt that he could be more valuable as an organizer than as a candidate. Again it was a question of timing.

Some people have wondered why Alan spent six years lost in the California political wilderness. Actually trying to forge a revitalized state Democratic party was a highly challenging, difficult task, and the stakes were very, very high. It required prodigiously hard work and concentration on Alan's part—analyzing, thinking, talking, planning, attending meetings morning, noon, and night; traveling constantly; pulling people together to organize clubs and councils of clubs; arranging conventions—local and statewide—to endorse candidates, and then campaigning for them; precipitating all sorts of decisions, and then seeing that they were carried out.

Alan had approached General Omar Bradley and Robert M. Hutchins about running for the Senate, but they had declined. No outstanding Democratic candidate for the Senate had surfaced save

Congressman Sam Yorty of Los Angeles. Yorty had secured promises of support from big contributors, labor, and Dime-A-Day. Yet his candidacy failed to enthuse the delegates. George Miller refused to endorse him, and most of the delegates from the north — and many from the south — followed Miller's lead.

"Cranston on the platform, and therefore in the spotlight most of the time, was determinedly neutral in his open conduct," wrote Carney. "He assured Yorty that if he received the endorsement he would support him to the limit. He insisted that he was doing nothing to *stop* Yorty."

Why the opposition to Yorty? A small, dapper man with light brown eyes and hair and a smiling, open face, he had had, as Congressman and state Assemblyman, a "liberal" voting record. But he had devoted most of his preconvention speeches to plumping for a big air force, more wings, more bombers, more training centers. While a legitimate issue, it did not stir the enthusiasm of the club members, who were more concerned with McCarthyism, civil rights, and the need for federal aid to education. They wanted an identity separate from the Republicans, to justify their whole political movement ideologically.

Alarmed by the rising opposition, the Yorty camp began to describe CDC as "Red," "radical," and "left-wing." This only heightened distaste for Yorty.

On Saturday night, Professor Peter Odegard, a distinguished political scientist at the University of California at Berkeley, was nominated as an alternative to Yorty. He had come, not as a candidate, but as a delegate to speak on issues at convention caucuses. Resentment of Yorty and all the desire of the delegates to make a free, enthusiastic choice of a man — because he shared their outlook and would make an outstanding senator — suddenly focused on the university professor. Delegation after delegation voted in caucus for Odegard's endorsement.

The chance of a ferocious intraparty primary battle between Odegard and Yorty supporters confronted Alan and other CDC leaders. The odds would favor Yorty, not CDC and CDC-endorsed candidates.

Alan, in the chair, felt he must remain neutral. But he knew that a CDC endorsement of Odegard might produce a multiple candidacy in the Democratic primary — which might in turn lead to Kuchel's election. Early Sunday morning, the other leaders — Joe Wyatt, Helen Myers, Dick Richards, and lastly George Miller, after great pressure from labor leaders — gave their support to Yorty.

Meanwhile the troubled Odegard sought out Alan. They walked the streets for hours that night, discussing whether Odegard should run. He asked Alan to assume the financial chairmanship of his campaign. Alan, who had great respect for Odegard, replied that he could not commit himself until the CDC endorsing process had run its course, and even then he would have to talk it over with other CDC leaders.

Odegard tried to call Edward Heller, northern California's top Democratic money raiser, but he couldn't reach him. There was no way he could discuss his candidacy that night with officials of the University of California or with his family. At last, Odegard reluctantly withdrew. He penciled a note to Alan, which was handed to him as he mounted the platform to open the final session. Alan read the note to the convention. A roar welled up from the pro-Yorty delegates, mingled with groans and shouts of "No" from Odegard's supporters. The CDC then endorsed Yorty.

With no Democratic opposition, Yorty won the nomination in the June primary—as did all CDC's endorsed candidates. There was no major intraparty contest. For the first time in a generation of cross-filing, the Democrats had fielded a candidate for every statewide office in the General Election. The CDC justly claimed a major share of the credit. The 1954 convention was the making of the CDC. It had managed the tricky and complicated process of designating candidates who became the party's nominees. For the first time since the days of Hiram Johnson's reforms, Democratic voters shut out cross-filing Republicans in the primary.

CDC raised a generous amount of money and put out 1,300,000 slate campaign pieces for their candidates. However, all the Democratic state candidates except for Pat Brown, the incumbent attorney general, were defeated in the general election. Brown was reelected easily.

A few months after the election, at CDC's "housekeeping convention," Alan spoke to the delegates. He lamented the November losses but cited the significant gains. He concluded by placing the CDC in the context of history:

> Jefferson once said that men inevitably divide into two parties—one for those who fear and distrust the people and wish to lodge all powers in the hands of the "higher classes," the other for those who place confidence in all people, cherish them and consider them the wisest instrument of the public interest. . . .
>
> Let us measure and act on all proposals before this convention in terms of two

tests: 1. Will they lead toward victory in coming campaigns? 2. Will they preserve and perfect the democratic ways of the CDC and thus keep faith with Jefferson's dream?

Much depends upon the wisdom of the decisions you are about to make.

The annual CDC convention two years later, in February 1956, was a different matter. With a new consciousness of power and a vastly enlarged membership, the delegates arrived in Fresno prepared to endorse only the candidate of their choice. Adding to the excitement, Adlai Stevenson and Estes Kefauver, both of whom had entered the state presidential primary, were on hand. National press and television crews, 1,500 accredited delegates, and as many guests and observers, gave the convention hall the appearance and atmosphere of a national nominating convention.

The overwhelming popular choice for the Senate and the leaders' choice were one: State Senator Richard Richards of Los Angeles County, a hero of the movement.

Sam Yorty, the only other candidate, provided the convention's most dramatic moment. Knowing that he could not receive the endorsement but planning to run in the primary anyway, he mounted the platform and angrily withdrew his name from consideration. Saying he refused to recognize the legitimacy of the convention, he indicted CDC as a closed, boss-ridden, illegal conspiracy against the unorganized Democratic voters of the state. While hundreds of delegates shouted abuse at him, the wiry, tense, dapper little politician smiled at the uproar and said, "I charge that this convention is packed, stacked, rigged, and wired for sound!"

His taunt was the unbearable insult to the delegates — that they were part of an undemocratic conspiracy — and they roared with rage. Alan, again presiding over the convention, pounded his gavel and shouted for order. Yorty turned to him, beaming, and said, "Let 'em boo!"

When Yorty marched out, borne away on a torrent of jeers, Richards appealed to the delegates in words they welcomed. He would campaign on the issues that stirred them. He would abide by their decision. His endorsement was whooped through. Fifty thousand dollars were raised on the floor for Richards, and the CDC treasury was stripped — a crucial decision. Now, when regular contributors saw that CDC could back its endorsements with money, they accepted Richards and made their usual donations.

Yorty remained in the race for the nomination, and Senator Kuchel, who was running this time for a full six-year term, cross-filed. But Richards won the three-man race in the Democratic senate primary, taking 53.3 percent of the vote.

Yorty's poor showing and Kuchel's failure in the Democratic primary proved that CDC endorsement was now necessary for victory in the Democratic primary. (In 1961 Yorty was elected mayor of Los Angeles where he became known as "Saigon Sam" because of his frequent trips and hawk-line position on Vietnam.) Despite the manpower and enthusiasm of CDC, Stevenson lost again in California. Senator Kuchel, in November, defeated Richards to retain his seat.

Early the next year, Alan told the CDC delegates at that year's convention:

> We have taken incredible strides in four years. In 1956 we led the nation in Congressional gains, sending two new Democrats to the House. Our most significant gains have been in the state legislature, the traditional foundation stone of a party's power.
>
> Today there are five hundred clubs with forty thousand members and immense political influence.*
>
> *It takes all of us to win.* . . . We have done all within our ability to help create the most harmonious situation within the Democratic Party in California in this political generation. . . .
>
> Unprecedented opportunities lie before us. At the moment of our own unparalleled unity, the Republicans seem on the verge of civil war. Never before were the stakes so high and so nigh; and never before were the Republicans divided so neatly into three factions, each with a leader insatiably hungry for personal power [Nixon, Knowland, and Knight].
>
> We have within the ranks of our party the material for the strongest statewide ticket in many decades. We seem certain to gain control of the state legislature for the first time in this century. . . .

"We must move on to new thinking, but not neglect old battlefronts," Alan reminded the delegates. He spoke of the needs of the poor, senior citizens, small businessmen, blacks.

> To do anything less than the most we can for those who are denied freedom is inhuman and ungodly.
>
> We must think anew about the whole matter of peace on earth. We must refuse

---

*For the time being, the fight to abolish cross-filing had been lost. Still, the Democrats in 1954 had managed to get party designations placed on the ballot after the candidates' names, an important victory.

to surrender totally to the tides of the arms race. It is our responsibility to seek a policy of peace to match our policy of power. *This is the most important matter upon the agenda of mankind.* If we fail to deal with it we, our children, or their children, will pay the price in a war of extermination.

The convention again elected him president. But he resigned December 6, 1957, to make his first race for public office. Joe Wyatt became the new CDC president.

On that occasion Alan expressed his appreciation to the Board, citing CDC's gains. Throughout the four years of his presidency, he had tried hard to follow Lao-tzu's ideals of leadership, deliberately avoiding personal publicity, and putting out almost no press releases. Instead he did all he could to involve every Democrat who wished a voice in public affairs and in the decision-making processes of the party. Lao-tzu's words had echoed in his speeches: "We have done this ourselves. . . . It takes all of us to win."

The stage was set for a sweeping Democratic victory. Meanwhile Alan made a fact-finding trip through the strife-torn South in February 1957 to Texas, Mississippi, Alabama, and Georgia. He visited Martin Luther King's church. He saw Ralph Abernathy. He talked with leaders of the new White Citizens councils and states' rights groups, with leaders of the NAACP, and with citizens of all shadings of opinion. He talked to Ku Klux Klansmen and churchmen, political leaders and legislators, newspaper, radio, and TV men. He visited a bombed church and two ministers whose homes had been dynamited.

When he returned he delivered an eloquent report on his findings to the Democratic Western States Conference. He gave a moving account of Rev. Martin Luther King's efforts to achieve nonviolence by applying the techniques of Ghandi to the teachings of Christ.

Alan expressed his conviction that the right to vote was a vital key to civil rights. He called on the Democrats to launch a new effort in Congress to enact legislation to ensure that every citizen should have an equal opportunity to vote in Federal elections.

★ ★ ★ ★ ★ ★ ★ ★ ★ ★ ★ ★ ★ ★
Campaign Slates
1957–58
★ ★ ★ ★ ★ ★ ★ ★ ★ ★ ★ ★ ★ ★

There is but one good fortune to the earnest man. This is opportunity; and sooner or later opportunity will come to him who can make use of it.

> David Starr Jordan
> First president of Stanford
> University (1891-1913)

But life, after all, is long enough to make oneself into something, if one only has faith enough and a sturdy will.

> John Uhl

Will Rogers once said, "I am a member of no organized political party. I am a Democrat."

While California Democrats were belying this statement, developing unity, pulling themselves together, and organizing to a fare-thee-well, their Republican counterparts — as though pursuing some mad law of opposite dynamics — were proceeding hell-bent in all directions. When Governor Earl Warren's ten years of strong state leadership ended with his appointment as chief justice of the U.S. Supreme Court, a vacuum was created in California Republican politics. The party was dominated by three figures: Vice President Richard Nixon, who had made an enemy of Warren and who had urged President Dwight D. Eisenhower to appoint him to the Court. This, of course, removed him from California's politics.

The second was Goodwin Knight, the governor who had succeeded Warren. The bland, likeable, rather bumbling "Goodie" planned to run for reelection. Popular and entrenched, he anticipated smooth sailing.

The third member, the dark, brooding, barrel-chested son of Oakland's publishing magnate Joseph R. Knowland, "Big Bill" Knowland, was the militantly conservative Republican floor leader of the Senate. Because his booming voice often filled the Senate chambers in ringing defense of the nationalist Chinese, he was known as the "Senator from Formosa."

Knowland yearned to be president and suited the part with his gloomy, aggressive good looks and air of command. To him, the governorship of California appeared as a logical steppingstone; in the summer of 1957, he startled the state by announcing his intention to withdraw from the Senate at the end of his term the following year. Asked why, he said, "After an extensive tour of California, I will declare my plans."

Alan's heart leapt when he heard the news. The Senate seat would be wide open. The timing might be right at last. He told a few friends in the party and some reporters that he might run, and suddenly he began to receive media attention.

Shortly after that, the Republican State Controller Robert Kirkwood (a former assemblyman from Santa Clara County) threw his hat in the ring for Knowland's seat. Eagerly, other Republicans eyed Kirkwood's seat as controller. Assemblyman Luther Lincoln announced for that post. Knowland had started a game of political musical chairs.

Richard Nixon, who had long regarded both Knowland and Knight with wary distrust as possible rivals for the presidency, feared their political power in his home state. There were press hints that Nixon, informed of Knowland's potentially disastrous scheme, encouraged it.

For Alan, as for most California Democrats, the obvious choice for governor was Attorney General Edmund G. (Pat) Brown. An Irish Catholic, a native San Franciscan (and like Father, a graduate of Lowell High School), Brown was possessed of a handsome family— including an ascetic and rather inscrutable son, Jerry—and an unbroken record of political success. After seven years as San Francisco's district attorney, he was elected attorney general in 1950, and, four years later, again was the only Democrat to be elected to statewide office.

Now fifty-three, he was rather heavy-set, with warm brown eyes twinkling through horn-rimmed glasses; a moderate with great political moxie but with a tongue that occasionally tripped him.

"In interviews, reporters learned to keep quiet and wait," said a political editor. "Brown was kind-hearted — he'd always go on and give us a little more. Sometimes, too much."

But he was also cautious. He hesitated to give up the certainty of reelection as attorney general for a far more chancy race. To Alan, all the signs seemed to point to a Democratic year. Against a background of recession, sputniks, and civil rights battles, President Eisenhower's popularity had declined, and the Republican party seemed to be in trouble nationwide. California suffered from population pressures. The Republican administration was in deep red ink.

Brown's decision was needed to clear the track for other Democratic hopefuls, some of whom were thinking of running for governor if Brown refused. Others had their sights set on the attorney general spot that would open up if Brown sought the governorship.

Alan was sure Brown could win. On July 9, 1957, he pounded away at his theme in a CDC speech in Los Angeles, which was widely quoted in the press.

> The winner of the inevitable knock-down, drag-out Republican battle for the governorship of California next year will be a Democrat — Attorney General Edmund G. (Pat) Brown.
>
> By all the logic, lore, and law of politics, it is too late for either Governor Goodwin Knight or Senator William Knowland to avoid one of the biggest and most destructive interparty wars in the history of the state.
>
> Retreat for either one in the battle for California would be an admission of fatal weakness. . . .
>
> If Knight surrendered his governorship for a Cabinet post, an ambassadorship, or the Senate seat abandoned by Knowland, it would constitute an intolerable step down the ladder of political power and would destroy his own more artfully concealed case of presidentitis.
>
> One will be knocked out in the primary, the other dragged out in the general election.
>
> The winner and new Governor will be a Democrat — Pat Brown.

Brown still was not ready. But he did admit that Congressman Clair Engle of Red Bluff had told him he would run for Senator Knowland's seat — if Brown ran for Governor. Engle, a small, shrewd, peppery, long-time friend of Brown, had been noncommittal previously.

"As far as Knight and Knowland are concerned," Brown told the press, "it doesn't make a particle of difference to me which one is the Republican nominee. My decision on whether to run is not dependent on what they do."

The reporters waited, as they always did, for Brown to say more than he had intended to, and sure enough he added emotionally, "If anyone thinks I'm going to let Knowland or Knight take this state by default, they're mistaken!"

Watching this at home on TV, Alan turned to some friends with a shrug and smiled, "The die's *almost* cast!"

At a press conference in Los Angeles in early September—to no one's surprise but to the jubilation of the Democrats—Pat Brown announced he was running for governor. It was the only time Alan had ever seen a nervous Pat Brown. He was finally making the break from the careful path he had always followed.

A little later Brown, Elinor Heller, and other of Brown's key advisers urged Alan to run for state controller instead of the Senate. Congressman Engle was a proven vote-getter, they argued, who would strengthen the gubernatorial ticket. The controllership—the second most powerful administrative post in the state—would provide Alan with valuable experience. Alan agreed to consider running for controller against Republican Assemblyman Luther Lincoln.

"What they were politely saying was 'no money,' " recalls Libby Smith Gatov, then national committeewoman.

In 1956 Engle had been Adlai Stevenson's California chairman. Though chairman of the powerful House Interior Committee, Engle made it plain that if Alan insisted on running for the Senate, he would not run, because he knew Alan would, without question, be endorsed by CDC and thus surely become the Democratic nominee. But Engle didn't believe Alan could win in November and told him so. They were sitting together by a swimming pool at a Bakersfield gathering of Democrats. "Alan sat there braiding and unbraiding his long toes when I told him what would happen to him if he ran for the Senate," Engle later told Joe Wyatt.

Alan felt he might win a Senate race, but that he also could lose— and hurt Brown's chances of capturing the governorship and leading California Democrats to what could be their greatest victory of the century. His optimistic and combative nature was in conflict with circumstances. While he debated with himself, he was encouraged to run by CDC activists, by some labor leaders, and by many friends.

Meanwhile the Republican drama played itself out like a Greek tragedy whose theme was human ambition and inevitability. Governor Knight's money sources dried up, while his shouts of rage shrank to a dismal mumble. He fell ill. He flew to Arizona to meet with President Eisenhower—a frustrating encounter, the press hinted. At last he capitulated and announced he would run for the Senate.

"They took away my money and my press," he reportedly told an associate.

Played out in the public view, this became known as the "Nixon-Knowland-Knight switch." Knight then compounded his troubles by declaring he didn't really want to be senator! Headlines on the "Republican rigging" went on for weeks. The voters resented this cavalier handling of their own democratic prerogatives and George Christopher, San Francisco's Republican mayor, issued a blast and filed for the Senate.

Moving about the state, consolidating his party support, Alan touched base with local Democratic clubs. His vigorous campaign style was reminiscent of his press mentors of the past, Fremont Older, Amster Spiro, and Frank Gervasi. Polls had shown that either Knowland or Knight could beat Brown. "But the situation has been reversed overnight," Alan said, predicting Brown would win. Alan attacked Knowland's major campaign theme, "right-to-work," as "the right to work for nothing or less!"

Balancing all the political factors, Alan decided to run for controller and promptly told Brown and the press that he would announce his candidacy soon.

"Alan's too nice," said Geneva the next day, resenting his self-sacrifice in giving up the Senate race. We were sitting in the fall sunlight on their patio on Hilltop Road in Los Altos. The soft light shone on her auburn hair, bare arms, and blue-green cotton dress, and on the yellowing leaves of the apricot orchard. Alan, in blue jeans and a checkered seersucker shirt, coiled up his garden hose and dropped into a canvas chair beside her, stretching out his long legs and sandaled feet.

"So you think I'm nice," he said smiling.

"He hides his disappointment well," she said.

"No, I could impose myself and take the CDC endorsement — nobody could take that away from me. I might win the Senate seat. But I don't want to abuse the role I've developed as CDC president. I think I'd be doing that if I rammed myself down the party's throat by walking off with a sure-thing CDC endorsement. Pat is going to win without question — unless something goes wrong. I don't want to be the guy that messes up our chance to win. I have a good chance to get a statewide office and the experience."

"They were afraid of you," Geneva said. "I still think you were too nice."

Alan went into the house to answer the telephone. He walked with a springy step, feeling he had made the right decision.

In early December, at a crowded, press conference in Los Angeles, Alan formally announced his candidacy for controller, saying he would fight

> to break the sixty-eight-year Republican conspiracy to circumvent the Constitution and control the controller.
>
> This conspiracy matches in its sinister implications the more recent Republican scheme to prevent a free and open election of the governor.
>
> The controller is an elective office according to the Constitution, but not since 1890 has a citizen become controller by winning an election. Every man to enter the office from that day to this has been a Republican who first got there through appointment by a Republican governor.

Having battled for openness and democratic procedures in his own party for the last five years, Alan declared he would "take the lid off this office" in 1958.

> I will show the voters why the Republican Party has so carefully kept the controller's office from public scrutiny.
>
> I do not suggest corruption in the conduct of the office. I do suggest contempt for constitutional government in the way the office has been filled and its importance concealed.

Noting that the controller fulfilled a task of trust, seeing to it that the funds of the people were spent only for proper purposes — and that he also sat upon sixteen boards and commissions, affecting virtually every aspect of life in California — Alan added emphatically:

> The controller has more influence on tax policy than any other man in the state. If I am elected, that influence will be exerted for simplification of tax forms and

slashing of red tape, for a fairer tax system, and for the lowest tax rate consistent with the public welfare.

Chagrined by Knight's announcement that he would run for the Senate, Robert Kirkwood was forced to backtrack and declare for re-election as controller. Only now he had a formidable challenger in Alan.

Assemblyman Luther Lincoln quietly withdrew in Kirkwood's favor. The Republican shuffle was complete. Again, the game of political musical chairs affronted the voters. But the Republicans offered a powerful slate:

> Goodwin J. Knight for Senator
> William F. Knowland for Governor
> Harold J. Powers for Lieutenant Governor
> Robert C. Kirkwood for Controller
> Patrick J. Hillings for Attorney General
> A. Ronald Button for Treasurer
> Frank M. Jordan for Secretary of State

Alan now faced an incumbent opponent who was one of the strongest vote-getters in the state. Kirkwood had been favored by fortune — tall, tanned, dark-haired and handsome, with a pleasantly wry mouth, and shrewd, blue, hooded eyes. By nature he was deliberate and self-contained. He and his wife and four children still kept their old family home in Saratoga. Governor Warren had appointed him controller from the State Assembly when he named Kuchel to the Senate.

The situation was further complicated by Alan's liking for Kirkwood personally. ("You've got to hate your opponent," Pat Brown once remarked to Alan.) He and Kirkwood had much in common. A political moderate, the youngest man on the Republican ticket — forty-nine to Alan's forty-three — the controller was a native of Alan's home county of Santa Clara and had attended local public schools and Stanford. He had even joined the World Federalists.

Having placed himself on "an equal footing" with other candidates seeking the CDC's endorsements by resigning as president, Alan went before a CDC convention that was shaping up as a free-for-all. Only Pat Brown was unopposed at the Fresno convention in January. It was described by Dick Bergholz, then the political editor of the *Los*

Angeles Mirror-News (and now with the *Los Angeles Times,*) as "the raucous 40,000-member CDC."

Former San Francisco Assemblyman George Collins, Jr., who had been the party's nominee for controller in 1954, challenged Alan. In a speech from the floor, he charged that the controllership had been offered Alan as a "swap" to get him out of the Senate race. Collins was usually a mild-mannered man whom Alan had known and admired for years.

Congressman Engle was opposed by Los Angeles Supervisor Kenneth Hahn and by Berkeley professor Peter Odegard, who was backed by the liberal wing.

The Engle-Odegard-Hahn Senate battle was the focus of the convention, and Alan was still being pressed to join the fray. He tried to explain: "People feel they need a proven vote-getter in the race. The controllership's important. We have a chance to capture that too."

All the hoopla of a national political convention was wrapped up in the three-day affair—banners, balloons dropping from the rafters, blazing television lights. More than three thousand officially sanctioned delegates and officials attended. Roy Greenaway ran the convention as he did in 1956.

Endorsing and electing candidates had been CDC's main preoccupation. Alan had done his utmost while president to keep its attention focused on winning nominations and elections—albeit with candidates who took strong positions on the issues. Now CDC was becoming issues-oriented, a stance that would later divide its membership and weaken its ability to unite on campaigns. The convention wrangled over a number of resolutions. One condemned the right-to-work proposal. Another advocated "adequately monitored" disarmament.

Finally the delegates voted on endorsements in sessions that extended far into the night. Dick Bergholz's story the next day, Monday, January 13, was headlined:

DEMO GROUP BACKS BROWN, ENGLE
AMATEUR POLITICOS BATTLE PROFESSIONALS
TO A STANDOFF IN FRESNO

"The amateurs," Bergholz wrote, "largely representing the liberal wing of the party, pushed through preprimary endorsements for two offices—lieutenant governor and secretary of state.

"The hard-headed veteran politicos in the party backed the winning candidate in the hottest convention race — U.S. Senator — and had a hand in the state treasurer's."

The delegates endorsed Alan overwhelmingly for controller. CDC endorsed Stanley Mosk for attorney general. But State Senator Robert McCarthy announced he would run against him in the primary. That meant CDC would have to concentrate its efforts on that race. Its other candidates did not face serious primary challenges.

The CDC slate read:

Clair Engle for Senator
Edmund G. Brown for Governor
Glenn M. Anderson for Lieutenant Governor
Alan Cranston for Controller
Stanley Mosk for Attorney General
Bert A. Betts for Treasurer
Henry P. Lopez for Secretary of State

Fearing that a liberal coloration would alienate his conservative support, Pat Brown made clear he intended to run independently of the slate in the June primary.

★ ★ ★ ★ ★ ★ ★ ★ ★ ★ ★ ★ ★ ★ ★ ★ ★

CHAPTER 13

Race for Controller, 1958

★ ★ ★ ★ ★ ★ ★ ★ ★ ★ ★ ★ ★ ★ ★ ★ ★

Alan threw himself into the race. Up and down the state he went, from the snowy peaks and rainy redwood forests of the north down through the great fertile valleys to the sagebrush-covered deserts and white beaches of the south. He was in his element, enjoying the extraordinary contrasts of the California landscape and its people, delighting in their vitality, their ideas, and basic good intentions.

He drove his own dusty Ford, often accompanied by friends, or Geneva and their small sons. He dressed conservatively—business suit, white shirt, dark tie—a new image for him. He looked trim, well-groomed, and extraordinarily happy.

Raising money, campaigning hard, he was on the attack, tough and hardhitting. He talked to small groups of people in meetings, at factory gates, in shopping centers. He visited newspaper offices and TV and radio stations. Gaining media coverage was slow work and an uphill battle.

Eventually the press picked up his attacks. In Sacramento Alan called for an end to "the Nixon-Knowland-Knight nightmare."

In Fresno he flung the challenge, "It's up to the Democrats to defeat men like Knowland and mice like Knight."

In Long Beach at the Congress of Industrial Organizations convention Alan hit at "the callous contradiction between Knowland's crocodile cries for union democracy and the steps he took to prevent a free choice for governor."

Alan sang Attorney General Pat Brown's praises more than his own. He campaigned for Brown as "a man dedicated to democratic progress." He fiercely attacked Brown's opponent, Senator Knowland.

"What's your chief handicap?" a reporter asked Alan.

"That few know the controller's importance," Alan said, "second only to the governor's. And why not? Each day $15 million pass through his hands. He sits on all manner of boards and commissions. Has more to say about taxes than anyone else. Also he's on the State Lands Commission. These men write leases for the oil companies."

The newspapers often picked up Alan's persistent reminders that for half a century the controllers had all been appointed when an incumbent retired, died, or was elevated to a higher office. An editorial in the Ventura County *Star Free Press* headlined, **"ELECTIVE? WELL, IN A WAY . . ."** The press, commenting on Alan's "whirlwind visits," took to pointing up this extraordinary fact.*

In April the Republican Associates, the GOP state organization, proposed that all state executive officers except governor and lieutenant governor be appointed. The Democrats gleefully quoted this proposal, citing it as more evidence that their opponents mistrusted the people. One Republican official objected, "That would void our system of checks and balances. We don't need a dictator type of government!" Kirkwood, contented himself with saying the job required experience and called for "stable policies geared to extensive growth."

Both Alan and Kirkwood had cross-filed. Alan was unopposed in his own party but was threatened even in the Democratic primary by the cross-filed Kirkwood. No Democratic candidate for controller had won during this century.

Alan sometimes ran into Kirkwood's wife, Jean, along the campaign trail. She always smiled at him, saying, "Don't work too hard! Don't campaign too hard!" But he rarely encountered Kirkwood, catching a mere glimpse of him once as the controller left an American Legion affair just as Alan arrived.

---

*CALIFORNIA'S CONTROLLERS, 1890-1957

Republican No. 1—Elected November 4, 1890
Republican No. 2—Appointed November 23, 1906
Republican No. 3—Appointed August 28, 1913
Republican No. 4—Appointed July 16, 1921
Republican No. 5—Appointed January 9, 1937
Republican No. 6—Appointed February 8, 1946
                  (Thomas Kuchel)
Republican No. 7—Appointed January 6, 1953
                  (Robert Kirkwood)

Alan struck blows for the freedom of the press whenever he could, citing his experiences with censorship under Mussolini. The press responded to this with rare attention. The *Los Angeles Times* headlined the story, **"OPEN DOOR POLICY FAVORED FOR BOARDS."** In the *San Francisco Examiner*, Syd Kossen quoted Alan as saying, "There's no justification for secret meetings of boards on which the controller sits!"

Alan reverted continually to his favorite theme of equal opportunity: "In sixty-eight years of Republican monopoly of the controller's office, no controller has appointed a single Mexican, Negro, or Oriental as an inheritance tax appraiser. And only one Jew — two months ago! I will disband the Controllers' Country Club."

By the end of April his campaign was in high gear. The state's money was running out, he charged. His favorite piece of campaign literature was a simulated check stating that $15 million of the public's tax money was disbursed by the controller every day.

"Millions are sitting in bank accounts that pay no interest," he pointed out. "Think of the schools this money could have paid for. Think of the increased aid to the aged and impoverished it might have financed."

The June primary election drew near. Alan had won a surprising number of newspaper endorsements, describing him variously as striking hard, traveling tirelessly, and as being an expert on world affairs, articulate, and highly qualified. Much was made of his newspaper and business background. Nevertheless, the majority of newspapers endorsed the incumbent.

The tide was running with the Democrats, however. In the governor's race, polls indicated a four-to-three lead for Pat Brown over Bill Knowland. Alan's race against Kirkwood was rated neck-and-neck. On the eve of the election Alan predicted victory for himself and said with mingled excitement, hope, and trepidation, "I will be the first man to become controller in this century by winning an election!"

On election night, June 3, Alan and Geneva went to the Los Angeles Biltmore with the other candidates to watch the returns.

All the candidates except one had cross-filed, and most of the Democratic candidates were unopposed in their own party except by cross-filed Republicans. It soon became clear that no one had won *both* party nominations. Alan and the other CDC-endorsed candidates — except for Stanley Mosk, whose contest with Bob McCarthy was in doubt—had all won their Democratic nominations. (Mosk eventually won.) The Democrats all settled down to watch the total vote come cascading in. By adding up the number of votes he had received in both parties' primaries, each candidate was able to assess his chances in the November general election.

Brown piled up an early lead and was declared overwhelming winner by a margin of over 600,000 votes. Joy reigned at the Biltmore when the totals each had won in both the Democratic and Republican primaries were added together. But more than four million Californians had gone to the polls and it would take many hours before all the votes were counted.

The lead in the total vote Cranston and Kirkwood had received in both primaries seesawed agonizingly back and forth into the following day. The final tally was chillingly close. Alan led by 3,571.

Despite the slim margin, Alan was elated. He shrugged off as a mixed blessing the special attention the media now paid his close race in the general election and prepared to campaign hard.

"It's the first time a Democratic candidate for controller has led in a primary since 1886, the year the gasoline engine was invented," he said on a southern swing through Fresno, Santa Barbara, and Riverside. "I got more votes than any Democrat ever seeking this office." Alan's literature portrayed the last Democratic controller as an ancient, bearded old man.

Moreover as one newspaper reported:

> The tremendous growth of California is reflected in the curious fact that Cranston won more votes than Washington, Adams, Jefferson, or any other candidate for United States president, in any election from the birth of our nation, through Pierce's victory in 1852. Cranston's opponent spent more than twice as much money, yet trailed in total votes.

Alan faced a popular incumbent with a powerful financial base. In addition, Kirkwood had a built-in organization working hard for him in every county of the state, his appointed inheritance tax appraisers. They were the secret weapon in the historic invincibility of incumbent controllers seeking reelection.

In San Francisco Alan rallied his troops, saying, "We can win all the state offices if we work." He added, "We face the most vigorous, ruthless, and rough campaign we've ever had." He warned that, because the future presidency was at stake, more money would be spent than ever before to prevent California from swinging into the Democratic column in a California election.

All that summer Alan drove himself up and down the length of the state at a furious pace. He crisscrossed it east to west. He came to know it well. He campaigned from ice-blue Pelican Bay far in the north eastward through the little forest towns along the Klamath River and the Eel, then southward on down the rugged coast past Cape Mendocino and Fort Bragg to the deep-blue Gulf of Santa Catalina at the Mexican border. He campaigned through the snow-capped Siskiyous and the Sierra down through the great Sacramento and San Joaquin valleys, all the way to the pale hot deserts of Borrego and the Salton Sea.

He followed a route from town to town, where his strong statements and speeches got him brief TV coverage on the evening news. Northward he sped from Sacramento up through Chico and Redding to Eureka and then down to San Francisco and on to Fresno, Bakersfield, Los Angeles, and San Diego. He concentrated on the population centers of the south.

The population of California was rapidly nearing fifteen million. How could he reach all these people? In 1958 TV had come on more strongly than ever before on the political scene but did not dominate campaigns as yet. The best TV advertising was the ten-second spot.

But the cost was staggering — five hundred dollars. A ten-second spot today would cost about four thousand dollars.

Billboards also had to be limited to a few words. Any more became a blur to speeding passersby. Anyone on the freeway trying to read too many words might crash. The message reduced to simply: ELECT ALAN CRANSTON — FIRST DEMOCRATIC CONTROLLER SINCE 1886!

"Speeches reach very few people," Alan told his largely volunteer campaign staff. "Only the most provocative and attacking phrases appear in the press. So speeches have become somewhat passé with the advent of the electronic media at least in races for offices like controller."

A friend who had a show in Los Angeles on the only TV station broadcasting after midnight wanted to give Alan a little free time. But his contract limited him to presenting only guests who talked about contact lenses, the product he was advertising. Alan found himself regretting, for the first and only time in his life, that he didn't wear contact lenses, but he persuaded his friend to put him on anyway.

"OK, I'll put you on," said the TV host, "but, remember, you can't mention you're a candidate, and for god's sake, don't use the word 'Democrat.' "

At midnight in the empty, barnlike studio, after Alan's friend had interviewed a beautiful young lady whose best friends didn't know until this moment of revelation that she wore contact lenses, he peered out beyond the cameras and announced, "Among the many people with us tonight is Alan Cranston. Won't you come up here, Alan Cranston? . . . This is Alan Cranston. Please tell us what you're doing, Alan Cranston."

"Good evening," Alan said. "I'm Alan Cranston. I'm running up and down the state making contacts and jumping in front of lenses!"

"Thank you for being with us, Alan Cranston. Good night, Alan Cranston," beamed his friend, who then explained, "That was Alan Cranston."

The audience must have been somewhat baffled by all this, but shortly before the election its sleepy members had heard the words "Alan Cranston" no fewer than eight times.

Alan took Geneva, Rob and Kim with him whenever he could. Geneva often chauffeured Alan from meeting to meeting while he worked in the car. The children and their German shepherd, Roy, went along.

One day in June, Alan was scheduled to speak at a Veterans of Foreign Wars' convention in Long Beach. Running late, the family raced down the sidewalk toward the auditorium. Kim, then six, tagged along in the rear. He spied a red metal box on a post, pulled the lever, and trotted on. A moment later, Rob, ten, exclaimed, "Mom, Kim just turned in a fire alarm!"

Geneva said, "Shhh! How could he? Stop teasing!"

Rob repeated his statement more loudly to Alan.

"How could he? When? Why would he?" Alan asked, rather crossly and somewhat distractedly. He was reviewing his speech notes as he strode along.

As the family reached the auditorium, breathless, they heard sirens whining in the distance.

"I told you!" shouted Rob triumphantly.

Kim's parents stared at him. "Did you *really* turn in a false alarm?" they demanded in unison.

"I thought it said 'FREE'!" he wailed in sudden terror. "I thought I'd get bubblegum!"

"FIRE — f-i-r-e — FIRE, dummo," explained Rob in disgust. He had to shout to be heard. The sirens were much closer.

"Gad," said Alan. "If we try to explain, they'll never believe us."

"They'll think we put Kim up to it to get some cheap publicity," Geneva gasped.

Several veterans emerged from the auditorium to investigate the commotion, recognized Alan, and whisked him to the podium. One of them, obviously impressed, said, "Hm, I gather you arrived with a police escort!"

As Alan began to speak, he looked over the heads of the audience and out through the open doors of the auditorium as three fire trucks screamed to a halt, helmeted firemen clinging to them. Alan watched in fascination as the firemen leaped to the street and moved about with huge hoses, gesticulating. His opening remarks were drowned out in the din. Part of the audience got up and rushed out.

Meanwhile, Geneva had grasped the children's hands, and they ran to a ladies' room near the entry. There they hid till they heard the fire engines lumber away. Then they rushed back to the car. Kim hid on the floor by the back seat shaking, expecting the police to come after him. Alan eventually rejoined them, and they sped toward San Diego. Kim got on his knees and peered out the back window — watching for policemen — or firemen. After that, anyone who called Kim a "veteran campaigner" was apt to receive a startled glare.

In September the weather turned cool, and the campaigns heated up. "It was a political battle of giants," wrote the *San Jose Mercury*'s Harry Farrell. The battles added to California's political vernacular. Knight described Engle as a "wisecrack at the end of a cigar." Knowland called Brown "the two-faced Santa Claus." Helen Knowland called Knight "macaroni spine." Knight resented Engle's billboards, which said, "California needs a *strong* Senator. The accompanying picture made the diminutive Engle look huge. "Actually, he's only a little fellow, way below six feet," complained Knight. Engle replied, "Up in the mountains where I come from, they measure a man from the neck up!" Besides these anatomical curiosities came a new cast of characters: "Buster Brown," "Weaseling Bill," and "Senator Straddle." Reporters called the campaign "Operation Big Switch" or "Big Fix." A Woodland paper called Alan "bird-brained."

In September Alan scheduled two last intensive swings throughout the state.

Commenting acidly on Kirkwood's latest statement that, "The state is faced with a deficit of at least $200 million," Alan told a Fresno audience, "They can't decide if we're knee deep or neck deep in red ink."

He amused his audiences with accounts of Republican infighting. He quoted columnist Herb Caen's one-liner: "Said Governor Knight about Senator Knowland: 'I won't say anything good or bad about that dirty louse!'"

Alan charged that the State Lands Commission, chaired by his opponent, had "lost all track of the land the state owned." Kirkwood denied "Cranston's cobweb claims."

In mid-September an important breakthrough in Alan's campaign occurred. One of his key supporters, Bart Lytton, a flamboyant savings and loan executive, suggested a novel tactic designed to strike at the very heart of his opponent's strength. Lytton was a former screen writer turned tycoon (whom Jesse Unruh once described as "a mad genius—in equal parts"). He had told Alan that the secret of success in business was to keep the opposition divided and off balance.

After carefully weighing the pros and cons, Alan sent a letter to Kirkwood's 119 appointed inheritance tax appraisers. Its text had been worked over for days:

> Since there now seems to be considerable belief that I will be the next state controller, I am writing to you to express certain thoughts relative to those whose status on the staff of the office is not on a civil service basis.
>
> The fact that I have not accepted the help so generously offered to my campaign by some of you who are on this status does not mean that I will not want experienced help in my conduct of the controller's office.
>
> It is my intention to maintain competent, trained, and qualified members on the staff if I am elected, for it will be my purpose to do the best possible job for the citizens of California. I simply feel it best that you who are not on a civil service status, like those on this status, refrain from taking an active part on either side in the present campaign for controller, regardless of political affiliation.
>
> I wanted to write you in this vein as soon as I became a candidate, but felt that such action on my part might seem presumptuous prior to the primary.

The letter demoralized Kirkwood's troops. The political activities of the appraisers, many of whom acted as unofficial campaign managers for the controller, were swiftly curtailed despite the frantic efforts of Kirkwood's top aides, who urged them to ignore the letter. One appraiser's office had been plastered with Kirkwood posters. They all came down the day after Alan's letter arrived.

The letter was soon in the hands of the press. It received wide coverage. One reporter wrote:

> Whether Cranston's letter constituted a threat, a warning, a statement of policy, or friendly advice was not clear. Appraisers were left to draw their own conclusions, since the letter could be read as advice not to campaign for either Kirkwood or Cranston.*

In October Pat Brown "wholeheartedly endorsed" Alan, citing his "ability and integrity" and crediting him for being "largely responsible for the reestablishment of the two-party system in California, through his leadership of the resurgence of the Democratic Party." Alan felt encouraged and buoyed, but it was no secret that Brown's campaign manager and other advisers were furious. They wanted Brown to run separately from the rest of the slate.

A year earlier, when he had urged Alan to run for controller instead of senator, Brown had promised his help. Brown had turned to his longtime friend and supporter, attorney Prentiss Moore, and said, "Why don't you take the lead in that?" Whereupon Prentiss switched from Brown's campaign to Alan's.

With his long experience in politics, the money he raised, and his toughness, Prentiss was invaluable. He was also symbolic of Alan's alliance with Brown. In Alan's words, "a savvy, daring guy to have on your side in politics."

Late in October another significant campaign breakthrough for Alan came with the endorsement of John Francis Neylan, a prominent San Francisco Republican with a reputation as an ultraconservative. Neylan, a regent of the University of California and William Randolph Hearst's former lawyer, had served as director of finance in Hiram Johnson's administration and had a long record of service to the state.

"Very few people," Neylan stated, "realize that the state controller is supposed to be the watchdog of the treasury and the independent

*The *Watsonville Register-Pajaronian,* September 16, 1958.

auditor for the taxpayers." Citing Alan's "excellent business experience and highest reputation for integrity and courage," Neylan added
that he was "confident Cranston would restore the office to the dignity
and importance it formerly enjoyed."

Neylan's support strengthened Alan with both the business community and the general public.

"We are in superb shape. The Republicans are losing ground," Alan
encouraged his supporters in San Francisco. "But it would be dangerous to be overconfident."

His apprehensions were shortly confirmed. On the eve of the election, in Chico, in northern California, Alan received a chilling phone
call from his campaign manager in Los Angeles, Teddy Muller.

"You're being smeared, Alan," she said, sounding hoarse and far-
away. "Precinct workers all over are bringing in awful pamphlets."

"What do they say?" He had anticipated a smear campaign, and he
held his breath.

"Lies and distortions," she quavered. "Garbled hints that you're a
Communist dupe."

"Who's getting them out?"

"Joseph Kamp. He seems to be well heeled."

In the cramped phone booth Alan sighed, squared his shoulders
and said, "Kamp's the worst sort of rabble-rouser. We'll organize a
counterattack immediately. Set up a press conference at eleven tomorrow. I'll be there."

At his Los Angeles press conference, Alan declared: "I will not
answer Kamp's lies and distortions directly until Kirkwood takes his
stand on this intervention by a notorious hate-monger of the extreme
right wing." Alan told reporters that Kamp was the first man in
history to be convicted of contempt of Congress three times and that
Kamp's Constitution League had been labeled a transmission belt for
Nazi propaganda in the mass sedition indictments during World
War II. In 1952 Kamp had claimed that "Jews and Communists" were
backing Eisenhower for president.

Kirkwood ignored the charges and countercharges. So did most of
the press. Kamp's pamphlet consisted of a twisted rehash of the events
of Alan's stormy Office of War Information days, plus assaults on the
Common Council for American Unity, and the United World Federalists. Alan found it hard to calculate the damage but some of his supporters were shaken. "I hope this doesn't affect Pat's race, or the other

candidates," he told Geneva wearily. "'A lie can travel round the world three times while the truth is packing its trunk.'" We're in the silly season now," he told a Los Angeles audience. "A phase of wild charges and silly speeches. Any candidate might expect to find himself accused of being a commie or a crook when he opens his newspaper."*

It was indeed the silly season: on election eve in San Diego a woman who saw the "Cranston for Controller" posters on city trash cans telephoned his campaign headquarters. She demanded that he come out and haul away the rubbish the wagon had passed up, because it was covered with insects. After a lengthy hassle, she said: "I thought that those posters said 'Cranston for Collector.'" Harassed and punchy, the Cranston team in San Diego tried to phone and tell Alan their latest news, but they were laughing so weakly and hysterically he couldn't make heads or tails of what they said.

Dan Frishman's column in the *San Francisco Examiner* noted:

> ROLL DEMO BONES: A non-voting adherent of Alan Cranston, the Demo candidate for Controller, obviously has learned something besides advanced calculus, togetherness and basket-weaving at Menlo Park's Peninsula School. Because he stormed into Daddy's study in Los Altos to say he felt pretty good about the election possibilities. "Kim is 7," he pointed out, "and I'll be 11 tomorrow. And besides our mamma rat just gave birth to seven ratlets!" You're faded, Robin.

Geneva told a reporter, "I was the only candidate's wife who had to arrange for a rat sitter. We hope to get back to the original two, after making a generous contribution to the Junior Museum."

Betting odds were 7-to-5 for Kirkwood.

The strain on Alan, Geneva, and the boys mounted. Alan took the family to spend election night in San Francisco, still the political center of the state before the population influx shifted it to Los Angeles.

Alan went into the *Chronicle* Building early that evening to get the returns. In a record turnout, Brown was winning by a landslide.

Alan saw with a stab of alarm that he was trailing. He recalls people making the kind of remarks that meant they thought he had lost— "'Good try,' 'Hang in there.' Frantically friends urged, 'Don't concede,' as though that would enable me to win. It didn't exactly en-

---

*Recently Alan was startled to be given a copy of a confidential letter from Vice President Nixon to Governor Knight, written in March 1958. This cited "a mutual friend's" suggestion that Alan might be charged with having been given his job in OWI "with the help of Commies."

courage me. I saw Senator Knowland there at the *Chronicle*, his face absolutely red. I'd never seen a redder face. I suppose it was the embarrassment he was suffering at losing heavily. . . . Later Knowland and I became friends."

Leaving the boys at the Pickwick Hotel, Alan and Geneva spent the rest of the evening at City Hall, tensely watching the returns with the other candidates. Pat Brown was euphoric.

"Don't worry," he told Alan. But Kirkwood continued to lead.

Tom Feeney, Alan's San Francisco County chairman, thought he saw a discrepancy in the returns. He demanded a recheck of the votes from the new machines in a few city precincts. It was discovered that Kirkwood had been credited with ten thousand too many votes. When they were subtracted, Alan pulled significantly closer. But he was still behind.

He phoned Mother at home: "It's close. Don't give up hope."

Finally he went to bed. Too exhausted and uneasy to sleep, he got up early and phoned the *Chronicle*. The reports were dribbling in slowly. He was still behind.

What made matters worse, there was nothing to do. He and Geneva took Rob and Kim to a large department store, the Emporium, to buy toys. Rob bought an overcomplicated, put-together toy. Back at the hotel he shrieked and stormed when he couldn't put it together. Alan and Geneva tried to help, but they couldn't put it together, either. Frustration.

The family went to a movie, *South Pacific*. In the middle Alan went out and checked again.

When he came back Mary Martin was singing, "Happy Talk."

"Boy, did I hear 'Happy Talk'!" he whispered. *"I'm catching up!"*

Later that evening Alan pulled ahead.

He phoned Mother. "I'm not sure, but I think I've won! . . . Mother, you're not crying!"

"Only tears of relief and joy!"

Alan won but by a mere 31,000 votes out of more than five million! (The final results were 2,553,020 to 2,521,497.) Clair Engle was overwhelmingly elected senator. All the Democratic slate was elected except for Henry Lopez, who lost to the aging, long-time Republican Secretary of State Frank Jordan. The Democrats captured the state legislature for the first time in the century and gained new seats in the House of Representatives.

Next morning when Alan and his family, radiant and exhausted, returned to their house on Hilltop Drive in Los Altos, their neighbors, the Baers, and I went over to see them. On this cool gray November morning, rain clouds veiled the blue of Black Mountain.

Alan put a symphony on the record player, and we sat by the fire. Geneva poured coffee from her copper coffee pot while the boys ran in and out, shouting excitedly. Roy, their German shepherd, barked at their heels. The firelight danced on the adobe walls while we looked out at the leafless orchard on the hill, talked about the move to Sacramento, and read the stacks of congratulatory telegrams.

"Of course it's not absolutely settled," Geneva said anxiously. Dark circles under her blue eyes showed her exhaustion as she stubbed out a cigarette.

"It's settled." Alan reassured her, "Don't worry." Relaxed again in jeans and a plaid shirt, he strode easily across the room to answer the phone. His whole appearance had changed. He held his head high and walked taller and straighter. The burden he'd thrown aside was almost visible.

For a full month Kirkwood refused to concede. He talked of demanding a recount. Geneva had been right.

At last, on December 10, the phone rang in the kitchen at Hilltop Drive. It was Kirkwood. Geneva had been washing dishes. She gave the phone to Alan, standing close by. After a moment he looked at her, raised his eyebrows, wrinkled his forehead, and nodded his head vigorously.

Alan thanked Kirkwood. "That's good of you," Alan said with warmth. "You fought a great campaign."

He hung up the phone and gave Geneva a long hug.

"Kirkwood's first words to me," he said, "were, 'I've decided not to pursue this any further.' It was nice of him. Had he won, he would have been the only Republican survivor — with a claim on the governorship next time around. He offered his help in the transition period."

"Did he? Oh, Alan, I wanted you to win. But I dread it!"

"Why?"

"Don't sound so surprised. Moving, changing schools, Sacramento, rivalries, tensions, teamwork. *More campaigns.* God, what is it going to be like? How can I measure up to it?"

"Of course you can measure up to it."

"Well, I don't know. Don't you sometimes long to be free? Just to have fun?"

"Sometimes I do," he admitted.

"But not often!"

"The main thing's not to look back," he said. "We can do this together."

Letters and telegrams poured in for weeks. From Adlai Stevenson: "NOW I READ THAT YOU ARE SAFE AND SOUND AND I AM OVERJOYED." From Bruce Bliven: "CONGRATULATIONS ON YOUR CLIFF-HANGING VICTORY." From Libby Smith Gatov (later John F. Kennedy's U.S. Treasurer): "FIFTEEN MILLION BEST WISHES AND HAPPY EIGHTEENTH WEDDING ANNI-VERSARY." From Ann Alanson (later Democratic National Com-mittee member): "CONGRATULATIONS TO A GREAT GUY, WHO MADE A SPECTACULAR STRETCH RUN."

The shortest said, "PHEW!" and was signed "Charter Members 'Cranston for President Committee.' "

Alan laughed when women's lib and male resentment surfaced early: "NOW THAT YOU WON DO I GET MY WIFE BACK? HOPEFULLY, MR. DOROTHY HENLEY."

But the letter that delighted him most came from his old friend Lee Falk, the cartoonist.

> Alan Cranston
> State Controller
> Sacramento, California
>
> Dear Controller:
>
> Justin Lunning of Georg Jensen's just gave me the above information and swears it's you.
>
> This is obviously a title taken from the works of George Orwell or Lewis Carroll. What do you control? Thought? Morals? Traffic? Weather? Butterfat content? Yourself? It's the kind of thing one would expect in that state of make-believe out there. "Let's have a controller?" — "What'll he do? — "We'll figure that out later. But let's have one, because it sounds so gruesome!"
>
> If you're not ashamed to admit what kind of a mess you've gotten into out there, write me about it. I have a few friends out

there, and maybe we can do something. Of course, I'm telling none of our mutual friends here about it. I have a vision of you striding the windy shores near Los Altos, ordering the waves to stop, and shouting, "You must! I am the Controller of California!"

Do write and tell me how you got into this sad condition.

I'm certain Geneva and the children are standing by you staunchly. In the meantime, try to rest.

Worriedly,

Lee Falk

Alan's tongue-in-cheek friend had made an important point. His new title did lead constituents to expect him to get all sorts of uncontrollable matters under control. Incredible and impossible demands were made upon him by expectant citizens. His first undertaking would be to try to borrow $30 million to deal with the state's rising deficit.

★ ★ ★ ★ ★ ★ ★ ★ ★ ★ ★ ★ ★ ★ ★ ★ ★

CHAPTER 14

The Controller Years 1958-59

★ ★ ★ ★ ★ ★ ★ ★ ★ ★ ★ ★ ★ ★ ★ ★ ★

Alan's recollections of the next hectic months tend to be kaleidoscopic. Right after the election Pat Brown invited Alan, Geneva, Rob, and Kim to join him, his family, other friends and staff members at the La Quinta Hotel in Palm Springs for a working vacation. Sitting around the swimming pool or in conference rooms or over drinks and leisurely dinners, the governor-elect began putting his new administration together. It was a time of blue skies and November desert sun, work and rest, hope and excitement, and idealism tempered with pragmatism.

Alan recalls, "Once Rob and Kim were wildly fighting Pat in the swimming pool. I was horrified at what they were doing to the future governor."

One day as Alan walked back from the pool with Pat past tubs of flowering oleanders and bougainvillaea, he tried to thank Pat for his support in the campaign. "I appreciate all your help very, very deeply, Pat," he said awkwardly fixing his eyes on a distant palm tree rustling in the desert wind.

Pat threw him a keen glance. He said warmly, "I'm glad you're part of this administration."

"It's a great administration to be part of. So broad and committed to trying to find ways to meet human needs."

Pat sighed. "We'll try to keep it that way."

"You'll have hard choices!"

For a moment they walked along together in silence, the hot sun warming their backs. Then Alan said, more lightly and easily but still with his feelings deepening his voice, "Prentiss Moore was tremendously helpful too. Thanks for your part in that also."

Pat glanced at him again saying soberly, "In the matter of your appointments, you've got to be very careful."

"Yes," Alan sighed too. "Prentiss once told me, 'The appraisal system's an unholy mix of a political bonanza and incubus. People think patronage went away with Hiram Johnson's reforms, but there's still this vestige. Repugnant to some — but there!"

Pat laughed, "Prentiss sized things up accurately as usual."

"I was glad to escape to Palm Springs," Alan said. "I was besieged by would-be appraisers." Then, relieved at having shared his feelings, he added, "It's also a rest. At first I could hardly sleep."

"There's a big job ahead . . ." said Pat. "The state's shaky financial condition. The north-south fight over water."

"Breaking the long deadlock."

"Too bad your race was so close," Pat concluded thoughtfully. "You're too modest. Your biggest problem will be finding ways to get better known. They'll be shooting at you because it was close."

Alan shrugged. "I know. I'll figure it out."

"Democrats as much as Republicans." Pat frowned. "The media will magnify our differences."

"Making me better known!"

"I know your heart's set on the Senate."

"Yes."

In late December, in order to attend a Board of Equalization meeting as controller, he was sworn in at an early ceremony by a family friend and Los Altos neighbor, state supreme court Judge John Wesley Shenk. We all attended the ceremony in the rustic little Los Altos Hills Town Hall.

Before Alan knew it, in early January 1959, he and Geneva were dancing and greeting their political friends and allies at the inaugural ball. Local committees, working to make this an affair of astonishing "pomp and opulence," had canopied the ballroom like a jewel box in gold and satin lamé and had decorated it with gold cherubs and urns, a profusion of English ivy and gold roping. A fifteen-piece orchestra, a grand march, and a formal announcement of the arrival of dignitaries, from the state officials and their wives to Lady Cedric Hardwicke of Hollywood, thrilled the guests, as did the rumored "surprises" — a five-foot replica of the seal of California, complete with its golden bear, poppies, and the inscription *Eureka;* towering ice replicas of the state capitol; a handsome bust of Governor Brown; and all California's historic flags. Democrats felt they were celebrating an historic occasion themselves — probably the biggest single takeover in state history.

Sober-faced and silent among those enjoying the festivities was Governor Brown's twenty-year-old son, Jerry, who had received special permission to attend from the Los Gatos Novitiate, where he was studying for the Jesuit priesthood.

The state officials' wives went all out to make this a full dress occasion, with a gorgeous array of couture gowns and furs. Geneva wore a long, brilliant emerald green gown of silk satin that enhanced her blue eyes and dark auburn hair. It had a "moulded bodice, having a matching chiffon scarf attached at one shoulder and draped across to the other and down the back, where it attached to the mermaid train with a rose."* Not owning any furs, Geneva had agonized over her wrap but finally had her dressmaker make a stole of matching green material, lined with foam rubber for warmth. "The stole looked beautiful," she told her friend Sally Hawley afterward, "but the rubber made it so elastic that if I didn't keep a tight grip on both ends, one end would fly out — 'PING!' — and fell the nearest bystander." She smiled. "It made an admirable weapon!"

When Pat Brown moved into the governor's famous southeast corner office in the white-domed State Capitol Building, Alan moved into the large southwest corner suite, just across the marble hallway. From the window of his office he looked across a little stretch of tree-filled park to the old Senator Hotel, where as a child he had often stayed on the way to Lake Tahoe. Just a stone's throw away on the nearest corner, at Twelfth and L streets, he could see a small stucco business building on the site of Aunt Grace Skeels's one-time Victorian mansion, where Father and Mother were married in 1903.

Alan, a member of Pat's "kitchen cabinet" and in the direct line of succession to the governorship, worked harmoniously with Brown on the governor's program. He did part from Governor Brown once briefly in 1963, firmly opposing a withholding tax on California wage and salary earners that Brown had proposed.

Sacramento Bee, January 6, 1959.

"I did my best to support Pat," he recalls.* "But I saw a mammoth bureaucracy, and my first impression was of the great danger that it could be unresponsive to citizens and to their elected leaders." His experience with the Sacramento bureaucracy foreshadowed his experiences with the one in Washington. It was almost impossible to fire a civil servant except for gross malfeasance.

The bureaucrats could say to themselves, "This too will pass," when a newly elected official arrived on the scene. Civil service covered the controller's staff so thoroughly that Alan could appoint ony two people of his own choice — his able chief deputy, Irwin Nebron, and his press chief, Dick Walton, to implement his new policies. He found himself, like it or not, dependent on a bureaucracy of several hundred civil servants in the controller's office and several thousand more with the numerous boards and commissions on which he served — a considerable challenge.

He was dismayed to discover that he couldn't even select his personal secretary. Eleanor MacArthur, who had become the controller's secretary years before as a patronage appointee, had acquired civil service status. Ralph McCarthy, the deputy controller, who was responsible for day-to-day administration, also had civil service status. But Eleanor turned out to be a fine and loyal secretary, and she and Alan became warm friends. Ralph proved to be an outstanding and responsive deputy. In time Alan developed a high regard for many bureau chiefs, commission executives, and other civil servants down the line, and he saw in them a parallel with the British system of permanent undersecretaries and aides who provide the government with expertise and continuity through the years.

"I did, though, continue to feel that it should be less difficult to reward excellent performance and to remove bureaucrats who performed incompetently," he concluded.

In Alan's very first week, the struggle for power and place among the elected officials in the administration began. Lt. Gov. Glenn Anderson, a close associate from CDC days, asked Alan to support him for chairman of the powerful three-member State Lands Commission on which Alan also served. The next day the third member, Bert Levit, a Republican who was appointed Brown's director of finance, asked Alan to support *him* for chairman of the Lands Commission.

---

*These and other quotations are taken from my taped interview with Alan in December 1973.

"I'm not sure I can," Alan said.

An hour later Alan received a call from Governor Brown. "Alan, you want to be chairman of the Franchise Tax Board, don't you?"

"Yes. The controller always serves as chairman of the Franchise Tax Board."

"I don't think Levit can vote for you for that," said Brown, "if you don't vote for him for the other." He was brief and tough in that conversation. "Think it over!" he said and hung up.

Alan called Lt. Gov. Anderson and said, "I guess I can't support you, Glenn." He explained why.

Anderson was also brief. "Oh!"

Levit was duly chosen chairman of the Lands Commission but with the understanding that Anderson would succeed him in August, when Levit planned to resign as finance director. Alan was in turn elected chairman of the Franchise Tax Board and pledged to work for tighter tax evasion laws and for greater ease to the taxpayers in filing returns.

A startling problem confronted the new members of the Lands Commission, the overseers of four million acres of oil-rich tidelands. The City of Long Beach was sinking. For eighteen years, oil companies had drilled for oil beneath the city, and the city—along with the naval shipyard—was sinking. Now the navy was threatening to sue and to pull out of Long Beach.

Alan flew south to the subsidence area and hiked over the tidelands with the press and various officials. "A crazy issue, absolutely weird," he recalls. "Navy officials were walking around on docks knee-deep in salt water. The yacht club had sunk thirty or forty feet and was down behind a dike that hid the ocean. The damage totaled something like $90 million. Five conflicting interests were involved—the oil companies, the navy, the city, state, and federal governments."

Alan was quoted berating Long Beach for delays in solving its problems and for its suicidal tendencies. Calling for immediate action, he declared that "the commission will be rigorous and vigorous in carrying out a policy of preventing further damage. We will tolerate no further drilling that might cause subsidence."

The state voted aid, and a crash repressurizing program was launched to solve the sinkage problem and protect the city and shipyard by pumping water into the earth to replace extracted oil.

"The Lands Commission gave me a unique opportunity to learn about resources, particularly oil," Alan recalls. He played a key part in a huge leasing offer in the Long Beach-Wilmington area, one of the largest single business deals in history. On one occasion while he was chairman of the Lands Commission, a lease was consummated whereby a major oil company actually agreed to pay—and did pay— the state more than 100 percent of the value of the oil sold by the state. "I dealt with the extraordinary, rugged men who run the oil companies—the majors and independents. Some of the hardest, shrewdest businessmen in the world. Fascinating, learning their individualistic ways, their bidding methods, the tactics they'd resort to in order to mislead rivals who were interested in the same oil sites.

"For the commission to represent the public interest, since the public owned the oil, was a definite challenge!"

On the whole, Alan was getting a cram course in financial management and in budget balancing by his second week in office. The need for prudence in spending and for restraint in taxation was a lesson he learned anew each day. The state's general fund—its basic operating fund—was exhausted. Alan formally wrote Governor Brown that the "unprecedented overall indebtedness of $100 million underscores the urgency for budgetary revisions to restore our state to a sound fiscal footing."

California, the Golden State, was attracting hundreds of thousands of new residents and scores of new industries. Brown called for higher taxes to "meet the problems of population growth and of providing new and more state services." Alan announced, "The long-range forecast is optimistic. The revenue from the governor's tax program should pull the general fund out of debt and come close to balancing the governor's budget."

Odd problems confronted Alan daily. What to do about old grazing leases still honored at one cent an acre? Or a title to some hapless citizen's property held up endlessly because of a missing ten dollars? Or interest that hadn't been paid on a particular obligation in 1899? What to do with the balance extant in a fund of $2,806.00 set up in the 1800s for fighting bands of roving Indians? What does one do with the contents of old forgotten bank vaults in the controller's custody, everything from gold coins to babies' skeletons? (Alan's deputy controller, Irwin Nebron, was photographed with embalmed, red-haired Siamese twins found in one vault!)

Outgoing Governor Goodwin Knight complained that his official capitol portrait failed to do him justice. He wanted a new portrait commissioned. "It doesn't look like me, or *at* me! I want a painting where your eyes follow you around." Alan held up authorization of three thousand dollars for a second portrait, while the legislative council considered whether the state should stock up on more than one painting of Knight.

It was incredible, the variety of matters a controller was involved in but they provided good experience in human foibles.

Mechanics in the capitol garage complained long and loud that Alan did not use his official car enough, and the battery was running down. "I want to conduct my official business in my office, not on wheels," Alan replied.

In March Alan was responsible for putting nearly four million state income tax returns into the mails. For months thereafter his press releases produced scores of press items on tax deadlines, extensions, overpayments, penalties, tax boosts, and tax take increases.

Alan also served on the Board of Control, which John Francis Neylan had created. In Alan's words:

> Bert Levit and a third person and I were members. I was horrified at what went on. People with some claim against the state came before the board and presented their grievance. Levit was very rough on them. Usually the claims were not valid. The board voted "no" on all claims almost invariably—sometimes, it seemed to me, ignoring the seemingly just claims of helpless people. Levit seemed to enjoy turning claimants down. Often he'd berate those unhappy citizens for taking the time of the board.
>
> I decided it wasn't a good place to spend my time. So I turned over that function to my deputy, though I got involved when something particularly meaningful came along. Like the Fry case.

In 1958 the girlfriend of John H. (Tennessee) Fry, a fifty-five-year-old black laborer, was murdered in San Francisco. Fry pleaded guilty to involuntary manslaughter and was sentenced to San Quentin. Six months later another man confessed to the murder and was convicted and executed. Governor Brown pardoned Fry on January 16, 1959.

Though Fry had always maintained that he was innocent, the public defender had persuaded him to plead guilty to the lesser offense to avoid the death penalty. Fry filed a claim with the Board of Control, contending he had been wrongfully convicted. The law under which Fry filed his claim provided for a "hearing" before the Board of Control, but no previous claimant had ever been successful. Alan changed that.

Carl Greenberg wrote in the *Los Angeles Times:*

> The wheels of justice, it has been said, grind slowly. But, every once in a while there's a spark in somebody that ignites a fury against injustice — and the wheels of justice not only start up but move with comparative speed. . . .
>
> Though he has weightier problems on his mind, like keeping track of most of the state's financial transactions, Cranston pressed for a full investigation that went on for months and included an unprecedented hearing in San Francisco.

The Board of Control finally voted to award Fry $3,000. The legislature upped this to $5,000, the maximum permitted by law. Alan's prodding also brought about a change in the board's procedures — a decision to have more thorough hearings in the future.

Since Fry's payment was based on his loss of earnings, an income tax problem arose. Greenberg concluded: "Maybe the state Franchise Tax Board can help Fry. Man named Cranston serves on that board, too." The state Franchise Tax Board helped Fry receive full reimbursement.

One day a routine letter came to the controller's office from one William G. Bonelli, requesting that payments start on a state pension of $445.45 a month, which he asserted was his due.

"Bonelli's pension will be paid over my dead body!" Alan announced.

Who was Bonelli? In 1954 the shrewd, sharp-tongued, rugged-featured former member of the state Board of Equalization (on which Alan now served) had been indicted on liquor license bribery charges in Riverside, California. He had fled to Mexico, where he battled against extradition. He had been a Phi Beta Kappa, a Son of the American Revolution, and a professor of political science at Occidental College — a remarkable case of a highly educated man getting into politics and becoming very corrupt.

The newspaper headings delighted the public:

STATE PENSION FOR A MAN ON THE LAM?
HE RETIRED IN SOME HASTE!
CRANSTON TELLS BONELLI: 'WANT YOUR PENSION?
COME AND GET IT!' QUESTION INVOLVES BONELLI's
LIVE BODY AND CRANSTON'S DEAD ONE.

Whenever it was a dull day the press reported on Bonelli's accumulated pension funds, which soon ran into thousands of dollars. It told and retold the story, which had everything to enthrall its readers — a stolen fortune (the taxpayers'), outraged virtue (their own), a hero (the government — or Alan) and a quite intriguing villain. Bonelli kept it alive with defiant missives and assorted sardonic holiday greetings.

He did Alan a huge favor unwittingly by making him better known (as Pat Brown had urged). It cast him in the role of an official able to *do something* about the Bonelli case. Its frustrations, and Bonelli's successes and tauntings, had long rankled in the public mind.

"It was a beautiful case of a story snowballing," Alan recalls.

★ ★ ★ ★ ★ ★ ★ ★ ★ ★ ★ ★ ★

CHAPTER 15

The Family and Sacramento

★ ★ ★ ★ ★ ★ ★ ★ ★ ★ ★ ★ ★

One of Alan's first and most difficult tasks as controller was to evaluate and replace many of the inheritance tax appraisers, who represented a view of government and politics widely divergent from his own. Equally difficult was his selection of new appointees. The very first appointment he made, a few days after he assumed office, was George L. Thomas, an able Los Angeles attorney. Thomas was black, the first ever to be named an appraiser, and Alan appointed him first to symbolize his intention of totally changing the hitherto exclusive nature of the controller's appraiser panel. He appointed the first female appraisers in California's history, and a number of Hispanics, Asians, and American Indians.

The pressures from applicants mounted. Pat Brown, facing similar problems, once told him wearily, "For every appointment you make, you create a hundred enemies—and one ingrate!"

On a certain Monday he planned to make one of his final replacements, removing a Sonora dentist who had long served as appraiser for Tuolumne County in the Sierra Nevada. Alan planned to replace him with a prominent young attorney. But on the preceding Sunday, Alan was scheduled to ride a horse in Sonora's annual Mother Lode Round-up Parade. Determined to keep his family with him as much as possible, he took them along.

As they were driving into the mountains, Geneva said, "It's going to be *hot*. But it's good we're together. You'll have to try and save weekends just for the family, Alan. Try and mix family and politics. Your little boys need you."

"I know, I'd like to," Alan said. "I can probably save Sundays at least. I'll save all the Saturdays and evenings that I can manage. But it won't be easy."

"I suppose this parade is important? How many people will see it?" Geneva asked.

"They say twenty thousand."

"Impressive."

Alan led the two-mile-long parade as honorary marshal. Riding past the grandstand, wearing his ten-gallon hat and western regalia, Alan spotted his family sitting with his Aunt Jessie Patton, who lived in this mountain town. Waving at him excitedly and pointing, the boys showed their delight in the hundred floats (one was a replica of a gold-rush era church) and the twelve-mule jerkline team, ancient hand-pumper cart, mobile calaboose, bands, stage coaches, silver-decked parade horses, horseless carriages, buckaroos, Mexican *vaqueros,* and Sioux Indians.

Geneva waved too and then fanned herself, indicating disgust with the heat — eighty-six degrees in the shade. (A seventy-four-year old and a four-year old had been stricken with heat prostration.) Beside her sat an unknown couple, a large stocky man with a tiny wife. "They were waving even more wildly than my family," Alan recalls. "They kept waving as though they were long-lost friends. I kept trying to figure out who they were."

Later in the stands, Geneva introduced them. They turned out to be the current appraiser and his wife; they had attached themselves to Aunt Jessie. "Aunt Jessie's delighted that they're so interested in you!" Geneva whispered to Alan.

"You *must* come see our wonderful house," the woman urged Alan. "It's close by in Columbia, a forty-niners' town, restored to its original state."

Alan begged off.

After the parade, Aunt Jessie persuaded the Cranstons to see the sights in Columbia on their own. But just as they drove into town, along came the appraiser's wife in her car. Waving frantically, she slammed on her brakes. Alan had to stop too. "We live just round the corner," she insisted. "You've *got* to come see our beautiful place. Your kids would *love* it. We've got some old pistols and things."

Rob pleaded, "Let's go." Alan reluctantly agreed. The Cranstons followed her to her house, which was indeed a unique showplace, furnished as it had been some eighty years before. The couples sat in the back garden, drinking sarsaparilla under a tree. Rob returned to the house again to inspect its curiosities. Shortly the wife excused herself. The Cranstons soon followed her into the living room and came upon an amazing scene.

Rob stood by a window, holding something up in the air. The woman, who was very tiny, even smaller than eleven-year-old Rob, was jumping up in the air, reaching, grabbing, clutching, trying to get whatever it was that he held in his hand.

Rob shouted, "Look what I found!" He threw something and Alan caught it. It was a matchbook. "ELECT BOB KIRKWOOD AS CONTROLLER!" it proclaimed.

"I found a whole *bunch* of them!" Rob shouted excitedly. "In that bowl over there!"

Her husband came in and was at once horrified. "I *told* you to get rid of those damn things!" he shouted at his wife.

The woman explained, "But if we'd used them in the campaign, they wouldn't be here, would they? We just use them to light fires."

Rob jumped around joyfully, "Oh, boy! What I found! Look what I found!"

Alan firmly subdued him. The couple apologized. The Cranstons apologized and made a rapid escape. Rob was proud to have discovered the matches and exposed their hosts, while Geneva was pink with suppressed mirth, and Alan was burning red to the ears with embarrassment.

Alan knew if he proceeded with his plan to replace the appraiser the next day, everybody in Sonora would believe that the petty state controller had removed him because he had Kirkwood matches in his house.

As Alan drove homeward down the highway, facing the glare of the setting sun, with the boys scuffling in the back seat and Geneva trying to promote peace, he sighed deeply. He decided to put off the move for several months.

Along with the complexities of the controller's job, Alan's new role brought changes in his personal life. Putting the Hilltop house in Los Altos up for sale, he and Geneva scoured the areas along the Sacramento and American rivers for a home. At last they found just what they were looking for — an old farmhouse with picturesque barns and oak trees, at 3819 Thornwood Drive, only fifteen minutes from the

Capitol. Hidden in a seven-acre rural enclave in Sacramento's north area suburbia, the square, two-story, white-clapboard house hugged the sloping land, which was bordered by a creek. Trees partly screened it from the subdivisions springing up in the olive orchard of the original ranch.

Enchanted with the place, they named it Animal Farm, and Alan later catalogued its occupants as "thirty-nine chickens, twenty-one ducks, four cats, two goats, one dog, one lamb, one horse, one pig, two occasional frogs, and just scads of birds."

Peaceful coexistence was the rule at the Cranstons' Animal Farm. "We're one big, happy family here," Geneva told a reporter.*

"Haven't you ever considered having, maybe, fresh from the farm lamb chops or southern fried chicken, if you know what I mean?" the reporter asked.

"That would be like saying which child should we eat for Easter," Geneva replied.

Under this live and let live policy, Snowball, their white sow, grew to 500 pounds. "Snowball was the good pig in Orwell's book," Alan recalled. Rob had captured her as a piglet in a greased pig contest.

The farm was screened by seven hundred trees that Alan planted. By the time he was nine, Kim became supervisor of Animal Farm, caring for the inhabitants and ordering all the cases of pet food, sacks of chicken mash, and bales of hay it took to keep the family happy for a month. He had regular daily customers for the chicken eggs to help cover his expenses. He was ably assisted by Roy, their watchful German shepherd. If the kidding got too serious between any two animals, including the cats, Roy leaped between them.

Cassius, a pugilistic rooster, developed the habit of ambushing Alan as he ran for his morning exercise.

"The Animal Farm collection began growing when we attended an auction in Roseville," Geneva recalled. "A man drove up in a pickup with all these tiny goats. He happened to say, 'They'll be good eating for Easter.' That was all Kim needed to hear. He bought one goat, Captain Billy Kidd, for three dollars." Visitors were sometimes startled to see Captain Kidd peering out from the upper branches of a large oak tree. He had climbed up on a series of ramps Kim had built to their mutual treehouse.

*Sacramento Bee, August 28, 1965.

The isolation of the old farmhouse lent itself to the family's observance of Hallowe'en which they found a welcome escape from the restraints and trials of the political life. Geneva threw herself into Hallowe'en with a vengeance, finding it an outlet for her creative talents and her sense of humor. She egged her "three boys" to new pranks and heights of bizarre inventiveness.

One evening recently Kim was recalling his childhood to me and I taped his recollections.

In Sacramento, we invited some neighbors to come over and help us create a haunted house. When you walked into the living room, you found a number of people doing odd things, like in a Charles Addams cartoon. An old woman sat in a corner all night in her rocking chair, rocking back and forth, cackling whenever kids got too close to her. Mom, in a witch's outfit, ran around scaring people. Upstairs in a bathtub was Irwin Nebron, the deputy state controller. The bathtub was filled with water and red dye. It appeared to be filled with blood. When Irwin offered cups of red Kool-Aid to kids as they walked into the bathroom, they all refused. Even I didn't take any.

Few people knew us or knew who lived in that house. So they weren't quite prepared for what they got. The house was somewhat weird in itself. I would go out and meet kids as they came down the street in flocks. I'd mingle with them, acting like one of them, and we'd enter and walk through the house. When we arrived back downstairs, they'd begin to wonder where the candy was. Just then Alan would come walking out of the kitchen, wearing a hobo outfit, old shirt, torn pants, old shoes, and with several days' growth of beard on his charcoaled face. He made mute sounds (a little more enthusiastic than groaning), and he pulled a garbage can with him, holding it by one handle. I said, "Maybe that's where the candy is," and I walked up and peered in, and Alan grabbed me by the heels and threw me into the can. A pillow in the bottom stopped me from going clear through. Screaming, a few kids threw their candy bags at us and ran. Alan dragged me off to the kitchen. I screamed, and Alan returned with the garbage can. Whereupon all of the remaining kids ran out of the house yelling, throwing their empty candy bags at us.

I sneaked out a side door and met another group of kids coming up the driveway. The kids going out told them, "You're crazy if you go into *that* house!"

With all the candy they threw at us, I didn't have to go trick-or-treating at all. It was great fun. So much easier than going door-to-door!

As I recall, the next Hallowe'en they came back with rotten eggs and water balloons!

Eventually the Cranstons outgrew their old, square, and occasionally "haunted" farmhouse and built a rambling gray-green modern ranch house close to the ancient stables among the oaks. Alan and

Geneva began inviting groups of legislators for informal Saturday lunches and dinners. There in a relaxed atmosphere of good food, fun, and fellowship, they discussed the emerging problems of the new administration.

The most alarming of these became the bitter and dangerous rivalry springing up between the powerful speaker of the assembly, Jesse Unruh, and Alan's long-time friend and ally, Governor Pat Brown. Unruh was thirty-seven, "over-sized and extra bright,"* fierce and rough as a bear. The Democratic assemblyman from southern California had played a key role in Pat Brown's campaign for the governorship. The southern California campaign had been under his direction. Brown rewarded him by helping him obtain the chairmanship of the powerful Assembly Ways and Means Committee, which controlled all finance legislation in the lower house. Thus it controlled much of the destiny of the governor's program.

"Brown has a bear by the tail," Alan remarked the day of Unruh's appointment. "I think he's a bit uneasy about Jesse himself."

Unruh, the bulky, pale-blue-eyed, sandy-haired son of a poor Texas sharecropper, had started up the ladder in the Assembly. He had fought every inch of the way. His mind was quick and tough. His aspirations were boundless. His German name spelled "unrest." For a long time he loyally supported the governor but gradually grew impatient. He had too many ideas of his own about the state and its future — and about his own future.

Ever since its last reorganization by Republican Governor C. C. Young thirty years before, California's government had grown haphazardly, mostly by additions rather than by functional consolidations. Governor Brown had to map policy with a cabinet two-thirds the size of the state senate and twice the size of the cabinet of the president. He could not get his whole cabinet into his capacious office.

Headed by Finance Director Levit, a new commission set up by the governor began drafting a plan for government organization. But the problem was complicated when legislation for that same purpose was introduced by San Francisco's Republican Assemblyman Milton Marks. Marks's bill threatened to strip the state controller of his tax functions, abolish the Franchise Tax Board, and denude the elective state Board of Equalization of most of its duties. Most of these func-

Ronnie and Jesse by Lou Cannon, page 9.

tions would be transferred to the Finance Department in a move which Marks claimed would save the state about four million dollars a year.

Similar legislation had perennially been introduced to no avail. But this time, to Marks's amazement, his measure was sent with a "Do-Pass" to the Ways and Means Committee. There Chairman Unruh, eager to diminish the power of other Democratic officials and to enhance the powers of the governorship — to which he aspired — declared he would do everything possible to support the bill. Alan, always concerned about too much centralization of power, quickly mobilized a counter-offensive. He appeared with a group of other officials before the Ways and Means Committee to oppose the bill. On the first day of the hearing, Unruh refused to recognize them and made them cool their heels while witnesses droned on with favorable arguments.

When the committee convened again, Alan and his exasperated cohorts were finally recognized. Alan argued that the estimated savings were wholly inaccurate, charging that the bill would create inefficiency and increased costs. Standing before the microphone, Alan, speaking deliberately, declared:

> This bill puts too much authority in appointed rather than elected officials. Auditors and collectors would be eliminated, leading to fraud and chiseling. The bill would strip the public of protection. There is no virtue in mere bigness. Too often there is a relationship between the magnitude of a government agency and the mileage of red tape it wraps around its procedures. It would be needless folly to increase the cost of collecting taxes and diminish the voice of the people in tax affairs, when we are asking the people of California to pay higher taxes.

Paul Leake, chairman of the Board of Equalization, argued:

> Fiscal authority must be independent from the governor's office, regardless of who is governor. This bill could give Brown the powers of a tyrant. There is the possibility of creating a dictator.

Assemblyman Edward Gaffney called it an Alice-in-Wonderland proposal that would make the governor a czar. Unruh, who had been glowering at the opposing witnesses, laughingly asked, in his powerful, rolling barrel-organ voice, "Do you fear these consequences under the present governor?" Unruh had shortly before characterized Brown as "a tower of jello." His question produced muffled snickers.

Weeks of tactical struggles followed. Eventually Marks beat a strategic retreat. Fearing his legislation would be killed if he let it go to a vote, he switched to calling for an interim study. But various other reorganization proposals were considered by Unruh's committee. The San Francisco *Examiner* published a cartoon of a couple of shabby middle-aged taxpayers scratching their heads over mounting piles of red tape. One said, "We like our *old* octopus best!" At last, the fight became a duel between Jesse Unruh and Alan, centered on a proposal tacitly supported by Governor Brown to reduce the role of the controller by cutting back his staff and transferring part of it elsewhere. Alan's civil service workers were outraged. The administrative deputy he had inherited from the Republican era, Ralph McCarthy, told Alan to fight the proposal, arguing that it was just a first step toward drastic weakening of the controller's authority. Deputy controller Nebron thought it was important for Alan to preserve morale and win the confidence of the staff. Alan, who had won on the major issue when Marks had given up, wasn't eager to continue the battle with Unruh on this relatively insignificant matter.

Alan recalls: "I wound up opposing the legislation. I had to fight Jesse in his own committee, where he had wanted to show his power as the new chairman.

"I beat him there on his home ground. Jesse was furious. He took it as a personal affront. It was his first and only defeat in his own committee."

After his victory, Alan bumped into Unruh in the shadowy, subterranean garage of the old El Mirador Hotel across from the Capitol. Jesse's pale blue eyes glared at Alan, and his wide mouth curved in a rueful grin. "You sure took the governor's pants off in my committee!" he growled. He lifted his ponderous frame into his car and drove off, having nimbly laid his defeat on the governor and not on himself.

As Alan drove away in the opposite direction and emerged into the sunlight, he thought, "How agile! He'll be tough to combat. Skillful and strong."

Looking back, Alan concluded he'd made a mistake tangling with Jesse on this issue, particularly on his turf. Jesse was a serious student of government. He had his own thoughts on reorganization, and he didn't relish being frustrated. Meanwhile Alan reorganized the controller's office on his own. He cut back on his civil service staff by shifting people to other jobs and not naming replacements. He expanded the number of appraisers by thirty-five, thereby reducing to a more reasonable figure the amount of money any one appraiser could earn, but without increasing the cost to the taxpayers. In another decision that was highly controversial among his principal advisers, Alan announced that, breaking precedent, he would publicly report the earnings of each appraiser each year. The decision was anathema to virtually all of Alan's appraisers. "We have no right to keep your public earnings secret," Alan told them.

Alan had, indeed, seen only the beginning of a long struggle with Unruh. Battle number two came when Jesse, seeing the CDC as a threat to his ambitions, sought to deny it the right to endorse candidates.

Jesse introduced a bill outlawing endorsements which sailed through the Assembly. Alan led the opposition in the Senate where it finally passed by a narrow margin. Unruh and his faction of the Party urged Brown to sign it. Alan and his faction urged him to veto it. Brown vetoed it. Jesse, vanquished again, was furious again.

Clearly Alan and Jesse were motivated partly by philosophical differences and partly by self-interest in this issue. Part of the underlying difficulty regarding the CDC was that it was made up of volunteers. Jesse used to say, "The trouble with volunteers is that you can't fire them." He wanted command and control. Alan wanted something quite different. Jesse feared, probably correctly, that the CDC wouldn't endorse him any time soon for statewide office so he wanted to cut it down. Alan believed that he and his allies could depend on CDC endorsements for the foreseeable future.

★ ★ ★ ★ ★ ★ ★ ★ ★ ★ ★ ★ ★ ★ ★ ★ ★ ★ ★
Brown and Chessman
★ ★ ★ ★ ★ ★ ★ ★ ★ ★ ★ ★ ★ ★ ★ ★ ★ ★ ★

Meanwhile Governor Brown was riding high. He began to be talked of as a possible presidential candidate in 1960. Alan, returning from a national Controllers and Treasurers Convention in Philadelphia (where he was elected vice president of the organization), told reporters of Brown's growing national reputation. He said, "Kennedy has greater support nationally than is widely believed in California. But there is a growing feeling that if a deadlock develops at the Democratic National Convention next year between Adlai Stevenson, John F. Kennedy, and Stuart Symington, then Brown is the likely man to emerge."

Brown told Alan later on, "Jesse Unruh made his reputation on my program, and I made mine on the way he handled it."*

The rivalry between these two men affected California's history, and Alan's life, for most of the ensuing decade.

Like the old Southern Pacific machine, Hiram Johnson's reforms, and Artie Samish's lobbying, the Democrats' "Responsible Liberalism" rose only to perish. From the very beginning, earthquake-like cracks appeared in its facade.

The *Sacramento Bee*'s long-time and sagacious political editor, Herbert Phillips, characterized Governor Brown's remarkable record in 1959 "for volume and scope of enactments in a single session (as) comparing favorably with Governor Hiram Johnson's in 1911." His Fair Employment Practices legislation brought widespread reform.

*The quote is also found in "California, the Politics of Confusion," *Frontier Magazine,* October 1962. Also in *Ronnie and Jesse,* by Lou Cannon, Doubleday, 1969, page 102.

Cross-filing was killed. Though creating bitter opposition, his tax bill was widely seen as fair and equitable. His budget was balanced. His California water plan and his master plan for higher education promised to become dramatic, historic achievements.

"We have steadied a rocking boat," Alan reported. National newspapers and magazines proclaimed Brown's "national stature."

Meanwhile Jesse Unruh, reaching an unprecedented summit of personal influence in the legislature, was charting an independent course. Though he guided Brown's budgets through the Assembly, he attempted to usurp the governor's initiative on a variety of state spending issues. Their first acrimonious public quarrel, however, occurred over the governor's handling of the Caryl Chessman case.

The whole country took note of Brown's death-row reprieve. Twelve years of well-publicized legal maneuverings had blocked Chessman's execution following his conviction as a bandit and rapist for a particularly vicious sex crime. Brown condemned capital punishment as a barbarous practice, contending it was not administered evenhandedly and did not deter crime. Searching for a humane solution during a period of intense agitation over the death penalty, Brown issued Chessman a stay of execution following an impassioned phone call from his son, Jerry.

Alan recalls:

> I was lunching at Del Coronado. Irwin Nebron came over and told me of Pat's action. I was thrilled by his compassionate act but thought the way it was done could be potentially politically disastrous.
>
> I shared Pat's view of capital punishment and went to work at once to try to lessen the political damage, speaking out all over the state against capital punishment. But I was unable to help him much. The issue cut deeply into his popularity with the public and strained his relations with many in the legislature. It proved to be the beginning of Pat's downfall.

Brown asked the legislature to consider wiping out the death penalty altogether. Furious at having this hot potato dumped into their laps, legislators summarily rejected Brown's plea. Unruh was especially outraged. "Jesse was mad, very mad," said an aide. "We just kept him in his office until he cooled down."

Like Brown, Unruh favored abolishing capital punishment, but he charged that Brown, who was not up for reelection until 1962, was "heedlessly sacrificing Democratic assemblymen in the 1960 elections." The Chessman case had made the death penalty a tremendously volatile political issue.

On May 2, 1960, the eve of the California primary, angry proponents of the death penalty were unappeased, and opponents were still more infuriated when, amid worldwide pleas for clemency, Chessman was executed in the gas chamber.

Brown himself attributed some of his ineffectiveness in controlling the California delegation at the Democratic National Convention — where John F. Kennedy was nominated a couple of months later — to "being badly wounded by the Chessman thing."*

Brown and Alan strongly supported Kennedy at the convention, but when Kennedy swept to nomination on the first ballot, California's votes were badly split — an indication of Brown's waning strength.

When John F. Kennedy was elected president in November, Richard Nixon carried the state by 35,623 votes. However, Jesse Unruh was credited with delivering populous Los Angeles County to Kennedy, and his status rose.

A few days after the election, Alan predicted that it would be Nixon against Brown for the California governorship in 1962 but declared that "I believe Pat Brown will win."

Richard Nixon, making his first political speech following his defeat for the presidency, told the California Republican State Central Committee in March, "I have no intention of running for governor in 1962."

Alan continued to tell audiences around the state, however, that Nixon *would* be Brown's opponent, and that Brown would win. "Nixon's repeated statements that he is 'not planning to run' are a matter of semantics. Nixon needs to stay in the public eye. His goal is the presidency. What better place would there be than as governor of California."

A slowdown in business across the nation had occurred at the end of 1960, and California felt the pinch. Sales tax revenues dropped. Unemployment rose. Most of the surplus of the General Fund went to putting the state's building program on a pay-as-you-go rather than a bond-financed basis. Little chance was seen for a state tax cut.

The biggest problem facing the state was its population explosion. It was widely predicted that California's population of fifteen million

*Lou Cannon in *Ronnie and Jesse.*

would double in twenty years. There was a rising demand for services to meet the needs of the newcomers.

Now the polls showed Brown's popularity at a new low: 17 percent behind Nixon.

Sharing coffee one day with the governor in his corner office, Alan offered some words of encouragement. Brown looked at him with a wan expression.

"I'm feeling exhausted. I may not run again," he confided.

Alan showed his surprise. "You must! I'm certain Nixon will be your opponent, and you can defeat him!

"I'll think it over."

Brown told others of his indecision. This set off a flurry of speculation in the press as to who might succeed him. The press reported that Alan Cranston, Jesse Unruh, Lt. Gov. Glenn Anderson, and Atty. Gen. Stanley Mosk were rivals in the fight to succeed Brown.

*   *   *

In 1961, three years into his first term as controller, Alan had the glow that comes with having been elected to public office and never having known political defeat. The press continued to speculate favorably about him as a potential candidate for higher political office.

From a September 15, 1960, editorial in the *Willows Daily Journal:*

> Cranston is scrupulously thorough and runs his office efficiently and with high employee morale. There was some resentment when he "inherited" the office from the popular Robert Kirkwood. But his entire staff is now 100 percent behind him, with the result that the office is run efficiently and economically, to the great advantage of California's taxpayers. Mr. Cranston's tact, plus firmness on matters of conviction have earned him the department's deep respect. This same quality has also won him the cooperation and admiration of legislators.

In the *San Francisco News-Call-Bulletin,* Ruth Finney wrote: "Most California Democrats when pushed for a senate candidate usually mention State Controller Alan Cranston."*

On February 21, 1961, the *Los Angeles Times*'s James Bassett described his appearance at a FDR-JFK fundraising testimonial dinner at the International Ballroom of the Beverly Hilton Hotel.

*February 24, 1961.

"Three years ago," said the tall, suave, eloquent Cranston, "Nixon, Knight, and Knowland seemingly had a death grip on California politics. But we are resolved that not one of these three shall ever again hold public office!" His remarks were greeted by applause so thunderous that nearby baked Alaskas collapsed like HHH's presidential boomlet.

Alan's frequent appearances on the statewide speech-making circuit led to predictions of an eventual power showdown between him and Pat Brown. One political editor* wrote: "To date there has been no sign of any friction between the two," and he forecast that Alan would run for reelection as controller in 1962 because California traditionally allocated its two United States Senate seats on a one-north and one-south formula. Senator Tom Kuchel's was the "southern" seat; Senator Clair Engle came from Red Bluff in the far north.

Kuchel had been appointed to the Senate in 1952 when Nixon moved up to the vice presidency. He had defeated Yorty in 1954 and Richards in 1956. Now he was minority whip, elected by the so-called "liberal bloc" of Senate Republicans. He was a popular middle-of-the-roader, attractive to California's independent voters.

Alan told reporters, "The Senate race is a long way off. Right now I'm trying to be a good state controller. I have enough issues to deal with and resolve without thinking about other fields."

All the speculation about Alan as a possible candidate for governor or senator cooled Republican opposition to him as controller. He was one of the last members of Pat Brown's team to be challenged by Republican candidates. At last a very conservative Republican assemblyman from Pasadena announced that he would run against Alan for controller. He was a silver-thatched savings and loan executive, fifty-nine years old, named Bruce Reagan.

*Harry Farrell in the *San Jose Mercury,* September 5, 1960.

CHAPTER 17

★ ★ ★ ★ ★ ★ ★ ★ ★ ★ ★ ★ ★ ★ ★
The 1962 Election
★ ★ ★ ★ ★ ★ ★ ★ ★ ★ ★ ★ ★ ★ ★

In late September 1961 Richard Nixon formally announced that he would run for governor. As Nixon ripped into the Brown record and the "mess in Sacramento," Brown's ire rose. Proud of what he had accomplished, the governor soon leaned toward accepting Nixon's challenge. He was strongly encouraged by Alan, who assured him that Nixon's candidacy was bound to activate a host of dedicated Democratic workers. Brown's announcement of his candidacy that January came as no surprise. He began to climb in the polls again.

Nixon won the Republican nomination two to one over Joseph Shell. In the Democratic primary, Alan ran for controller unopposed—his first unchallenged race. Senator Thomas Kuchel faced a right-wing challenge from Lloyd Wright, but won handily. Alan noted that Wright's campaign was chaired by a rapidly rising newcomer to Republican politics, actor Ronald Reagan.

The contest between Brown and Nixon dominated the general election, and was watched with fascination by the entire country. Campaigning tirelessly, as much for Brown as for himself, Alan felt reasonably confident of his own reelection.

Once, aghast after looking at one of Alan's weekly schedules, Ted Baer asked him, "What makes you campaign such long hours and cover so much ground each day?"

Alan's dark eyes looked sunken and tired, but they brightened when he said: "Because when I stagger across the finish line, I want to know that I've been everywhere and done everything that it's humanly possible for me to do!"

He virtually ignored his own lesser-known opponent and talked mostly about the administration's gains. "The water controversy is on the way to a solution. The state's fiscal position is stronger than it has been in years. The master plan for higher education, the smog control bill, enlightened election reform, and civil rights legislation — these typify the accomplishments of the incumbent administration."*

Both Brown and Nixon presented positive programs for solving state problems, but negative charges dominated the news. Brown accused Nixon of inexperience with state issues and having eyes on the White House. Nixon claimed Brown played partisan politics, indulged in nepotism, and appointed incompetents to office. The loan by Howard Hughes to the Nixon family became an issue, while Nixon resurrected his traditional campaign charge that his opponent was soft on communism.

At a campaign affair at a Hollywood home, shortly before the election, a woman asked Alan to come outside into the dark garden for a secret talk. There she said, "I'm working in an ad agency handling the Nixon campaign." She handed him an envelope and fled, leaving him in the darkness wondering what the envelope contained. He returned to the home, found a bathroom, and locked himself in. The envelope contained original photographs showing Pat Brown bowing down to a little girl with cerebral palsy. As he bent over her and she looked up smiling, his hands were clasped in what looked like a praying position. This photograph had been taken in the Assembly Chamber in connection with a cerebral palsy fund drive. Also enclosed was a cropped, composite photo showing Pat apparently bowing down to Communist Mao Tse Tung, who had been substituted for the child. ("I believe Harry Bridges was shown beaming in the background," Alan recalls.) The composite photo was to be used in a pamphlet attacking Pat Brown as a Communist sympathizer. A similar tactic had been used in the Nixon campaigns against Helen Gahagan Douglas and Jerry Voorhis.

Alan turned the material over to Harry Lerner, a public relations man in the Brown campaign. The moment the Nixon campaign unveiled their pamphlet, the Brown campaign counterattacked, releaseing the doctored photos, and disclosed their opponent's duplicity. The pamphlet backfired badly — showing there was no new Nixon yet!

Pat Brown became exhausted and groggy toward the end of the strenuous campaign. Often he awoke in a strange motel feeling like

*From Alan Cranston's "Sacramento Commentary," his occasional column. 2/4/61.

a zombie, unable to remember where he was or why he was there. Once, he told Alan, he had awakened with a start and discovered a small female figure beside him in the motel bed. Frantically he struggled to regain full consciousness. Then his first hair-raising thought came: "My God, Nixon's put a woman in bed with me!" He leapt up and sprang toward the door, just as his wife Bernice rolled over, opened startled eyes, and exclaimed huskily, "Pat, *what* is the matter with you?!"

Once on a very hot day before a Los Angeles parade, Alan unexpectedly came face to face with Nixon, waiting beside an open car. Standing together, they spoke briefly. Suddenly Nixon poked his finger hard into Alan's chest and exclaimed, "You're not sweating!" Alan felt as though he had been stabbed.

Toward the end of the bitter campaign, Alan received two secret requests from influential people asking him to use his position as chairman of the Franchise Tax Board to give them a glimpse of Nixon's income tax returns. One was from an individual purporting to represent Pat Brown. The other was a prominent publisher of a daily newspaper. The requests were, of course, improper. Upon investigation, Alan learned that at various times in the past, some members of the board had indeed taken a quiet look at the tax returns of certain individuals. Apparently, in at least one instance, a member of the board had used the tax information to dissuade (blackmail) a potential opponent from running against him.

"The temptation in the case of Richard Nixon was, of course, great," Alan recalls,

> since along with almost everyone else, I believed he was running for governor in order to seek the presidency, an outcome I viewed as disastrous for the country. I thought the national interest was deeply involved in a Pat Brown victory over Richard Nixon. But I turned down the requests, and I put through a resolution at a subsequent Franchise Tax Board meeting, instructing the staff to refuse to give any board member information about anyone's tax returns, unless instructed to do so by the full board in an open, public meeting.
>
> I was outraged when Nixon as president reportedly instructed his aides to use tax returns to harass his political opponents!

Shortly before election day, the Cuban missile crisis occurred. Alan recalls, "We wondered what political consequences, besides other fatal consequences, this might cause. I remember sitting in the Subway

Terminal Building, watching TV with a big crowd, as John F. Kennedy made his first dramatic announcement that the Russians were moving missiles into Cuba and that we were going to stop them. The results seemed almost incalculable."

> As the campaign came to a close, it looked as if we were winning, but we still couldn't believe we had Nixon hanging on the ropes. We expected some bombshell at the last minute. Nixon had reserved Sunday night for a TV show. I remember pulling into a motel, interrupting my own campaign, getting a room, and settling down to watch for a bombshell. Nixon was very wooden, sitting there with his family. He really had nothing much to say. No surprises. After two or three minutes, we relaxed, knew the show was a dud, and felt the campaign was over.
>
> It was in the course of that show that Nixon demonstrated where his mind had been all along. He mistakenly alluded to his campaign for "president of California."

The final count showed California had undergone "another of its swift and mystifying reversals of sentiment."* Having given Nixon the edge for president in 1960, it rejected him for governor in 1962. Brown received 3,037,109 votes; Nixon, 2,740,351. Brown had accomplished in California what John F. Kennedy had failed to do, and was again being hailed as a giant-killer. Alan watched with countless other Californians as Nixon — tired, shaken and unshaved — appeared on TV at a press conference the morning after the election. He declared that he had "retired" from politics and chastised the press, all save Carl Greenberg of the *Los Angeles Times*. He accused the reporters of "shafting him." When he concluded with the now famous "You won't have Dick Nixon to kick around any more," the political pundits mostly agreed that Nixon was through with politics. "His mask was off," Alan said to me thoughtfully.

Senator Kuchel had defeated Dick Richards by a massive margin — 3,180,483 to 2,452,839 — but all the incumbent statewide officials had won.

Alan led the ticket. He won by the biggest margin in the state's history in any statewide race — 1,258,314 votes. His total vote, 3,372,691, was the largest ever given a candidate in a contested statewide struggle in American history.

*Herbert Phillips in *Big Wayward Girl*, page 210.

★ ★ ★ ★ ★ ★ ★ ★ ★ ★ ★ ★ ★ ★

CHAPTER 18

The Senate Seat
of Clair Engle

★ ★ ★ ★ ★ ★ ★ ★ ★ ★ ★ ★ ★ ★

In the summer of 1963 Alan, Geneva, and their boys spent almost two months in Europe, touring twelve countries with *Europe on $5 a Day* as a guide. Upon their return in August, they learned that Sen. Clair Engle had been hospitalized for brain surgery. Speculation was rife as to who would succeed to the vacancy that many assumed might occur.

Five years earlier, Alan had stepped aside in the Senate race for Clair. Thus he was not surprised to find on his first day back, August 26, that Governor Brown had sent word he wanted to see him. In Brown's inner sanctum, the true "corner office" of the Capitol Building, Alan found the governor hunched over his vast walnut desk, immersed in legislation and letters requiring his signature. Light filtered through the trees in Capitol Park, played over the deep-piled orange carpet and walnut paneling, and glanced off Brown's horn-rimmed glasses as he looked up with a serious face. He half rose from his swivel chair and extended a hearty handshake.

"Welcome back!" he exclaimed in his husky, Irish voice. "You look great! But you're thin!" he said enviously.

As they chatted briefly, Alan noted that Brown's face looked tired and harassed.

"Now there's some tax legislation here," Brown said warmly. "I want to know what you think . . ." he began, and they settled to business. After ten minutes of concentrated work, Brown pushed some papers toward Alan with a sigh of relief. "I agree. You'll know how to proceed."

Picking up a sheaf of papers, Alan started to go. But the governor took off his glasses, rubbed his forehead, and said, "Wait . . . Jesse Unruh is still fighting me at every turn. He wants to head up President Kennedy's campaign for reelection in California. The White House staff, O'Brien, O'Donnell, are all pushing it."

Alan grimaced.

Brown continued. "It's too bad we can't be a team. But . . . Jesse has decided he wants to be governor. Can't wait till I'm ready to leave. So he obstructs and opposes and fights and schemes and balks me and scuttles my program. It's fierce! Some days I'm almost ready to quit — but that's just what he wants me to do!"

"Don't quit!" Alan exclaimed.

"I know you'll help," the Governor said heartily. His face had reddened when he mentioned the speaker. Now it fell into anxious lines. His lower lip and jaw protruded as he stared out at the trees in Capitol Park. Alan waited, knowing Brown still had something to say.

"Alan, you've heard about Clair Engle's brain surgery three days ago?"

"Just heard. It's hard to believe."

"Clair and I have always been close. Last week he was speaking on the Senate floor. Absolutely no warning! A horrible shock!"

"Awful!" Alan said feelingly. "Clair's always been such a scrapper. I'll bet he pulls through."

Brown sighed heavily. "Speculation's running wild. Nobody tells us about his actual condition. What his prognosis is. His wife won't let his doctors discuss his case. He may be all right. But a scramble's already on for his job. Everybody's asking who will run next year if Clair can't, whom I'll appoint if he resigns or dies." He shook his head. They exchanged a look of commiseration. In the sudden silence, alert to what the governor would say next, Alan heard the muffled clatter of a typewriter off in another room.

"Help me all you can," muttered Brown.

Alan nodded sympathetically. "I'll see what I can find out," he said. "Don't be discouraged." He went out, leaving the governor looking relieved at having shared his problem.

As Alan crossed the corridor back to his office, past scenes raced through his mind — Pat being helpful in the days of the rise of the CDC, always cooperative, yet avoiding turmoil, and wisely staying away from party battles. In his cautious way, he had done everything Alan had asked. Alan felt a great obligation to him.

Two weeks later at an evening reception for top Democratic officials at the Senator Hotel in Sacramento, Governor Brown drew Alan into a corner of the crowded high-ceilinged room.

"About the Kennedy campaign," he said, "I'm urging the White House to name me overall chairman, with Tom Lynch and Stanley Mosk as northern and southern heads."*

"Great," said Alan. "Do you think they will?"

"Yes, I *think* so. But Unruh's still pushing them hard."

A tall, broad-shouldered man bore down on them, carrying drinks. But Brown turned his back and half-faced the corner. "I've heard about Clair, confidentially, he said. "His doctors found an inoperable brain tumor. He's speechless and partially paralyzed. He's undergoing X-ray treatments at Bethesda to shrink the tumor.

"But Lu loves the Senate and wants her husband to stay. She says that she may—she *may*—publicly state that he can't seek reelection. In about three weeks! So our hands are tied! Meanwhile the jockeying's incredible!"

"I know."

"The Republicans are watching it too."

"Yes. Bill Knowland might try a comeback."

"Hm," said the Governor warily. "If I have to appoint a senator . . . whoever gets it will have to stand for reelection next year. The Republicans'll go all out to recover the seat." He sighed. "I'm under terrific pressure."

Impulsively Alan touched Brown's arm, looked intently into his face, and said, "You know, Pat, you owe me a Senate seat!"

Brown looked back alertly and thoughtfully. "Yes, Alan," he said. "I know your interest. In '58 you stepped aside for Clair. Now the other contenders are all from the south . . . Mosk, Unruh, Glenn Anderson . . ."

"Jimmy Roosevelt, Yorty."

"And the other seat's southern with Kuchel, of course. The old north-south tradition. I think . . ." his eyes through his glasses were friendly and warm. He smiled at Alan earnestly and left it at that.

*Lynch was San Francisco's DA. Mosk was the attorney general and Democratic national committeeman.

Alan exclaimed, "I wish it had come about in some other way! Clair and I've become good friends. And he's been a fine Senator."

"Yes," said Pat. "It's a tragic mess! Unruh sees the controllership as a possible steppingstone to the governorship." He glanced at Alan sharply. "Would you like to see Jesse as controller?"

What Pat seemed to be suggesting, if a vacancy occurred due to Senator Engle's plight, was a possible double play: Alan appointed to succeed Engle in the Senate, Unruh appointed to succeed Alan in the controllership. The thought of his panel of appointed appraisers being left to Unruh's tender mercies — and its power being used against Pat and himself — shot through Alan's mind. He answered firmly and without hesitation, "I would not!"

The governor shook his head in perplexity. An aide approached him, and he allowed himself to be drawn away. Later on, Alan was to wonder if that last exchange with Pat cost him a Senate seat in 1964.

On September 15 Sydney Kossen, the *San Francisco Examiner's* political editor, wrote that Alan was "the hottest Democratic prospect to replace Senator Clair Engle." He cited Alan's successful performance as controller but noted Alan was really more interested in national and foreign affairs.

On October 3 Alan took time out to send a bulky letter to Jack and me, vacationing in Ireland. "Things have been extremely wild politically," he wrote. He enclosed the Kossen clipping with a pile of others.

On the first he scribbled, "No change in Clair's condition. All signs indicate I'm in front if there's to be a succession — so naturally, all rivals are firing at me. Meanwhile, great maneuvers are under way to grab the controllership. Unruh wants it! I don't think he'll get it."

The *San Francisco News-Call-Bulletin's* veteran columnist Jack McDowell had noted on September 11:

> Geographical points give Cranston the edge. The California tradition, generally respected by both parties, has been to choose one U.S. Senator from the North and one from the South.
>
> Electability is a major point because the appointee would have to be running for election almost immediately.

Other articles pointed out that Cranston had led the ticket and broken all previous records in the last election.

Alan aslo enclosed a Rowland Evans and Robert Novak column from the September 30 *Washington Post*. On it he scrawled, "Jesse launches a model campaign in an odd way!" While Unruh would love to be senator, the column said, he feared he could not be elected. The controllership was the job he coveted, because it was relatively sheltered from political attack and publicity. "King-sized Jesse Unruh is plagued by being colorful and quotable in an age of political blandness."

Alan's final clipping, Arthur Caylor's column in the October 2 *News-Call-Bulletin*, reported that President Kennedy had "finally decided to settle a terrific inside struggle for power—perhaps for political survival—between Unruh and Governor Brown." He had named Atty. Gen. Stanley Mosk and San Francisco D. A. Tom Lynch, an ally of Brown, whom he described as "close as his morning shave," to head his state reelection campaign. Unruh was not mentioned. The Republicans would be disappointed, Caylor wrote—they would have liked nothing better than to see Unruh become the Democratic big shot in California. "Then they'd have a real issue in 'bossism'."

*   *   *

On November 22, 1963, the assassination of President Kennedy in Dallas rocked the world. This was devastating news to Alan, Brown, Mosk, Unruh, and other Democratic officials who had known and admired him, worked and campaigned with him, and strongly supported his leadership. Of them all, it was later Alan, in ways utterly unforeseen, whose career was the most profoundly affected by the tragedy.

As the curtain rose on a newly unfolding drama—the administration of President Lyndon B. Johnson—a pathetic figure appeared on stage, California's Clair Engle. Pale, frail, and semiparalyzed, barely able to speak, he attended the funeral of President Kennedy in a wheelchair. There California Democratic State Chairman Eugene Wyman gently asked his plans and was told only that a decision would be made in January.

In December two potent Republicans, actor George Murphy and financier Leland Kaiser, announced their candidacy for Engle's Senate seat.

On January 6, 1964, speaking in a weak and hesitant voice, Senator Engle announced in a TV film that he would run for reelection. "I'm in the race to stay," he declared haltingly.

The Democratic high command was confused, uncertain, alarmed, and incensed. Brown exclaimed to Alan, "It's pitiful the way Clair's being used!"

Later that week, attending a meeting of the Democratic National Committee in Washington, Alan, Brown, Mosk, and other officials wanted to see Engle, hoping to find out the truth about his condition. Engle's wife (and former secretary), Lucretia, announced that she planned to invite a series of Democratic dignitaries to their home for cocktails, dinners, and informal discussions.

Libby Gatov was one of the first to see Engle in his 100-year-old house, four blocks down New Jersey Avenue from the Senate. The Democratic National Committee member, who had served as John F. Kennedy's U.S. Treasurer, was a woman of considerable beauty, political savvy, and finesse. She had been chosen by the frustrated Democratic leadership as their spokeswoman. She emerged from the Engles' home grim-faced.

"I don't see how Engle can wage a fight for reelection," she told the press. "I'm sure this will be a contested primary. I dread the strain a campaign would impose on Engle."

She recalled later, "I cried on my way back to the hotel in the cab. Clair was in his wheelchair and looked better than I had expected; bright-eyed as always. But there were great gaps in the conversation when he was silent, unable to answer. He laughed often and utterly *inappropriately.* That was the thing that was so terribly disconcerting."

Alan visited Engle and felt the same pity and frustration. He, too, noted the strange laughter. Like the others, he declined to make any public comment, leaving that to Elizabeth Gatov.

Pat Brown called next, intending to persuade Engle not to run if he was too ill. He had an embarrassing confrontation with Mrs. Engle, who was infuriated when Brown implied that Engle should resign so he could make an appointment. She refused to let the governor see her husband. Following this episode, the governor demanded a full public medical report.

Dr. Roy Sexton, Engle's doctor, declared that "it would be professionally and administratively impossible to comply with the governor's demand." Angrily, Governor Brown announced the race was open to all comers.

During these anxious weeks, Engle appeared only twice on the Senate floor, one arm in a sling, the other holding a cane, to cast key votes for the Johnson administration's program. Lucretia Engle told the *San Francisco Examiner*'s Mildred Schroeder, "Politics is cold-blooded and ruthless. Since September I've been pouring tea for a parade of saliva testers. It disgusts and amuses me. We'll let the people decide."

Meanwhile, to the shock of Democratic leaders, a private Gallup poll showed Jimmy Roosevelt well ahead of Cranston, Engle, and Mosk.

Alan pondered his moves and made a difficult decision. On January 19 at a CDC directors meeting in Fresno, he announced that he would run for the Senate if Engle was unable to campaign vigorously or serve effectively. And Alan would also have to win the endorsement of the CDC convention.

"We're all acutely and inwardly torn by a basic conflict," he told the group of directors. "On the one hand, there is loyalty to a good and conscientious public servant—a friend. On the other, there is a deep and sensitive understanding of the overriding obligation to the millions of people in this state, and this nation, to insure strong leadership." The CDC leaders responded with warmth and encouragement. Alan proceeded to write a letter to Engle, urging him to authorize his doctor to make public a report on his condition. He said that if the report indicated Engle could run, he would do all he could to support him. Back came a letter signed by Engle declining to release a medical report and declaring, "I'm sorry to see you've joined the ranks of the saliva testers."

"As I read that letter," Alan told me, "I lost my hesitancy over the race. Bang! I made the decision to run. Right then I said, 'I'm going!'"

On February 11 the big, unruly CDC opened its convention in Long Beach. Two thousand delegates representing 75,000 club members jammed the registration area. Attendance exceeded 7,000. CDCers were agitated over Unruh-backed legislation in Sacramento that threatened CDC's future. But the impending race for the Senate seat held by the ailing Engle riveted everyone's attention. Mosk's candidacy had the behind-the-scenes backing of Unruh, but one place where the powerful Jesse had little influence was inside CDC. Congressman

Jimmy Roosevelt was coming up fast. He had his father's charm, smile, and speaking ability; if you closed your eyes when he spoke, you could hardly believe you weren't listening to FDR. With his magic name and his own ten-year liberal voting record in the House, he threatened to stampede the convention.

The Cranston forces won a long stiff preliminary scuffle when the convention voted to make a single endorsement among the nominees for the Senate seat, instead of endorsing all contenders.

On Saturday morning, Governor Brown's speech hailed CDCers as the most powerful volunteer force in America."

When Alan's name was placed before the convention, it set off a huge floor demonstration.

Then came a moment of tragic drama. Senator Engle was nominated in a series of impassioned speeches. He was not present to accept his nomination. But the presiding officer of the convention, crew-cut CDC president Tom Carvey, put through a prearranged telephone call to Engle in Washington. An expectant hush fell over the convention as Engle's halting voice greeted the delegates over loudspeakers. He briefly accepted their nomination and added, "I'm in this r-race to stay."

Carvey quickly asked, "When will you be out to see us in California?"

There was a long breathless silence. Then Engle's voice was heard again: "Well, it's a problematical, and-a, and-a . . ." There was a brief, strange, cackling laugh. Then the halting voice stumbled on: "It's, it's—a problematical."

Carvey exclaimed, "Senator, we all love you. God bless you! And get well!"

There was no reply. The full convention rose to its feet and applauded for a full minute. Many in the audience wept. The three-minute episode had a searing impact. Delegates called it brave, pathetic, and heartbreaking.

Roosevelt delivered a fiery, ultra-liberal acceptance speech, immediately following Engle's telephone drama. He was more effective than Alan in arousing the liberal emotions of the delegates. They roared in response, interrupted him constantly with cheers and applause, and capped his performance with a prolonged standing ovation.

Mosk was not nominated. He had decided not to seek the CDC endorsement.

The battle was on, and it was very intense. The outcome was far from certain. For Alan and his supporters, the suspense mounted. Most CDCers stayed up most of the night, working for their Senate favorite, partying, or roaming the halls.

On Sunday morning, in an atmosphere of great tension, the balloting took place. Alan took an early lead, and slowly his votes piled up. His loyal supporters worked the floor throughout the roll call. They knew the ways of CDC far better than Roosevelt's slimmer band of partisans. Their skill, along with Alan's years of work in the vineyards and his hold on the affection and respect of so many party activists, overcame the lure of Roosevelt and his appeal to CDC's deepest liberal instincts. The final count showed Alan had won:

Cranston	1,197 (53.4 percent)
Roosevelt	727 (33 percent)
Engle	281 (13.5 percent)
	2,212

Holding hands with Geneva, Alan mounted the platform wearing the lei of white carnations a frenzied supporter had looped around his neck. He thanked the delegates and told them, "My happiness and edge of exhilaration are blunted by the tragic circumstances involving Senator Engle. I predict a tough and bitter fight. Without your endorsement, I would not run. With it we will win!"

Many of the delegates wept as they cheered. Alan descended to the floor of the convention with Geneva and marched up one aisle and down the other, exchanging greetings, handclasps, hugs, and kisses with the excited throng.

Soon the Long Beach paper was out with a banner headline: **CRANSTON DEFEATS ROOSEVELT!** Roosevelt, Engle, and Mosk gave no sign of quitting the race, and the convention adjourned.

The next night, Alan and Geneva were sitting in the living room of their Sacramento home. The phone rang. It was Jimmy Roosevelt.

"Alan," he said, "I've decided to support you for the Senate. I won't run. I'll do anything you want to help you against anybody else who runs."

Overwhelmed, Alan thanked him warmly.

Libby Gatov soon announced her support, a significant symbol of party solidarity behind Alan. Newsmen surmised the governor's support would soon follow.

In a public statement, Brown cited Alan's impetus and good start but didn't quite endorse him. Mosk withdrew. Alan was exhilarated and hopeful. It seemed to him and to most other observers that he now had clear sailing for the Democratic nomination in the June primary and probably for the November general election as well.

On March 5 in San Jose, he filed for the Senate race — accompanied by Geneva, Robin, and Kim; our eighty-five-year-old mother; his eighth grade teacher and grammar school principal, Miss Margaret Wibel; and about fifty friends, relatives, and supporters. The cameras caught him in the midst of a sea of smiling faces, holding Mother's hand as they exchanged a serious look.

A newsman asked if he would accept support from Jesse Unruh.

"I'd be startled to receive it!" Alan replied to general laughter.

That same day Governor Brown issued a strong statement of endorsement: "Alan Cranston has the vigor, the vision, and the ability to carry on for Clair Engle and for California. His experience in fiscal and foreign affairs equips him uniquely for the Senate."

Alan was very happy, closer than ever before to realizing his dreams. Though Engle was still in the race — with the probable backing of Unruh — Alan dared to let himself hope, and almost believed, that the nomination was his.

"Cranston entered the primary as one of the most-liked Democrats in the state," Kimmis Hendrick wrote in the *Christian Science Monitor* (January 13, 1965).

Victory celebration. Alan defeats Max Rafferty and is elected Senator, 1968.
Jesse Unruh is on Alan's left.

Roy Greenaway

Murray Flander

ALAN'S SENATE STAFF:

Mary Lou McNeely

During an all-night session of the Senate, 1970.

A quiet moment in the Oval Office.

With the congressional delegation to China, 1978. Teng Hsiao-ping on the right.

Eleanor and Jack Fowle

Alan and Norma Cranston

Alan, Eleanor and Murray Flander

Alan at the opening day of a Moscow school, September 1981.

★ ★ ★ ★ ★ ★ ★ ★ ★ ★ ★ ★ ★ ★ ★ ★ ★
Primary Race: Cranston–Salinger
★ ★ ★ ★ ★ ★ ★ ★ ★ ★ ★ ★ ★ ★ ★ ★ ★

There was none of the customary lull after the CDC convention. The political firing escalated rapidly. Republican Assemblyman William Bagley of San Rafael, Alan's sometime friend and ally, launched a new attack on the state inheritance tax appraiser system and thus on Alan—who sensed Jesse Unruh's hand behind this development.

In a long, angry press release that hit newspapers throughout the state, Senator Engle accused the governor of a ruthless attempt to destroy him. "Brown is trying to bury me, but I will not be buried. . . . I didn't oblige him by dying." Engle's statement, filling several newspaper columns, concluded: "Like Caesar, I feel this is 'the most unkindest cut of all.'"

Distressed, Brown told reporters, "Engle could not have written this statement. When I last saw him, he could hardly talk."

Assemblyman Tom Carrell, an ally of Unruh, swore he had seen Engle dictate the release.

Engle's administrative assistant and press secretary both resigned, saying Mrs. Engle and a secretary had prepared the memo at night and released it without their knowledge.

"If Engle could have made the statement, I would be for him!" the governor exclaimed. "The Senate has stopped Engle's secretary from voting for him and instructed Engle, if he is voting aye, to put his hand to his eye. If he is voting no, he'll put his hand to his nose."

Los Angeles Mayor Sam Yorty conferred with Stanley Mosk and threatened to enter the race, saying, "Both of us feel there should be a candidate other than Cranston if Engle can't run."

Alan shook his head over the reports. He continued campaigning, parried questions, and refused to discuss Engle's health. His support was widespread. He felt reasonably confident about his chances, despite the rising clamor and the furor created by the uncertainties, charges, and countercharges concerning Engle.

Against this murky background, on Thursday, March 19, twenty-four hours before the deadline for filing, Governor Brown received a call from the White House. It was Pierre Salinger, President Johnson's press secretary.

An aide heard Brown shout into the phone, *"You what?!"*

"I'm flying to California tonight to file for the Senate race!" Salinger repeated.

The governor suddenly felt and looked as though he had been slugged. He tried to persuade Salinger to run for an open congressional seat in San Francisco instead.

"No. It's definite. I'm leaving right now," Salinger said.

That same afternoon, Salinger had told Lyndon Johnson. The president was surprised but hardly as stunned as the governor. Johnson impulsively asked, "What's the filing fee?"

"I think it's $450," Pierre replied. Johnson wrote out a check for that amount and wished him farewell.

Lee Falk said at the time: "I doubt if Johnson had analyzed the Senate race. Perhaps he jumped at the chance to rid himself of Kennedy's former press secretary. More likely, though, he wanted to continue the press relations he was enjoying during his honeymoon period. Also, he thought about running with Pierre on the same ticket in California, and he had respect for the Kennedy magic."

Brown's finance director, Hale Champion, a close friend of Alan, walked in to tell him the news. "Someone's trying to yank the rug out from under us," he said. "Pierre will be tough."

Alan felt as if he had been winning the 440, about to snap the tape, when suddenly he had smashed into an invisible wall of brick. Champion departed, shaking his head, looking glum.

Momentarily alone in his corner office, Alan thought swiftly. On the nation's TV screens, Salinger's dark, cherubic face was almost as well known as President Kennedy's own countenance had been. His role was legendary. He had been at Kennedy's elbow throughout the Cuban missile crisis. He had refused to go on the fifty-mile fitness walk, endearing himself to thousands of sedentary Americans. He had been the butt of the President's humor—"Portly Pierre." He was amiable, tough, and proficient—a folk hero. Newsmen liked him. He was one of their own. Besides the famous name, he had the glamor of service to two presidents. Glamor politics would be his game.

He would have powerful allies in California—Unruh and Mosk. The campaign costs would be staggering. Anger swept over Alan.

The June 2 primary was eleven weeks away. There were certain weaknesses that Salinger could be tagged with—carpetbagging, "boss-ism," inexperience in office. Alan's optimism reasserted itself. "I'll just have to fight still harder," he thought. For an instant, "Who lives by the sword" shot through his mind. "No, what's that quote from Tennyson, in *Ulysses?* 'Strong in will, to strive, to seek, to find, and not to yield.'"

He picked up the phone and called Irwin Nebron, the deputy controller, to tell him the news. While waiting for him, Alan thought of the long days and nights when he and Pierre and Don Bradley worked together in local campaigns all over California. He remembered dropping in to see Pierre at Kennedy headquarters in Washington long before Kennedy had the 1960 nomination nailed down. Pierre had invited Alan out to dinner. Alan had a conflict on his schedule and had to decline. "What if I'd spent that evening with him?" he thought. "No, he'd still be running."

He recalled visiting Pierre in the White House press room. Pierre with his feet on his desk, relaxed, puffing his cigar. Anger swept over Alan again. He brushed it aside.

Salinger arrived in San Francisco at 4:30 the next morning. By Friday noon he had raced around with friends, acquiring the necessary seventy-five signatures. He paid his $450 filing fee and called a press conference at the Fairmont Hotel. Standing beside him, Alan was concerned to learn, was Don Bradley, who had worked for Governor Brown and had managed his 1962 northern campaign and Engle's in 1958. Bradley, the Democratic State Central Committee's executive director, denied that he would manage Salinger's campaign, saying, "My boss is for Cranston." The press was skeptical. So was Alan.

Accompanying Salinger as his press aide—having just quit his job as White House associate press secretary—was Andrew Hatcher, one of California's best known black Democrats.

Reporters asked Salinger if he was truly eligible, having lived in Virginia the last nine years.

"If I didn't think so, I wouldn't be running," the San Francisco-born candidate replied. "The law stipulates a candidate must be an inhabitant. I am one, starting today."

Had he conferred with Attorney General Mosk?

"Yes, we met in the White House Thursday. I won't tell you what we discussed."

Had he conferred with Speaker Unruh?

"Jesse and I have had some talks. He's supporting Engle."

The press reminded him that Unruh was "neutral." But Salinger deftly turned aside sticky questions.

Grinning, he declared that his candidacy was "a genuine draft . . . a draft inspired by the candidate himself." Leaning against a table in the crowded conference room, the thirty-eight-year-old Pierre beamed at his friends and former colleagues in the San Francisco press. Rotund, energetically waving his cigar, with his wavy black hair and heavy black eyebrows, he oddly resembled a baby disguised as a cartoon politician or an old-fashioned political boss.

Reporters variously described him as "short, chubby, cigar-chomping Salinger"; "195 pounds of confidence"; "wrapping the mantle of the slain president around him. "Comparing him to Alan, someone called the campaign a "horse-race between fat and fit."

Salinger heatedly denied reports of strained relations between himself and President Johnson, and he denied that a rift between the president and Robert Kennedy had motivated his decision.

Kennedy was rumored to be planning to run for Senator in New York. Was this a trial balloon or the birth of a California-New York axis?

"I won't speculate," Salinger said amiably.

The unexpectedness of his decision to leave the White House and seek the Senate nomination, his dash to California, his whirlwind steps to meet the filing deadline—all this was political drama, great for page-one press copy.

Alan issued a statement welcoming Salinger into the race. "It's a free and open primary. The more candidates running, the wider the people's choice." He added, "I find it significant that Salinger, with the best sources of information available to him while in the White House, has apparently determined that Senator Engle's health does not permit him to carry on in the Senate."

Governor Brown loyally told the press, "Pierre is an able young man and an old friend. But I was for Alan Cranston before Pierre got into this and I am still for Alan." Privately the governor was furious; his enemies were delighted by the problems the Salinger candidacy posed for the governor.

Secretary of State Frank Jordan refused to put Salinger on the ballot. This made more headlines. The candidate filed a brief. Still more Salinger headlines. A few days later Alan's heart plummeted to the ground when he saw black six-inch headlines: **SALINGER WINS!**

The state supreme court had swiftly approved his candidacy—even though he could not vote in California. Angrily, Brown said, "I wish the justices had written a formal opinion on a matter as important as this."

State Senator George Miller, Jr., complained that the decision could lead to cross-country carpetbaggery. "If Salinger wants to be a Senator, let him return to Virginia and run against Harry Byrd!"

CDC President Tom Carvey spoke despairingly of "New York celebrities roving the states from primary to primary."

The first polls were ominous. Pierre was twelve points ahead of Alan. Senator Engle was far behind them both, totally out of the race.

"Pierre has no place to go but down, and I have no place to go but up," Alan told reporters.

On April 1 Don Bradley officially became Salinger's campaign manager, bringing with him a band of political pros who had been waiting for him to find a campaign to head.

Geneva told Alan bitterly, "You're playing against a stacked deck!"

The governor angrily severed his connection with Bradley. Now the party split like the Red Sea. Politically, in every county in the state, friend parted from friend and ally from ally as the battle lines formed.

"Shades of the Nixon-Knowland-Knight power play!" muttered one of Alan's friends.

Campaigning up and down the 1000-mile length of the state, doing his utmost to hold old sources of strength and to enlist new support, Alan warned that a bitter intraparty fight could ensure the election of a right-wing extremist. "The probable Republican nominee is George Murphy, a Hollywood song-and-dance man, who would rather be far-right than senator!"

He continued his jibes at his opponent. In San Francisco he said:

"Salinger has been grabbing headlines. He entered the race in a rather dramatic way from a rather dramatic place — Washington. But whether this can be translated into votes is another question. I am campaigning at a grassroots level. Pierre is campaigning at a publicity level."

Opening his Los Angeles headquarters, Alan told a crowd of four hundred backers, "Salinger's real motive for running may be part of the raw power play now forming to seize control of the party from the working Democrats of California. His only preparation for the state's highest federal office is a three-year stint as a high-level public relations man."

"Tall, trim, and confident," the press described Alan.

He told a crowd in Fresno, "Pierre has never had to decide on issues, nor act on those issues. The issue is bossism. The people who can vote — unlike Salinger — will defeat bossism."

Salinger conducted a whirling dervish campaign with crowds, autographs, and great media attention. His cigar became a campaign symbol. He smoked up to twelve a day. Someone called him "a walking smoke-filled room."

Exasperated, Geneva told *San Francisco Chronicle* reporter Michael Harris, "California voters won't be swayed by Salinger's slightly-clad 'P.S.-I-love-you' publicity cuties. I'm convinced that Alan's appeal lies much deeper."

Family members pitched in, too. Mother conducted a clipping service. Jack raised vast sums for TV. Armed with a map and driving a Hertz on the Los Angeles freeways, I garnered newspaper coverage for Alan by attending over forty coffees and teas.

On April 24, in Washington, D.C., Alan ran the gauntlet of Pierre Salinger's long-time associates at the National Press Club. Columnist Doris Fleeson wrote: "They concluded that the Senate race would be a lot closer than people thought. Cranston submitted himself to that forum to counteract the legend that he was a worthy but colorless politician, fated to lose to Salinger in star-crazed California. He attacked his election problems with lucidity and a light touch."

Racing up and down the state, Alan amused his audiences with a typical drumfire of anti-Salinger one-liners: "I'm the candidate who lives and works in California." Smiles creased his face when the crowds applauded each sally. "I pay my taxes in California. I'm against representation without taxation. Furthermore, I'm against reapportioning the Senate to give three votes to Virginia and one to California." He likened Salinger to Nixon in one respect: "Both came back to California after many years away and promptly misjudged the leadership and direction of the Democratic Party."

At a Cranston event at Fisherman's Wharf in San Francisco, Alan was up on the stage gaily singing with the rest:

> Alan's campaign's a roller,
> Can't you see him in a bowler?
> Who'll be the next controller?

Assemblyman Byron Rumford, a black leader considered a likely replacement, danced onto the stage.

The authoritative Field poll, which had shown Pierre leading 33 percent to 21 percent over a month before, now gave Alan 33 percent. Portly but plunging, Pièrre was down to 27 percent from the 53 percent he had initially claimed in a private poll.

The press reported a rising tide of support for Alan. The AFL-CIO and five hundred labor leaders endorsed him, as did the California Federation of Young Democrats. The *San Francisco Chronicle*, the *Sacramento Bee*, and a number of other leading papers came out for him too. A flying squad of California congressmen flew to the coast for a one-day "We Like Alan" swing.

Salinger tried to portray Alan as a dry-as-dust, bureaucratic egghead, describing him once as "the eager tax collector who'd make a fine mortician." He tried to overcome his own image as a roly-poly bon vivant by talking seriously about the Cuban missile crisis. "I looked down the nuclear gun barrel with John F. Kennedy," he proclaimed.

The press took to referring to "Cranston" and "Pierre," the latter having the connotation of the stock comic character of French pantomime, Pièrrot.

In late May, the *Examiner* reported, "Cranston is walking, riding, running, and flying down to Tuesday's primary finish line with all the confidence of a winner. Cranston, who had plenty to worry about when Salinger entered the race like a mid-March thunderbolt, seems unworried now. 'We're winning,' he said."

The two engaged in two television debates. By that time neither was very comfortable with his public image. Salinger, who was known around the White House for his good cheer and quick humor, cracked only half a smile twice in the whole hour. Alan, who had suffered from the charges that he was a humorless intellectual IBM machine, smiled slightly and shyly before answering each question.

Charges and countercharges filled the air. Unruh denied he was backing Salinger but made it clear he was fighting Cranston.

"Expect a smear a day now that Unruh has taken over active control," Alan told a labor rally in Oakland.

State Senator Jack Schrade, a right-wing Republican and sometime ally of Unruh, charged that Cranston had put the "campaign arm" on inheritance tax appraisers whom he had appointed.

"These charges are false," Alan said. "They are made by a candidate who is losing, who turns to slanderous charges. I have made no efforts to raise funds from my appointees. They have been put under no pressure. Some contributed to my campaign, and some did not."

Salinger took up the inheritance-tax-appraiser charge.

Bradley told Libby Gatov, the national committeewoman, "I'd rather be a bastard than a loser!"

Alan slapped a two-million-dollar libel suit on Salinger, his campaign manager, Don Bradley, and two former inheritance tax appraisers (Alan had previously fired one and had refused to reappoint the other) accusing them of a "conspiracy to make false, malicious, and defamatory statements to influence the outcome of the primary."

Embarking on a flying tour of the state, Alan said, "The voters of California see the smears for what they are—the wild and irresponsible charges of a losing candidate." Asked if they would hurt him, he said, "Not at all."

At Bakersfield on May 28, asked whether he would support Salinger if he won the nomination, Alan said, "I would be supporting him and suing him."

An editorial in the *Palo Alto Times* of May 30, 1964, stated: "Despite the smear attempts, Cranston's honor remains unsullied."

The contest now became a savagely fought race where the battle for power had large stakes extending far beyond the personal success or failure of either candidate.

Salinger constantly resurrected his days of glory with the late president. He insisted that he knew more people in Washington and could get past more doors.

"It is one thing to get in the door," Alan retorted. "It is another thing to know what to do when you're inside."

On the eve of the election, Unruh and Mosk announced their support for Salinger. Field's final poll showed Alan ahead by two points. This was after months of campaigning, traveling thousands of miles, shaking thousands of hands, and making an infinite number of phone calls.

In Santa Barbara Alan rushed in to a TV station to do a program. His campaign aide ran to the nearest phone. Tom Moore, the campaign manager, went to another one. Their driver raced to a third. The station manager blew up. "Damn it, you've tied up all my lines! This is *not* a campaign headquarters!" he yelled. *"Get off my telephones!"*

For the last two weeks of the campaign Alan asked Lee Falk to join him on the campaign trail. Lee knew newsmen all over the state, and his humor and companionship helped Alan to throw off the tensions during even the darkest happenings.

When Lee arrived from New York, suave, perceptive, and sartorially elegant as always, he bit off the words sardonically, "Well, Alan, this is it?"

Lee found the campaign exhausting. Worse than that, he found no chance to write his scripts. Cartoon sequences began bursting the seams of his mind. Late one night he asked to be dropped off at our home in Los Altos. On our dining room table with lightning fingers he typed several weeks' scripts of his four serials, the daily and Sunday "Mandrake" and "The Phantom."

Amazed at his performance, I asked incredulously, "You type with only three fingers?"

"One, mostly," he muttered ironically, looking up in a trance, still typing at the speed of light.

In the final hours of the campaign, Pierre's people mailed four million postcards. Each bore a blue-bordered photo of Kennedy and the legend, "In his tradition," and a sample ballot with an "X" after Salinger—a tremendously costly but effective piece of propaganda.

The evening of June 2, we all flew south to Los Angeles. Shortly after the polls closed we arrived at the Biltmore Hotel, where in a huge room the election returns were to be shown on large boards. The first newsman Alan encountered asked him, "Are you conceding?"

Startled, Alan asked him what he was talking about. Some early returns had started to dribble in, and Salinger was out in front.

"Of course I'm not conceding," said Alan. "It's much too early. Who knows where these tallies came from? They're probably the absentee ballots, and they never prove anything."

I was laughing at one of Lee Falk's jokes, not paying much attention, when Geneva said sharply, "It looks very *bad!*" At that moment Alan turned and looked at me. I read the same recognition in his startled eyes.

As the returns continued to come in, they steadily worsened. At times the race grew closer, but gradually Salinger's lead increased. It became apparent that he would win.

The rest of the evening remains a blur. We trailed Alan to gatherings of friends and supporters. Riding wearily around the city in taxis, we accompanied him to his official media interviews—where Alan acknowledged that the tide was adverse, but refrained from admitting defeat. Finally, toward midnight, we went to a barnlike hall where hundreds of Alan's friends and supporters waited, disheartened and tearful. His message was brief and poignant. He had lost. He thanked them from the bottom of his heart. Now the fight was against Murphy in November. His words were as cheery as he could make them, but his friends, accustomed to his buoyancy, were stricken. Then he left with Lee Falk and Irwin Nebron to make his televised concession speech.

Dazedly, Jack and I left the hall. In the darkness outside we encountered the chairman of the state Board of Equalization, Alan's southern campaign manager, and his attractive wife. We stared at each other wordlessly. As we passed, the wife, one of the nicest and most elegant women in politics, simply muttered, under her breath, "Oh, s— —!"

At the Palo Alto Republican headquarters that same night, Catherine Elwood, an old friend who had been a Rockefeller delegate, was watching unhappily as Goldwater's votes piled up. Suddenly Alan appeared on the TV screen, making his concession speech. She saw the lines of fatigue in his face and the stunned dullness in his dark eyes. He spoke in a voice harsh with weariness and unsteady with the effort to keep up a good front for the Democrats. He offered Salinger his support.

Catherine felt a lump rise in her throat. She turned to a coworker standing close by and was astounded to see tears rolling down the girl's cheeks.

"I hate a good loser!" her friend muttered through clenched teeth. "I hate a good loser!"

Eventually, Alan returned to his hotel where Kim, overwhelmed by Alan's disappointment and defeat, lay down on the floor of his parents' room and sobbed himself to sleep.

Exhausted, Alan lay awake, thinking. He was fifty. The Senate seat had eluded him. He feared it would be finally won, in the wake of the Democratic shambles created by the divisive primary, not by Salinger but by George Murphy, who had walked away with the Republican primary. That would mean consistent votes, from a Democratic point of view, against peace in Vietnam . . . human rights . . . jobs. Murphy might stay on in the Senate for years.

Alan knew he'd had everything going for him — the support of the CDC, Governor Brown, most of California's Democratic congressmen, organized labor, countless friends, most of the press, and twenty-five years of varied and responsible experience in public affairs. His whole life had prepared him for the job of senator.

Why the loss to Salinger? What more should have been done? Alan asked himself what mistakes he had made.

For the first time, a CDC-endorsed candidate had lost in a statewide primary. How ironic that the first CDC loser was founder and first president.

Brown's popularity was sagging, and the governor was badly wounded by Salinger's victory. Alan vowed to do all he could to help remedy that.

He faced a campaign debt of about $350,000. It had to be paid off. How?

About four in the morning, Alan finally got to sleep. Then there came a sudden knock on the door. Lee Falk stood outside. Despondently he said, "I'm leaving." They shook hands grimly and he left.

Geneva was awake and said, "Alan, you can always see the bright side of things. Can't you think of any redeeming features to cheer us up?"

Alan thought for several moments. Finally he said, "No, I can't think of anything. There's not a single good thing about it. It's all bad."

In the morning, Alan phoned Salinger, congratulated him and

offered his support. Their conversation was brief but not unfriendly.

In the peculiar severity of American politics, Salinger had defeated Alan by 143,788 votes out of 2 million cast.

Alan resumed his comforting role with the family and with his friends. But in his eyes, for a while, there was a depth of sadness that had not been there before.

The defeat seasoned him for the years ahead. And the experience was not without its clear lessons.

"I learned that the animosities incurred in head-on battles are usually not worth it," he recalls. "I hadn't sought conflict with Jesse Unruh, and probably he hadn't sought it with me. It began more or less by accident. And it hurt us both."

Unruh probably had more to do with Pierre entering the race — and winning — than anyone else.

CHAPTER 20

★ ★ ★ ★ ★ ★ ★ ★ ★ ★ ★ ★ ★ ★ ★ ★
1964 to the Reagan Landslide
★ ★ ★ ★ ★ ★ ★ ★ ★ ★ ★ ★ ★ ★ ★ ★

Alan retained his sense of humor and even then enjoyed telling the following story.

President Lyndon B. Johnson was introducing his new press secretary, George Reedy, to a crowd in Sacramento during his 1964 campaign. After casting an arch look at Pierre Salinger, he added, "The reason he's still my press secretary is that there aren't any Senate vacancies at the moment."

Afterward, the president lunched in the governor's cabinet room with Brown and a select group of the governor's close friends, advisers and campaign contributors. As food was being served, Brown rose and welcomed Johnson with a few warm, laudatory words. Then he suggested that while they ate, and before the president addressed them briefly, each individual present should stand up and introduce himself or herself to the president.

"You're all very important people," said Pat, expansively. "Instead of me introducing you, just get up, one after another, and introduce yourself to the president of the United States. Tell him in a few words who you are, what you do. Why don't you start, Ben?"

As the first guest pushed back his chair, got to his feet, stated his name, and started to describe himself to the president, Alan swiftly formed two impressions. First, all the other guests were barely listening, if they were listening at all. Each, like Alan himself, was thinking over what he would say about himself when his turn came. Second, the president wasn't listening either. At least, he didn't appear to be. He wasn't even looking.

181

Instead, Johnson was bent over his food with lowered eyes. With single-minded attention he was bolting down his lunch with astonishing swiftness. Although he was seated, his huge frame was that of a man in motion. While his right hand and arm forked up food from his plate, his left roved the table territory before him: now sweeping up a roll, dipping it in butter, carrying it to his mouth; now grabbing a glass of water to wash it down; now snatching the napkin from his lap to dab his lips and chin; now plucking an apple from a bowl to take a huge bite. All this, and more, was done at top speed.

To their chagrin, the leaders of California with increasing self-consciousness were introducing themselves to a man who didn't exactly seem to be there. Occasionally the president shot a glance at someone as he spoke; usually, he didn't find time between his bites.

When Alan's turn came, he announced, "Mr. President, I'm Controller Alan Cranston, chairman of the Committee to Keep George Reedy in Washington."

Johnson glanced up. He shot Alan a piercing look, smiled comprehendingly, and again riveted his eyes on his plate.

Soon a seemingly satiated and satisfied Johnson was called upon to speak to a somewhat abashed but nonetheless attentive audience. Then the lunch broke up, and as the president was about to be hurried away to Air Force One, Alan approached a friend who was one of LBJ's aides.

"Why on earth did the President bolt his food like that during all those introductions?" he couldn't resist asking.

"The poor man never knows when or if he's going to eat," explained the White House assistant. "If he's politely attentive through the opening formalities at an affair like this, like as not he's suddenly introduced — not with a long speech that gives him time to have a few bites and get ready, but just, 'Ladies and Gentlemen, the president of the United States' — and he's up and speaking without any fuel for that big frame of his. The moment he's done, he's told he's behind schedule and has got to take off. One day he missed breakfast, lunch, and dinner that way. He cussed us all out and swore it wasn't going to happen again."

Alan worked hard for Salinger's election in November. He also paid off his campaign debts in full. Salinger apologized publicly for his false campaign charges and Alan dropped his $2 million lawsuit.

Jesse Unruh, whose relations with Pierre deteriorated after the primary, remarked that "Salinger's victory was simply the voters' tribute to the dead president."

When Senator Engle died in July, Governor Brown announced he would appoint Salinger to fill the brief remainder of the unexpired term. It was a logical appointment. After all, the Democrats of California had nominated Salinger and incumbency was generally viewed as a political advantage. Only the astute Jesse Unruh looked at it differently. "Let Brown offer it to you," he told Pierre, "but turn it down — publicly. Say you want to get to the Senate on your own, by winning the election, not by the grace of someone's appointment. You'll be a hero. If you take the appointment, it'll look too easy. Let Brown give the honor of serving in the Senate to some big contributor till you get yourself elected." Pierre listened to others, accepted the appointment in a meeting with the governor in his office, and immediately walked across the hall to see Alan. "I came because I knew how you feel," he said. "I want to thank you for your support, and to tell you I'm your friend. I *am* your friend."

"Thanks, Pierre," returned Alan. Then, holding both of his large hands out, fingers spread, he added, "I had it right in my hands! That's what hurt."

The appointment hurt Governor Brown in an odd way. Many of Alan's loyal supporters were enraged by the Salinger appointment. They thought Brown should have stayed with Alan and appointed him. Actually, Alan couldn't have accepted. He'd have had to resign as controller, and he could have served in the Senate only till year's end, when the term expired.

Ironically, Salinger's popularity began to sink after the primary. The appointment clearly did him damage — a development no one but Unruh had foreseen. His Kennedy image began to fade away. Slowly he began to assume a new image — that of an interloper and carpetbagger. At the same time, polls showed that Alan's popularity was rising. A Field poll that summer showed him ahead for governor if Brown did not seek a third term.

In November, while Johnson was defeating Goldwater in California in a landslide, Salinger lost to George Murphy by 200,000 votes. In his book *With Kennedy,* he attributed his defeat to his support for the highly controversial Proposition 14, for open housing. Alan agreed that white backlash was the knottiest problem in California politics that year. But he attributed Salinger's defeat mainly to the appointment, to Murphy's skillful handling of the carpetbagger issue and artful avoidance of all controversial matters, and to Murphy's acting abilities capped by his superior performance, grave demeanor, and general appearance in a widely watched television debate. Others felt the bruising primary battle was a major factor in Salinger's downfall. Many observers believed Alan would have defeated Murphy.

In January 1965 Alan and his family bought their beloved Krag Ranch, a hundred and more acres of rolling, oak-studded land and stream in the Mother Lode country of Nevada County. The family signed an agreement, drafted by Alan, promising as much as possible, to keep the land in its natural state, preserving its aesthetic values. The same standards had been applied at Villa Warec. Krag Ranch is still beautifully natural, its oaks and streams intact.

This turning to the land was one slight sign of a momentary change of Alan's focus in the wake of the debacle with Salinger. There was another: he took up oil painting. And a third: he resumed sprint running on a more serious and regular basis.

Then Alan threw himself back into all the challenges of the controllership and began to prepare to run for reelection in 1966. On January 9, 1965, he announced he would indeed run for reelection as controller, explaining that he was making an early statement to lay to rest rumors that were drifting about the state of a reshuffling of the Democratic ticket. At that moment he was without a prospective opponent in either party.

Brown, on the other hand, was faced with a double challenge if he attempted to win a third term. Mayor Samuel Yorty of Los Angeles plainly planned to try to knock Brown off in the primary. Two Republicans, actor Ronald Reagan and former Mayor George Christopher of San Francisco, prepared to battle for the chance to fight him in November.

The struggle for power between the Brown forces and the Unruh forces intensified. Despite Alan's reelection announcement, the press often mentioned Alan as the state's most popular official and a possible candidate for governor—which did nothing to improve Alan-Jesse relations.

"Jesse had his heart set on the post," Alan recalls. "I did not. I had my heart set on the Senate. But I didn't disavow all interest in the governorship in case that opened up and the Senate didn't. I did flatly say, 'I'll support Pat if he runs.' Jesse equivocated, hoping to thrust Pat aside."

It was in the midst of this jockeying, rivalry, and tension that Alan ran into Jesse Unruh at a "Moose Milk Lunch," an event put on by lobbyists every Thursday at the El Mirador Hotel in Sacramento. That was in the days before Proposition 9, the Campaign Reform Act.

"How old are you?" Jesse asked jovially.

"Fifty-one."

"I'm forty-three," said Jesse. "There's time enough for both of us to have our turn at it."

Alan was tempted to say, "OK. Me first, you second." But he didn't. He grinned, said "OK," and let it go at that.

Recalling that encounter, Alan once said to me, "The strangest thing about my constant combat with Jesse was that, despite it all, at times I couldn't help liking him. There were moments when I hated him. But his sense of humor was irresistible, and even when he had me most upset, I couldn't help but admire his immense political skill, his craftsmanship."

On March 15 Alan invited members of the press into his office informally to meet his new press chief, Wes Willoughby. During this informal meeting, Alan, sitting on the edge of a sofa with both feet folded under him, deliberately said, in the most casual tones, that if any of the fellows had brought pencils along, he might have something worthwhile to say.

"Pat Brown has flatly and irrevocably decided to run for reelection next year," Alan told the newsmen. "He told me so last Thursday, knowing I would pass it along. He made a flat statement without reservations. This should end the infighting between him* and the legislature and cut off for at least five years the discussion over the succession."

The reporters abruptly shot to their feet and rushed across the hall to Brown.

"I'll comment on the Cranston statement when the first snow falls on the Sierra this year," the governor said with a twinkle. He added significantly, "Alan's a very close friend of mine—politically, governmentally, and socially. I can tell you this—there's still one good fight left in the old man!"

*Meaning Unruh.

Republican Assemblyman John Veneman grumbled, "Why do we have to contact the weather bureau for the governor's own announcement!" Jesse Unruh's comments were unprinted—or unprintable. When the snow fell that fall, Brown formally announced his candidacy for a third term.

1966 was a troubled year. CDC was declining. Early in 1965 Alan became convinced that the organization was becoming ingrown and was in need of new and charismatic leadership. He had fought successfully for the election of Simon Casady, the bright and fiery editor and publisher of an El Cajon newspaper, to the presidency of the CDC. But soon after taking office, Casady proceeded to launch an all-out fight against the entire Democratic leadership over the issue of the Vietnam War, leveling violent attacks on President Johnson, Governor Brown, most of the California Democrats in the House of Representatives, and other leaders.

Originally, CDC had been organized as an umbrella to hold all the diverse party elements together, and when Alan was president, he had believed in letting everyone have his say. But he held things together by keeping differences on issues subordinate.

Now a deep split developed within CDC, and between the CDC and other elements of the party. Many California Democrats who opposed the deepening American involvement in Vietnam feared that Casady's bitter assaults were counterproductive, and that while having little or no affect on U.S. policy in Southeast Asia, they might succeed only in destroying the Democratic Party in California.

In January of 1966, Hale Champion, on behalf of the governor, urged Alan to join Brown in ousting Casady. Alan, though he was no supporter of the Vietnam war, agreed. Casady was deposed after an horrendous struggle.

Shortly after that, Brown and Cranston sought and won the endorsement of the CDC convention, but delegates booed, hissed, and walked out on Brown by the hundreds, and a lesser number gave Alan the same hostile treatment—in startling contrast with preceding years.

In the June primary, Alan won the nomination for reelection as controller by a landslide vote, leading his opponents, Bert De Lotto and Paul Burke, by almost a million votes:

Cranston	1,244,113
Burke	286,337
De Lotto	108,811

A moderate Republican assemblyman, Houston Flournoy, who had only decided to file at the very last moment, narrowly won the Republican nomination for controller. In a summer Field poll, Flournoy, an associate professor of government at Pomona College, was identified by only a small percentage of those interviewed, and Alan had a wide lead over him — 55 percent to 26 percent. This was generally viewed as a safe margin. Flournoy immediately began to attack Alan on the appraiser issue, but Alan never responded, simply ignored him, and the controller's race drew little attention.

Alan had devoted more attention to Pat Brown's primary contest than he had to his own race. He attacked Yorty. The Los Angeles mayor skillfully exploited every Brown weakness, and though he failed to defeat the governor, Yorty's slashing onslaughts wounded Brown badly. The final margin between the two was dangerously close:

Brown	1,021,029
Yorty	712,156

Reagan defeated Christopher in the Republican primary — and led Brown in the first polls. Conservative Max Rafferty, the nonpartisan state superintendent of public instruction, meanwhile won reelection by a whopping margin, capturing 1,590,000 votes.

Confident about his own race but fearing for Brown — and considering Pat's race much more important than his own — Alan stumped the state defending the governor. He campaigned hard for himself, but in almost every appearance his emphasis was on the importance of a Brown victory.

And disturbed by a rising tide of right-wing extremism in the state, Alan issued a scathing twenty-six-page white paper on the John Birch Society, charging it with racial hatred and religious prejudice. He called on Reagan to disavow Birch support, and actually confronted him directly in a highly publicized meeting at the Sacramento airport when he handed Reagan a copy of the white paper. Alan lambasted Flournoy — in one of the few occasions when he acknowledged the existence of his opponent — for labeling the Birch issue "irrelevant." Alan pointed out that a neo-Fascist influence had been evident in the Birch Society since its founding in 1958 and said, "I saw fascism happen in Nazi Germany, and I never want to see it happen here."

Max Freedman reported in the *Los Angeles Times:*

It could not have been easy for Cranston to make his recent important statement on extremist groups in California. . . . He accepted the risk because he believes that the extremists make their greatest gains when the moderate and responsible people are silent or timid.

Cranston began by citing documentary proof that the Communists and the John Birchers often say the same thing. . . . The extremists have probably made life a misery for Cranston since he denounced them. But other public officials will no doubt follow his courageous example. A concerted exposure of the false assumptions and dangerous methods of the extremist groups is the best way to discredit them utterly.

The Birchers indeed attempted to make Alan's life a misery — as had been anticipated by some of Alan's advisers. Heated discussions led to the decision to issue the white paper. Wes Willoughby, his press secretary, recalls that he personally urged Alan to make the attack; the Birch Society was his own pet hate, and he did the research on the project. Curt Roberts, the experienced head of the public relations firm handling Alan's campaign, advised Alan not to go ahead because he knew it would coalesce the Birchers against Alan. Hadley Roff, Alan's campaign manager, agreed with Roberts, saying, "Why be a focus for all the hate?" But Alan felt that it was right. And so the paper was issued.

There were other controversies. In August the California Democratic Party split asunder in a battle royal at its Sacramento convention. Running for state chairman, Assemblyman Charles Warren of Los Angeles, whose campaign Alan led, defeated by a mere four votes the southern chairman, Carmen Warschaw, the Harvey Aluminum heiress and colorful "Dragon Lady," who was supported all out by Unruh and equivocally by Governor Brown.*

Next day, Carmen and her husband Lou Warschaw threw Alan out of the free campaign space they had provided him in their Subway Terminal Building in Los Angeles.

Alan viewed this latest diversion with concern, but he carried on his campaign for Brown and against Reagan. Later in a wide-ranging and candid exchange at the Stanford Political Union, he assessed the governor's political leadership, calling him "a great human being and a great governor, but a poor political leader," in reference to what he called the disarray and diffusion of power in the party.

---

*The convention also elected me Democratic State Women's Chair.

He urged support for Brown for another reason as well. He saw Reagan and what he represented as a long step backward, and he insisted, "The British are not about to elect one of the Beatles prime minister, the French aren't going to elect Maurice Chevalier premier, and by the same token, I don't think Californians, if they think it through, will elect an actor without previous government experience to the governorship."

However, the tides were running against Brown, and shortly before election day the polls indicated Reagan would win by a substantial margin. Virtually all political observers and insiders conceded that the contest was over.

A confident Reagan then turned his attention to Alan and, secondarily, to other members of the statewide Democratic ticket. He didn't relish the prospect of Alan looking over his shoulder from the controller's office, nor of Glenn Anderson serving as his lieutenant governor. He pumped money into their opponents' campaigns and urged the voters to give him a full Republican team in Sacramento. Sam Yorty joined the attack against Alan.

A few days before the election, Alan ran into Jane Tolmach, a close friend and ally from Ventura County (recently mayor of Oxnard), a shrewd and successful local political leader. "I hate to say this, Alan," she declared dejectedly. "Not only is Pat going to lose, but so are you and everybody else on the ticket. I feel it in my bones." That was Alan's first and only warning of what was to come. According to a late poll he was still way out in front.

On November 8, 1966, Ronald Reagan won a massive landslide victory—by about a million votes. One television commentator had declared Alan to be in trouble early in the evening, but while all other statewide Democrats except Atty. Gen. Tom Lynch were losing, he held a reasonably comfortable lead throughout election night. The morning-after headlines proclaimed, **"CRANSTON, LYNCH SURVIVE REPUBLICAN LANDSLIDE."**

Alan flew north with Geneva and Win Griffith, his chief deputy, to hold press conferences in San Francisco and Sacramento. They were met at the San Francisco airport by a grim Hadley Roff. "It looks bad," he said. "Flournoy's gaining, and a lot of votes haven't come in yet from Orange County. The place has been fogbound, and the official tallies haven't all been delivered from the polls."

Alan's group avoided the press and lunched silently with friends and campaign aides at the Red Knight restaurant. Hadley returned from a phone call to announce, "Flournoy's pulled ahead. You've lost."

Stunned, Alan thanked his supporters and tried to cheer them up. There were tears in Geneva's eyes. Then he, Geneva, and Win drove to Sacramento. They were very tired and in a slight state of shock. They wondered about the future of California, and their own. Alan remembers that all three laughed uproariously at several aspects of the situation, but he cannot for the life of him recall, now, what was so funny.

They walked into the controller's office, passing a panel in the reception room containing the pictures of all save the very first of California's controllers. Win impulsively turned and, with a loud clatter, slammed all the pictures to one side, making space at the end of the row for the photograph of the newest controller — Houston Flournoy.

The final count was now in. Flournoy had won by some 50,000 votes out of more than 6 million cast. Alan had carried every northern county; Flournoy every southern county.

Reporters and a sad group of aides and friends were waiting in Alan's inner office. Wes Willoughby recalls that — feeling partly responsible for the catastrophe because of his insistence on the Birch attacks — he approached Alan, fighting back tears. Alan gave him a bear hug. Then he turned to the press, who were expecting only a concession statement — and perhaps a declaration, after Alan's two straight defeats, that he was retiring from politics. He exclaimed, "I'm going to run for the Senate in 1968."

The reporters listened, astounded.

> I am considering running because the conservative GOP elements that have elected Reagan will try to wipe out Senator Kuchel, a moderate. Kuchel might well be defeated in the 1968 primary by the right-wing Max Rafferty — or by Chuck Connors, or John Wayne, or someone else brought up from somewhere.
>
> Mayor Sam Yorty, who opposed Brown in the primary and refused to support him in the general election, is considered a likely candidate for the Democratic nomination for Senator.
>
> I am determined to see that California's choice for the Senate at the 1968 general election is not between Rafferty or some actor and Sam Yorty.

A reporter asked whether the debacle left Unruh as the real leader of the disheveled party.

"No," Alan said.

He will only be the leader of one legislative house, assuming he's reelected speaker. There's still one Democrat holding statewide office, Attorney General Tom Lynch. And I assume Hugh Burns will still be the leader of the Senate. But the real state- wide party leaders, I think, will be Chairman Charles Warren and northern Chair- man Bob Coate."

Wes Willoughby, who is now with the San Francisco Redevelopment Agency, recalls that "The press understood that Alan's defeat was not a personal one — not a popularity contest between Cranston and Flournoy. It was part of the Reagan landslide. Alan's attacks on Reagan and Yorty had caused them to devote themselves to defeating Alan and that was enough to tip the scales."

Don Bradley, who had served again as Brown's campaign manager, acknowledged that "Alan had raised a lot of money for his own cam- paign and turned a substantial amount over to Pat. "It was the most purely unselfish political act I've ever seen," Don commented.

Murray Flander, then the owner of a newspaper in Coalinga that had received Alan's John Birch Society white paper expose, agreed that, "Alan was sacrificing himself for others." And Joe Houghteling, that dry and ascerbic political analyst, observed, "One candidate's support for another usually doesn't 'rub off' unless it is downward sup- port, not upward. Alan's support for Brown was upward. He fell on his sword for Brown."

CHAPTER 21

★ ★
The 1968 Senate Primary
★ ★

Alan and Geneva took stock of their situation, weighed the pros and cons with their boys, and decided to move to Los Angeles where Alan had been offered a well-paying job as president of a low-cost housing firm, Better Homes for America, Inc. Leaving their friends and the Animal Farm was hard; they had to give away most of their pets.

In January, they bought a rambling, yellow brick house on a brushy hilltop overlooking suburban Bel Air, near the UCLA track. The house had no grounds or garden, but it did have a sweeping view of wooded Stone Canyon, the heart of Bel Air. The south was a pleasant change with its perpetual sunlight, poinsettias and hibiscus, beaches, deserts, brush-covered hills, and the boney, bare, blue mountain peaks of its Sierra Madre. The sprawling city was lively, its architecture exciting.

Jerry Carroll of the *Evening Outlook* interviewed Alan the day they moved into their new house.

> The former controller, dressed in a checked shirt and blue denims, helped his wife point out where the furniture went.
>
> Moving men had to use a shuttle truck to transfer the household furniture, books, papers, and other memorabilia of eight years in Sacramento from a van up a steep drive to their house. The agent had hinted that hazards of brush-fires and earthslides had brought the cost down.
>
> Alan humorously told the reporter that they had brought three cats and their dog, Roy, with them, leaving behind a menagerie of animals including sixty chickens and as many ducks. "We also had a great big pig named Snowball. But she got married and ran away."

Asked if he thought his party had recovered from its internecine warfare, he said, "No, but unity is always more obtainable in adversity." He added: "It was a tidal wave which swept the country from Alaska to Florida, sweeping Democrats out and Republicans in.

"In California I think it was an accumulation of grievances and objections to decisions we made. It's difficult to make all those decisions day after day and not alienate people, as Reagan is now finding out."

Alan said that private life was giving him a new sense of freedom, a greater opportunity for personal choice, and he wasn't interested in any federal appointment. "I don't mind having six million bosses," he said, "but I'm not sure I would want to have just one."

The move had actually endowed Alan with a triple political benefit: he had been born and reared in northern California; he had served in statewide electoral office in central California (Sacramento), and now he had a base in southern California.*

Offstage, Geneva was dejected. In her darker moments she expressed to friends her disenchantment with politics and its cruelties and her feeling that Alan had quixotically thrown away the election.

Alan became vice president of the Carlsberg Corporation, dealing in land investments. He was now earning more than he had earned as controller. He had also arranged to write a column for the *Los Angeles Times*, the *San Jose Mercury*, and many other papers throughout the state, dealing with issues that most concerned him: peace and the preservation of democratic freedoms in particular, along with his general concerns about government's increasing inefficiency and its mounting budgets. In one column he wrote:

> There's a sweeping law now affecting our daily lives in California that was never enacted by the legislature and never approved by any governor. It is the law of diminishing returns.
>
> Under Malthusian rules, the population explosion was forcing our taxes upward relentlessly, while causing a shortening supply of breathable air, drinkable water, and tillable soil.
>
> We're getting diminishing returns from our tax dollars, less control over events through our social and governmental institutions, and less ability as individuals to plan and live our lives as we wish — because so many millions of people, so many billions of dollars, and so many trillions of actors are now involved that public and private affairs alike have simply gotten out of hand.

*From Ralph Nader's *Congress Report*.

Alan continued to study California politics closely, concerning himself especially with the two Senate seats held by Republicans. Senator Murphy was probably beatable, but that race was three years away. Senator Kuchel was widely deemed unbeatable, but Alan—and Max Rafferty—did not share that view. Alan knew that obtaining adequate financial backing for a Senate race would be difficult, unless he could reestablish himself politically.

Then, on March 23, 1967, like a burst of light, the *Los Angeles Times*'s state poll by Don Muchmore headlined: **KUCHEL LEADS IN U.S. SENATE RACE; CRANSTON RUNS SECOND.** Cranston led Yorty 46 percent to 35 percent. Senator Kuchel led Max Rafferty 44 percent to 27 percent. Alan had learned to be distrustful of early polls, but his spirits rose.

He wrote an Easter greeting to Mother, now in her ninetieth year and still living at Cypress Drive in Los Altos.

> This poll was on the front page of the L. A. *Times.* The Democratic primary figures are somewhat good—but Kuchel looks tough.
>
> We had a pleasant, quiet weekend. Went to track meets. I'm now running on the track about three days a week with Kim.
>
> More soonest. Muchest love, Alan.

By mid-September the same L. A. *Times*'s poll was headed: **CRANSTON AND KUCHEL LEAD.** At the same time the Field poll showed that Kuchel led the field. But if Rafferty were nominated, he could be defeated by Cranston, Unruh, or Yorty.

Who was Rafferty? With a background in education, first as a football coach and later as a school superintendent in Needles, he had been catapulted into sudden fame with a single, extraordinary demagogic speech that he proceeded to deliver all over California, excoriating Communists and the "permissive society." The Birchers and the Republican right wing had seized on him as a candidate, poured money into his campaigns, and twice elected him superintendent of public instruction—to the dismay of more enlightened educators.

Time described him this way: "Rafferty was a master of the politics of nostalgia. His rhetoric was punctuated with such anachronistic expletives as 'Confound it!' and 'Horsefeathers!' He considered 'law and order' the one great issue. His targets included novels, newspapers, students, demonstrators, the Supreme Court, dope addicts, TV commentators, urban rioters, and pornographers."

Alan weighed all the possibilities. Conservatives had won three con-
secutive major victories in California: Barry Goldwater and George
Murphy in 1964 and Ronald Reagan in 1966. Alan was convinced that
Rafferty stood a good chance of winning the Republican primary in
1968. He felt that Rafferty in the U.S. Senate would be a disaster for
the state—if not for the nation. Alan felt, too, that if he didn't strike
soon, his name recognition would fade, his ability to raise campaign
money would dwindle, and his supporters would start looking
elsewhere.

But friends who had been through Alan's 1964 and 1966 campaigns—like Ann Alanson, then the national committeewoman;
Libby Gatov, the former U.S. treasurer; and Robert L. Coate, the
northern Democratic state chairman—hated to think of his facing a
possible third defeat. They urged caution.

"It's tough to raise money," said Coate. "The Republicans won't
have that problem!"

I asked a veteran professional, Tom Saunders, manager of President Johnson's Northern California campaign, if he thought Alan
should run. The abruptness of his answer took me aback: "I think
he'd be out of his mind! The Democratic establishment is tired of
Alan."

Win Griffith among others urged Alan to run for Congress. Alan,
however, felt that he was better equipped than ever before to run for
the Senate. Some people still regretted his decision to step aside for
Clair Engle in 1958, but Alan didn't. He was unfailingly optimistic,
and he had developed the habit of seeing the good things in a decision
once made. "One can learn much from books," he has remarked, "but
the real master is experience. A mistake or error in judgment can
always be put to good use."

But he moved with extreme caution. Once he phoned me and said,
"Probably I'll take a chance and run for the Senate. If I don't, I
couldn't be considered in 1970. It's a reasonable chance. If I lose . . ."
he paused and added soberly, "Well, then . . . the parade will have
just gone by."

There were rumors of other candidates. As Democratic State
Women's Chairman, I worked closely with Bob Coate raising funds for
the party. One day I said, "I'm enjoying working with you. I'd like to
do still more. But sometimes I wonder if you're on a collision course
with Alan for the Senate?"

He looked at me thoughtfully. "No," he said. "Alan deserves a chance at the Senate. I've got plenty of time."

Coate kept his word and sought to discourage other Democrats from entering the race. The conventional opinion was still that Rafferty's chance of beating Kuchel was an extremely poor one. But a Field poll in early 1968 showed that Rafferty, though well behind, had gained percentage points on Kuchel. That not only moved Alan nearer to making the race, but it caused other Democratic big guns, such as Yorty and Unruh, to consider running. Cautiously Alan delayed his final decision.

An effective, young, liberal Beverly Hills Democrat, state Senator — now Congressman — Anthony Beilenson entered the race.

Shortly before the last day for filing, Alan penciled a note to Mother:

> The Senate pot is boiling — don't know yet what I'll do. I'm talking with Unruh tomorrow in Sacramento and to Yorty on Friday. Muchest love, Alan.

Alan had planned his strategy. Convinced that everlasting conflict with Unruh was both foolish and fruitless, he had decided to make peace with him — and to stake everything, his entire political career, on a gamble. Jesse was now clearly the unchallenged leader of the party. He had enemies and detractors, but he was dominant. Alan believed he could beat Jesse in a primary, but he knew it would be bloody and he doubted that he'd be in shape to win the general election after yet another struggle with Jesse. He knew, too, that Unruh would have to give up his powerful base as speaker if he ran for the Senate. That could cost him the governorship — always his dream. If the Republican Senate nominee turned out to be Kuchel, Jesse would almost surely lose and be out of office. He thus had much more to lose than Alan, who was already out.

Alan arranged to see Unruh and Yorty on successive days. Seated in Unruh's office in the capitol on Thursday, Alan thought Unruh looked almost as massive as his massive desk. Columnist Art Hoppe's frequent allusion to him as the "Dread Unruh" flashed through Alan's mind.

"Well, Alan?" said Unruh, extending a huge hand.

"Well, Jesse?" Alan parried, closely studying the somber face and hooded eyes of his long-time adversary. Then he said this, "Jesse, I want to run for the Senate. But if you run, I won't — and I'll support you."

"I appreciate that, Alan. We've tangled enough, haven't we?" Unruh sighed and abruptly came to the point, saying in his oddly mellifluous voice, "It's a funny race. Kuchel seems bound to win. He's too far ahead in the polls. Rafferty's a nasty customer. Why would anybody want *him?*"

There was a pause. Alan had worried that Jesse might keep him in doubt about his intentions, leaving him dangling in uncertainty, off balance as long as possible. Then Jesse went on: "I've decided, I'm not going!"

Alan's heart leaped. At that precise moment his decision was made. He would run. Now he had a clear shot at the nomination—except for Yorty. "Thanks a helluva lot for telling me, Jesse," he said. "You didn't have to." Then: "What do you think Sam will do?"

"I don't think you have to really worry about that too much," replied Unruh. To Alan's surprise and delight, the speaker opened a desk drawer, and pulled out a private poll he'd commissioned.

It showed Alan far ahead of Yorty in the Senate race.

"That's fantastic!" exclaimed Alan. "Thanks a million for showing that to me. Do you mind if I tell Yorty about these figures?"

"No," replied Jesse. "Just don't bother to tell him where you got 'em."

"Right," said Alan, "and I'd appreciate if you'd keep it to yourself that I've decided to run."

"OK," said Jesse. "I probably won't support you in the primary, but I won't oppose you. If you're nominated, I'll back you." Alan departed with one war forever behind him. Another loomed. He met with Sam Yorty at Los Angeles City Hall twenty-four hours later. The small, dapper mayor welcomed him pleasantly and launched into a rather scattered discussion of city problems and his last trip to Vietnam. After a bit, Alan changed the subject rather abruptly, saying, "Sam, let's talk about the Senate race."

"What about the Senate race?" inquired the mayor innocently.

"I've made up my mind to go," said Alan firmly with a smile. "A poll shows I'm well ahead of all possible Democratic candidates." He told the mayor the exact figures in the Cranston-Yorty match-up.

"I don't know what I'll do," said Sam. "I may run. I may not. Why are you telling me all this?"

"The press has reported that you may run," responded Alan. "I don't want to seem to be throwing down the gauntlet to you, in case

you decide not to run. I'll be glad to wait about making an announcement, while you're deciding what to do. Filing doesn't close for twelve
days."

"Well," said Sam. "If I go, I go. If I don't, I don't."

"I'm in no rush," said Alan. "I'll just wait a few days."

There was silence. Yorty gazed thoughtfully out a window. Then he
swung his eyes back to Alan: "You just go ahead and announce whenever you feel like it, kid."

The next day, Mayor Sam flew east and met with Richard Nixon, a
sometime ally. Alan spent the next several days putting together a
campaign structure. Then at successive press conferences in Los
Angeles, San Francisco, and Sacramento he announced his candidacy.
He declared, "I am entering the primary because I think I can serve
the interests of California more effectively and knowledgeably than
anyone in the race or likely to enter it."

He called for the United States to get out of Vietnam "with honor."
He refused to choose between his party's rivals for the presidency. How
could he remain neutral among Lyndon Johnson, Eugene McCarthy,
and Robert Kennedy? he was asked.

"They all want peace," Alan said.

Turning to domestic issues, he spoke clearly: "Rancor will rise
between the races until the nation sheds the burden of Vietnam and
turns its full resources to the problems at home.

"We must deal forcefully with riots but even more forcefully with
the causes of riots. If we—you and I—had suffered first slavery and
then lack of equal opportunity, we wouldn't put up with it. No one
worth his salt would put up with it!"

Subsequently, Yorty bowed out of the race.

The Vietnam War was dividing the American public as no other
international problem had done since the clashes between interven-
tionists and isolationists before World War II. Alan opposed the war—
against the advice of some of his professional advisers, who thought he
could draw votes in southern California with a more hawklike stand.
On the Republican side, Senator Kuchel was considered a hawk and
Rafferty a superhawk. There was little public interest in the Democratic primary where Alan was opposed by Beilenson and Public Utili-
ties Commissioner William Bennett. The media concentrated on the
Kuchel-Rafferty race and, more, on the intense battle in the presiden-

tial primary. Alan and Beilenson, his main adversary, had agreed to refrain from mutual attacks. Alan found it difficult to raise campaign funds. Nobody felt he needed much for the primary—in that he seemed a sure winner. And conventional wisdom had it that his opponent in the general election would be Kuchel, who was considered unbeatable. Labor, and many Democrats, traditionally supported Kuchel.

A phone call Alan made to Allyn Kreps, a brilliant, tough, giant of a man who was a partner in the prestigious law firm of O'Melveny and Myers, was typical of the situation. They had met twenty years before and worked closely together in the World Federalist movement. Allyn had then been a high school student, almost twenty years younger than Alan.

"Allyn," said Alan, "I need your help in my campaign."

"Alan," said the no-nonsense Kreps, "You don't need any help in the primary. And Kuchel's a good senator. I intend to support him in the general election."

"Kuchel won't be my opponent," replied Alan. "I'm going to have Rafferty on my hands."

"If you draw Blue Max," said Kreps, "I'll take a leave of absence and devote full time to your campaign!"

On primary night, June 5, in a large room at Los Angeles's Ambassador Hotel, Alan, Geneva, and the boys along with friends, supporters, and staffers watched the returns on TV. It soon became obvious that Alan was overwhelming his opponents and that Robert Kennedy was forging ahead of Eugene McCarthy and Hubert Humphrey. Everyone's attention focused on the race between Kuchel and Rafferty, who were running neck-and-neck.

Kennedy was coming down to the ballroom to make his victory speech. We strolled across the lobby and stood in a vast, excited throng to watch him come on stage, flushed with victory and flanked by family and friends. Among them stood Jesse Unruh, Rosie Grier of the Los Angeles Rams, and Paul Schrade of the United Auto Workers. We were thrilled by Kennedy's exultant and challenging speech.

He and his entourage exited backstage, and Alan returned to his own reception. I stopped to speak to a friend. As I was returning, I was caught in the jammed corridor when shots rang out nearby. I ducked into another hallway to escape a suddenly panicked crowd. Someone raced past, shouting, "Where's a doctor?" I tried to escape into a room filled with TV equipment, but a cameraman barred my way, brandishing a chair over his head. With a sense of dread, I escaped through a darkened room, across the lobby, and back to Alan. I found him and the others watching the screen with stricken faces, and I learned that Senator Kennedy had been shot. More somber than I'd ever seen him, Alan presently called off his party, thanked his friends, and bade them goodnight. We were told later that a dark-faced young man, Sirhan Sirhan, had visited our reception earlier in the evening and had mingled about after having been ousted from Max Rafferty's party nearby.

A small group of us went up to Alan's and Geneva's room and continued to follow the Kennedy tragedy on TV. Tony and Dolores Beilenson came by, apologizing for being tardy in congratulating Alan. White and shaken, they explained they had been with Kennedy in the kitchen when the assassination took place.

They had seen Paul Schrade fall with a head wound and Rosie Grier wrestle the assassin to the floor. Jesse Unruh had taken charge, climbing on a table and bellowing, "Protect him! Keep him alive! We don't want another dead Oswald!" They had watched men tenderly carry Kennedy away. The police had detained them for questioning. The Beilensons stayed with us, silently watching the news, most of the rest of the night. Once a few of those sitting with us tried to go home, only to find that the police wouldn't permit anyone to leave the hotel.

About four o'clock in the morning when a tear-choked Frank Mankiewicz made the sad announcement of the seriousness of Kennedy's condition, we returned to Bel Air. The Kuchel-Rafferty race was still hanging by a thread. Nobody slept.

By breakfast time, we knew Rafferty had won. He had nosed out Kuchel by 1 percent of the 2 million votes cast by Republicans — a narrow margin of about 66,000 votes.

Alan's political intuition had not failed him. He was in the race against Rafferty.

★ ★

CHAPTER 22

1968-The Rafferty Campaign

★ ★

There is nothing so frightening as ignorance in motion.

—Goethe

For all of us who heard Robert Kennedy's call to seek a newer
world, that guiding voice is silent, but the call is no less urgent,
and we can still do better.

—Jesse Unruh, July 11, 1968

Soon after his victory in the primary, Alan met once again with Jesse
Unruh. He needed to nail down Jesse's support against Rafferty.
Jesse needed a clear run two years hence for the governorship. It was
a standoff.

Once again in the speaker's office in Sacramento, Alan saw that
Jesse had changed visibly since Robert Kennedy's death. Two months
earlier, Unruh had strongly urged Kennedy to enter the California
primary and had led his state campaign. There was deep sadness in
his face.

The two reminisced for a moment, and Alan said simply, "Jesse, all
our fights and animosities weren't worth it."

Jesse soberly agreed. Alan sought Jesse's advice on various aspects of
the campaign. Jesse gave it freely and thoughtfully. He readily agreed
to give Alan his wholehearted support.

Then Alan proceeded to reassemble his campaign organization. His
first step was another phone call to Allyn Kreps:

"Allyn, I seem to remember a promise you made when I called you up a while ago."

"I remember. I'm ready—full time. I was planning a vacation in Alaska with my family. I'll cancel it."

Allyn started out as Alan's personal aide. He was at once convinced that the campaign structure, adequate enough for the primary, needed a total overhauling. Soon he took full command. Lu Haas, who had formerly worked for Governor Brown, resigned a top position with HEW in Washington and returned to California to become press chief. A powerful financial committee was formed, led by the remarkable Mark Boyar and including Richard Silberman, later one of Governor Brown's closest associates. Eli Broad and Art Carlsberg, both active in the primary, stayed on in top posts. The executive committee included Paul Ziffren, Libby Gatov, Don Bradley, Roy Greenaway, Roger Kent, Chuck Bender, and other Democratic leaders. This time Alan had a united party behind him and the strongest campaign structure ever. Sandy Weiner, a Republican campaign consultant, was engaged to help round up support from moderate Republicans who could not forgive and forget Rafferty's wild smear campaign against Kuchel.

The campaign began. Alan, now a seasoned campaigner, was as usual inexhaustible.

Given the apparent mood of the California electorate at the time— the fact that the media, and just about everyone else, invariably called Alan the liberal candidate and Rafferty the conservative didn't help the campaign. Actually, the labels were simplistic and inaccurate. Alan tends to approach spending issues cautiously. He has profound respect for history and is wary of government intrusion into private life and business. He likes to quote George Bernard Shaw's definition of a liberal: "someone with both feet firmly planted in midair."

Rafferty's supporters welcomed the two labels, and responded by asserting that "Max has both feet on the ground." At Lee Falk's suggestion, Alan answered by quoting the comedian Joe E. Lewis: "Show me a man with both feet on the ground, and I'll show you a man who can't put his pants on!"

Lee Falk recalls an incident that occurred when he came out later for the Rafferty campaign. "A national magazine had run a story, calling it the hottest campaign of that election year. Rafferty was called dynamic, suave, clever, amusing, and spirited. Alan was dubbed 'the Colorless Cranston.' It went on to say that Alan 'talked in a high-pitched, monotonous voice, tended to sprinkle polysyllables over uncomprehending listeners, and—like Humphrey—talked twenty minutes when the schedule called for ten.' At this time, Alan was much better at ad lib answers to questions than at speeches.

"After this story appeared," Lee said, "our friend Alan Lomax, America's foremost folk song scholar and collector, called me and said, 'This story about the "dull Cranston" is terrible. We have to do something about it. I have a friend, a very famous communications expert, Dr. Birdwhistell at Stanford, who says he can work with Cranston a day or two and redo his image.'

"'Come now,' I said, 'that's ridiculous. Nobody can do that.'

"But Lomax insisted Birdwhistell could do what he said and made me promise to tell Alan. I flew to California next day, was met by a campaign aide, and was driven to a campus stadium where Cranston was appearing before thousands of students. It was just a few months after the assassination of Robert Kennedy and the defeat of Eugene McCarthy. Alan had suddenly surfaced in the public view, and especially before the students, as the last great progressive hope.

"As we approached the stadium, I could hear the roars of the crowd from half a mile away. It sounded like a football crowd.

"When we arrived, the stadium was jam-packed with shouting students. There was a stage or platform in the middle of the field. Alan was standing there with Senator McCarthy, who was campaigning for him.

"I was whisked through the crowd to this platform. Alan had just arrived and was waving his arms to acknowledge the roars of the crowd. The sound was deafening; the students roaring 'Cranston! Cranston! Cranston!', waving banners and flags bearing his name. When I got to the platform, we shook hands, yelling in order to be heard.

"'How are you?' shouted Alan.

"'I'm fine,' I said. 'By the way, Alan Lomax called me about that magazine story that called you "colorless."'

"'What?' yelled Alan. The crowd was shouting *'Cranston! Cranston! Cranston!'* It was like being in a wind tunnel.

"'Dr. Birdwhistell at Stanford,' I said, shouting to make myself heard. 'He says he can make you colorful.' Students were stamping their feet. The platform was shaking. I finally got this great message across to Alan about Dr. Birdwhistell.

"He looked at me with kind of a funny grin, and he said, 'I'm afraid it's too late!'"

It soon became apparent that California's Democrats and Republicans couldn't have nominated two candidates who contrasted more starkly. Where Rafferty was a spendthrift with language, Alan economized it to the point of penury. Where Rafferty became almost sensually involved with his audiences, Alan maintained the emotional distance of a man in complete control of himself and who intended to stay that way. By midcampaign the press had dubbed the race the bitterest in California history. The *Christian Science Monitor* complained that, while a campaign of great importance was going on in California, one couldn't get a clear view of the candidates because of "all the garbage in the air."

But others, who were disturbed by what they called the campaign's negativism, failed to understand what Alan eventually sensed was to be the determinant issue—exposure and defeat of demagoguery. Of the three issues he considered most important in the senatorial battle, including peace in Vietnam, and peace and security in America's streets, the third—Max Rafferty himself—became by far the most crucial. Alan was concerned that in an age of rampant social crisis, under the dark and menacing shadows of possible nuclear war, and in the midst of the new electronic phenomenon of instant and total communication, Americans no longer had the luxury of a cooling-off period between word and deed. There was increasing danger of high-speed responses to intemperate speech instantaneously communicated. The way serious issues were approached was becoming almost as important as the substance involved. It was, again, a matter of means shaping ends. In a very real sense, Rafferty's inflammatory language became the overriding issue of the campaign.

Alan's objectives were twofold. First he had to establish forthright positions on the war and on vital domestic problems—positions that would solidify his general support and arouse the vast armies of conscience that Robert Kennedy and Eugene McCarthy had marshalled in California. Second, he had to attack and destroy Max Rafferty's credibility. Rafferty had to be seen as a man unfit for public office.

The common denominator of American anxieties in 1968 was violence, in Vietnam and in our cities. Alan staked out his position early and unequivocally in Sacramento at the Democratic state convention that August. There he made a blistering attack on administration foreign policy, calling for the end of a war he labeled a "moral outrage . . . a military and political failure." His demand for a bombing halt, a negotiated peace, free elections with all parties represented, and a phased American withdrawal, quickly became his major substantive issue and remained so throughout the campaign.

In a state that was widely thought to be in the throes of a deepening political reaction, the decision to campaign on peace in Vietnam represented a substantial political risk. Despite early opposition from some key campaign advisers, who feared that the Sacramento speech would invite charges from Rafferty that Alan was a Communist or something akin thereto, Alan was adamant. He was convinced the war was tearing America apart. He had an abiding concern with the danger of nuclear war. He had been a leader in the world law movement. If he was going to be elected to the U.S. Senate, it would be as a peace candidate. And if he was to be defeated, it would also be as a peace candidate. It was his speech and he would give it — not once, as it turned out, but "forever." In various forms and forums, it became "The Speech" of the Cranston campaign.

What Alan and his advisers failed to comprehend at first — and what Rafferty *never* realized — was that a personal attack questioning Alan's patriotism was precisely what might be needed to nail down a Cranston victory. When the attack finally came — as inevitably it had to, considering Rafferty's nature and history — it proved to be not a disaster for Alan, but a bonanza.

After advocating reduced violence as the way to end the Vietnam War, Alan moved to tie Rafferty's policy of greater violence in Vietnam to his advocacy of police repression at home. He made an issue of Rafferty's predilection for simplistic and violent solutions to complex problems.

Alan overcame Rafferty's built-in advantage with the white middle class on "law and order" by focusing on the outrageous price his opponent seemed willing to risk paying to get it — a police state. Likewise, he focused on the dangerous price Rafferty was willing to pay in pursuit of American military victory in Vietnam — atomic holocaust.

Many Californians who generally agreed with Rafferty's conservative objectives decided they couldn't accept his price in violence.

Alan reminded the voters in every speech that "Rafferty has advocated the shooting of looters, military court martials for civilians, a national police force independent of presidential control, and abdication of civilian control of the war to the military for them to escalate as they might see fit. Rafferty is the spokesman for the politics of violence."

Communicating to the voters the violent consequences of Rafferty's views required a strategy that repudiated what are often considered cardinal rules of politics:

> Don't give your opponent free publicity.
> Never refer to him by name.
> Pretend that he doesn't exist (except by innuendo).

If Rafferty's major weakness was his character, attention had to be single-mindedly fixed on him through direct and blunt attack. The task was to strip back his linguistic facade to reveal its demagogic foundation.

On Labor Day, Alan kicked off the formal campaign and began his public expose of Max Rafferty, swiftly creating a first-class problem for the Republican. Rafferty had gained his first wide attention in the town of La Canada years before with a speech on patriotism, denouncing the education profession for teaching trivia and for making youths "spineless, luxury-loving, spiritless traitors and booted, sideburned, duck-tailed, unwashed, leather-jacketed slobs whose favorite sport was ravaging little girls and stomping polio victims to death." His new managers decided to give him a more moderate tone. Without inflammatory rhetoric, however, a demagogue comes across as a hollow shell. Rafferty was left in an awkward stance, with nothing to say.

There were no defenses to Alan's charge that Rafferty's only solution to violence at home and abroad was more violence. Rafferty's wild statements were all on public record. The only avenue open to Rafferty was counterattack. So he fell right into Alan's trap, returning to his old form and launching smears that surpassed in vitriol even those of his campaign against Kuchel.

Rafferty had beaten Kuchel by saturating the state with a series of false smear ads — too late for Kuchel to have time to respond effectively. The tactic would surely be repeated against Alan; thus a prime objective was to establish, before the distortions came, that Rafferty was not a man to be believed. Accordingly, a plan masterminded by campaign chairman Allyn Kreps was put into operation. A group of young volunteer lawyers assembled a document called "MAX RAFFERTY'S NINE BIG LIES: Rafferty's Primary Campaign of Smear and Misrepresentation Against Thomas Kuchel." It was put out by GOPocrats for Cranston, a brainchild of Sandy Weiner's and mailed to every newspaper in the state, as well as to moderate Republicans. Almost overnight, a host of editorials and cartoons appeared, portraying Rafferty as an unconscionable liar and mudslinger for such outrageous nonsense as the accusation that Kuchel had voted to give American tax dollars to Red China to build steel mills.

A perplexing issue of great concern in the Cranston camp revolved around Rafferty's repeated and insistent demands for a debate. Alan's advisers were convinced a debate would be unwise, but nobody could figure out how Alan could avoid it without looking timid. Someone finally proposed a simple stratagem: the truth.

Thereafter, each time Rafferty demanded a debate, Alan responded by saying, "How can you debate a liar? If Max Rafferty will stop lying about me and admit his lies about Tom Kuchel, I'll be glad to debate him."

Rafferty soon tired of encountering the word "liar" every time he used the word "debate," and he subsided. How well Alan's strategy was working became apparent one night when Kim told him about an incident at a Santa Monica shopping center.

Kim and a crew of friends were asking shoppers if they could put "Cranston" bumper strips on their cars. A man drove into the parking lot with a "Wallace for President" strip on his bumper. He looked like a hopeless case, probably pro-Rafferty, but Kim decided to tackle him. He held up one of his strips and asked, "Can I put this on your car?"

"No," the man scowled. "I'm just for George Wallace — don't care about anybody else."

Kim persisted, "You know Cranston's running against Rafferty."

"Rafferty?" the man snorted. "Put it on the car! I can't stand liars."

Another main theme of Alan's campaign was exposing Rafferty's extreme right-wing support. The *St. Louis Post Dispatch* revealed that substantial national funding for Rafferty came from the right-wing direct mail specialist Richard Viguerie. Richard Smart noted, "John Rousselot, a top Birch Society officer, prepared a book of materials for use in ads attacking Cranston.*

A break occurred when H. L. Hunt of Texas, thought by some to be the world's richest man, proudly proclaimed that he had been instrumental in Kuchel's defeat. Alan jumped to the attack: "Wealthy forces behind Rafferty are as free with their money as Rafferty is with the truth. California is not for sale to right-wing Texas oil billionaires! I demand that Rafferty state whether he has received money from Hunt!" Rafferty denied he had received such money, but it was soon proved that he had.

In October, Gov. Lester Maddox of Georgia announced his choice for George Wallace's vice presidential running mate: Rafferty found the endorsement a serious liability.

The revelation of the true nature of Rafferty's support and his lack of candor, as it came to light, lent more credence to the attacks on his credibility.

Then as so often happens in politics, something totally unexpected and momentous occurred. Rafferty had made patriotism, duty to country, and courage issues in all his campaigns and this one as well. He had resoundingly denounced draft-card burners as "creeps, cowards, unwashed, long-haired Communists." But the *Long Beach Press Telegram,* in a series of articles by a crack investigative reporter, David Shaw, revealed that superpatriot Rafferty had never served in the military. He appealed a 1-A classification and got a 4F exemption in World War II — for flat feet. Rafferty, according to his ex-wife, said that if his claim to have flat feet didn't work, "it would be easy to have an accident and shoot a toe off."

The reporter wrote, "The standing joke in Trona (where Rafferty taught school during the war) was that 'Max Rafferty celebrated V-J Day by throwing his cane away.'"

The county superintendent of schools told reporter Shaw, "I don't blame anyone for not rushing off to enlist. No one wants to be killed.

*Richard Smart, *Defeat of a Demagogue* (unpublished), a perceptive analysis of the campaign.

But if Rafferty was classified 1-A and then appealed, I find what he says now about patriotism and military service a bit inconsistent with what he did himself."

Alan did not personally attack Rafferty about his cane. But Trona's joke about the famous educator and flag waver caught on statewide, and the public was amused and edified by what seemed a new kind of Aesop's fable. The zeal of Rafferty's right-wing supporters diminished. They were patriots, and their faith in their candidate was badly shaken.

The Field poll showed Alan's lead widening to twelve points. The *Palo Alto Times,* the *San Francisco Chronicle,* and the *Los Angeles Times,* the largest paper in the west, endorsed Alan. One thousand prominent Republicans endorsed Alan in full-page ads.

At last the anticipated smear came. Rafferty announced, "Cranston's advocacy of a bombing halt is perilously close to treason." In the 1950s somewhat analogous charges by Sen. Joe McCarthy had destroyed careers and forced victims to run for cover. Now Alan, gambling that public opinion was now more sophisticated, did all he could to give Rafferty's charge maximum publicity. He "welcomed" into "Max Rafferty's Treason Club for Distinguished Americans," twenty-seven prominent U.S. senators and McGeorge Bundy—all of whom supported a bomb-halt policy. He also lashed out at Rafferty for espousing a policy of "professional demagoguery and amateur militarism."

In the first week of October, the polls showed a further drop. Panic struck the Rafferty camp. The candidate's cry of treason, Alan's confident repetition of it as the final proof of "how wild a man Rafferty really is," a negative press reaction, Rafferty's increasing tendency to flail about on television, all dictated drastic action.

The Nixon staff had begun to mute its support of Rafferty in the closing days, but on October 7, the Reagan apparatus took over. Governor Reagan's presidential hopes were dead for this election, and his key financial backers went to work for Rafferty. Lyn Nofziger resigned as the governor's press secretary to become Rafferty's communications coordinator.

Nofziger tried but failed to muzzle his candidate, who was now being referred to inside his own campaign as "Supermouth." But the second part of Nofziger's strategy seemed to hold greater promise. Suddenly he had Rafferty running against a favorite Reagan scapegoat, Eldridge Cleaver—and seeking to draw an absurd association between Cleaver and Cranston. The Black Panther Leader, along with campus revolution in general and the University of California in particular, had been prime — and popular — Reagan targets.

Nofziger instructed the Lawlor Advertising Agency to drop everything else and to prepare an entirely new media campaign directed against Cleaver, with Alan portrayed as his ally. According to a Rafferty campaign official, this strategy originated in the Governor's office and was handed to the campaign organization as an ultimatum. The new line quickly emerged.

The public was inundated with ads playing on people's fears of social revolution. One asserted: "Do you want Eldridge Cleaver and his four letter obscenities speaking to your children? Alan Cranston does." A television commercial showed Cleaver exhorting a large audience, "You riot, baby." This was followed by a voice asserting that Cranston supported Cleaver.

Lu Haas told me in an interview: "We first heard about the ads in a call from Fleming Atha, a friend and supporter in Bakersfield. 'My God, have you heard this commercial?'

"We called the station, asked them to read the ad over the phone, and it was outrageous! We sprang into action to stop the commercials. Kreps set up a telephone chain of young lawyers who phoned stations all over the state, warning that the ads were potentially libelous and that management had a personal responsibility to consider the contents. We sent telegrams to every radio and TV station. We sent press releases everywhere with the text of our telegram, disavowing any connection with Cleaver and demanding the commercials be stopped. We scared the hell out of them.

"Stations don't usually scrutinize their commercials that carefully. But now they looked and decided, 'Oh, no!' The ads violated U.S. Supreme Court rulings against material that shows a reckless disregard for the truth. The rest of the ads never got on the air.

"Rafferty and his people fought back charging that Cranston had 'terrorized the media.' He turned the free speech issue back on Alan, and again it looked bad."

Finally, Alan returned home to Bel Air to await the outcome. He was reasonably confident, but it was impossible to gauge the effects of Rafferty's last-minute smears and spending — estimated at $2.9 million. Alan's campaign had spent $1,092,208 (San Francisco *Chronicle,* December 10, 1968).

On election night, Alan and his supporters gathered at the Biltmore Hotel to await returns.

Rafferty took an early lead based on absentee ballots, traditionally Republican. Soon Alan caught up. Slowly, slowly he forged ahead. *At last he knew he had won!*

Shortly before midnight, with most of the votes counted, he had 3,615,261 to 3,275,679 for Rafferty—a margin of less than 400,000 out of nearly 7 million votes cast.

We went downstairs to a long room jammed with a thousand supporters who converged on Alan—laughing, cheering, crying, all wanting to hug him or shake his hand. Alan took Geneva's arm, his other hand held mine. With Jack beside us, we began a difficult, tortoise-like progress toward a platform at the far end of the room — it looked miles away—with a forest of TV cameras, mikes, and lights. The press of bodies around us opened a path, then crushed us again, the crowd moving together like a surging wave. The wave crested, and I was literally lifted out of my shoes, which Jack somehow managed to retrieve. I felt terror. But Alan moved purposefully forward—tall, tanned, eager, and smiling, his face showing a strange mixture of utter calm and total excitement — towing us in his wake.

The wave crested again and hurled us up onto the platform. The cameras churned. Jesse Unruh lifted Alan's arm aloft in triumph.

Geneva rolled her blue eyes at me, seized my hand to steady herself as people continued to shove, and gasped in her husky drawl, "I always wanted to win but — but I never knew it would be like this!"

News photos show Alan's joyful face, surrounded by a sea of tense ones.

He began to speak. He thanked his supporters from the bottom of his heart. "My campaign was based on reconciliation, not retribution," he said. "It was based on a theme not of law and order, but of order and justice under law. To those who opposed me, I will forget that opposition. I look forward to representing all the people." His words were drowned out by an ovation.

Even in those first hours of exhilaration and triumph, Alan was not unmindful of others. That night, lying awake at his home on the hill, he thought of all that he wanted to do in the Senate, and of all those who had helped him get there. There were a few individuals without whom he could not have won—Allyn Kreps, Prentiss Moore, Mark Boyar, Jack Fowle, and a handful of others; he counted six in all. He would tell them he knew that as soon as possible. And then there were *all* the others!

Next day, the final returns showed that Alan had defeated Rafferty with 52 percent of the vote, against 46 percent for Rafferty, and 2 percent for Peace and Freedom candidate Paul Jacobs. Nixon had carried California and the nation over Humphrey. The Republicans captured the State Assembly, and it was anticipated that they would depose Jesse Unruh as speaker.

Tom Sorenson, Alan's northern campaign manager, who had been in Robert Kennedy's primary campaign, wrote to me later, "It was the worst of years and the best of years . . ."

Dick Smart wrote later: "Alan's victory dealt a severe blow to extremist strength in California, damaged Governor Reagan's prestige, united the strife-torn Democratic Party, and laid the basis for a strong assault on Reagan in the 1970 gubernatorial campaign. But more important than any of these results, Cranston's campaign holds some clear lessons for all Americans, who, in an era of deepening social crisis, are determined to resist demagoguery posing as deliverance."

The *Almanac of American Politics 1972* reported, "Thus conservative California elected a senator who opposes the Vietnam war, large military expenditures, and most of the domestic policies of the Nixon administration."

The following day Alan held press conferences in Los Angeles, San Francisco, and Sacramento. At the Los Angeles Airport we joined a long line of people waiting to board the plane to San Francisco. Pete Somers, Alan's campaign aide, told him he had arranged to board him ahead of the other passengers. Alan declined this comfortable privilege and stood in line with everybody else much to the surprise — and edification — of some of his younger relatives who were accompanying him to San Francisco.

CHAPTER

★ ★ ★ ★ ★ ★ ★ ★ ★ ★ ★ ★ ★ ★ ★

First Senate Term

★ ★ ★ ★ ★ ★ ★ ★ ★ ★ ★ ★ ★ ★ ★

History is past politics and politics present history.
— Sir John Robert Seeley

Soon after the election Alan flew to Washington with Lu Haas to see Senator Kuchel and to prepare for his entrance into the Senate. They took a cab up Pennsylvania Avenue past rows of maple trees turning red and gold in the fall. The bright November sunlight shone on the flags, the pigeons, and the marble buildings. The driver played a lilting country tune on his radio.

As they swung left on Constitution Avenue, they looked up through the trees at the tiered white Capitol dome — as white as the sky was blue. Lu, a veteran of many campaigns and political hassles in California, waved his hand at the beautiful sight.

"There it is!" he said. "Alan, tell me; when you were working late into the night to fight cross-filing, to organize the Democratic party, trying to put together a statewide Democratic slate, to get north-south cooperation within the party; and all those many hours you spent as state controller, making the department more efficient, attending the committee meetings required of you, did you, during those times, ever have the slightest idea that you would be here, looking up at the Capitol, as California's senator?"

Alan answered succinctly, "Yes."

"Just that one word," Lu recalls. "It was so typical of Alan. And I thought, 'How dumb a question for me to ask!'"

215

At a victory celebration a friend said: "Alan, this is only four years late!" He was thinking of Salinger.

Alan said, "You mean ten years." He was thinking of Engle.

That showed precisely the same focus Lu Haas had noted.

On his first day, Alan and Lu lunched in the senate dining room. Hugh Scott, the Republican whip, came bustling over and shook his hand warmly. "I want to thank you for saving the Republican party from Rafferty."

Alan and Geneva moved to Washington. Ray Lapin, then the head of "Fanny Mae", the Federal National Mortgage Association, and a longtime friend, invited them to stay with him in his Watergate apartment until they could find a place of their own. Ray recalls Alan's coming down to breakfast in his bathrobe early the first morning and finding Ray reading the *Washington Post*. "Good morning, Senator!" said Ray, standing up to greet him.

Alan smiled and threw his arms around Ray in a bear hug. "I'm a Senator!" he said.

Knowing how self-contained Alan is, Ray says that he felt like crying. Then Alan added, "How about keeping on calling me Alan?"

Later that day, taking his place at his rosewood desk in the Senate chamber, Alan looked about the great grey and gold room. It seemed smaller than it had from the gallery—so much closer to the vast ceiling. He glanced up at the golden oval of lighting, at the marble busts of the vice presidents in their niches who had presided there, at the reporters and visitors thronging the gallery—Geneva, Robin, and Kim were there—and down to his own desk, where previous Senators who had sat there had carved their names in the drawer. He looked up at Hubert Humphrey, sitting in the vice-president's chair, the presidency forever lost to him. He watched Senator Mike Mansfield, the majority leader, and Ted Kennedy, the newly elected majority whip, and Russell Long, whom Kennedy had deposed as whip moments before. Then he began to study the others around him. All—or most—had been through the same hellfire and brimstone he had been through on the way to the Senate. He was determined to find common ground with each of them.

The first letter he wrote from his office was to Mother: "For twenty minutes today I presided over the Senate! Didn't say a single word!"

One of the first letters he received came from a favorite constituent:

Senator Alan Cranston
Senate Office Building
Washington, D.C.

Dear Senator:

I was one of your strongest supporters and one who believed in your integrity —
perhaps even your manhood. I sent you a check for $25 for your campaign.

Inasmuch as you are now safely ensconced in office I think you would be doing a
handsome deed by returning my $25. However, if you insist upon running again at
some future date, just send me the money and I will hold it in escrow until I find
out definitely what your plans are for the future.

Sincerely,

Groucho Marx

Alan replied:

January 30, 1969

Dear Groucho:

I was relieved to learn that you believe in my integrity and my manhood, just as
you will be relieved to learn that your $25 check, which I promptly cashed, was
good.

So much for my integrity, my manhood, and your twenty-five bucks.

Gratefully,

Alan Cranston

As Senator, Alan's first contact with the military was a briefing
presented by some very high Pentagon brass. It was routine but
thorough and impressive to the newcomer. The briefing focused on
U.S. military weaknesses and consequent equipment, manpower, and
budget needs. Afterwards Alan rode back to the Senate in a car driven
by an enlisted man. A colonel sat with him in the back. As they

approached the Capitol, the colonel asked: "Now is there anything else we can do for you, sir?"

"I don't think so," said Alan.

"Well, if you ever want anything, just let us know."

"Thanks."

The colonel persisted. "Just anything you need; don't hesitate, sir."

"Actually," said Alan, "I do need a helicopter."

There was a strained silence. Alan could imagine the startled colonel, utterly taken aback, thinking to himself, "Oh, my God! What kind of a senator do we have here?" He finally stammered, "I think maybe that could be arranged . . ."

Envisaging compromising reports flourishing in Pentagon files, copies proliferating, and one leaking to the press, Alan hastened to explain that he was only joking. But it wasn't easy to convince the colonel. He never smiled.

As he got out of the car, Alan made one last effort to lay the matter to rest. "Actually," he grinned, "I'm afraid of helicopters."

A few days after entering the Senate and two days before President Lyndon B. Johnson was due to leave the White House, Alan went to see him.

"There are two kinds of senators, workhorses and show horses," the president, who had served twelve years in the Senate, told him. "I hope you're going to be a workhorse."

*   *   *

Every senator's career depends to a great degree on the quality of his staff. Alan put together a staff that the Washington press corps describes as one of the best on Capitol Hill. But Alan still chuckles over an incident that happened very early at his Los Angeles office. A very bright fifteen-year-old named Richard was so fascinated by government that he worked as a volunteer every day after school and full time in the summer. At first he just emptied wastebaskets and ran errands, but he soon graduated to answering the telephone. After a while he was actually answering questions and helping people who phoned. His voice hadn't changed yet, however, and constituents often thought they were talking to a young woman.

Richard became deeply involved in helping solve the retirement problems of an army colonel who called up every day or so and addressed him as "Miss Richard." One day the colonel came to the office for additional help. He entered at the very moment when the nine-year-old son of a staff member, who had also dropped in, was sitting at the front desk, the receptionist having stepped out momentarily.

The small boy received the colonel with aplomb. The colonel said he had some questions about his retirement pay, and the nine-year-old said he knew nothing about that subject. The bemused Colonel asked if he could see "Miss Richard." The nine-year-old picked up the phone, summoned the fifteen-year-old, and introduced him to the colonel: "I think you want him. His name is Richard."

The nonplussed colonel recognized Richard's voice and found his answers satisfactory. He left, shaking his head.

Every senator starts with a basic staff allotment equal to that of every other senator. The chairmanship of a committee brings with it additional staff, but otherwise staff size is based upon the sovereign equality of the states. Some allowance is made for the size of the population of each state; but this by no means takes into full account the great discrepancies between states. California, the most populous state, has 22,000,000 people; Alaska is the smallest with 403,000. That's a fifty-five-to-one ratio, but the staff ratio is approximately two-to-one today. If staff were apportioned to a senator on the basis of population, as it is in the House, Alan would have a staff of 774. Alan has 63 people on his senate staff, while Senator Mike Gravel, a fellow Democrat who came to the Senate when Alan did, has 28, almost half as many. Alan's constituency is the largest any legislator has ever represented.

To help him handle the myriad small and large issues, problems, complaints, demands, questions, ideas, and everything else that is generated by the immense constituency of California — and all else that a senator is expected to do, must do, or can do — Alan is fortunate in his administrative assistant, Roy Greenaway, a long-time associate who eats, sleeps, and breathes his work. His occasional professorial manner and whimsical expression belie a mind that is incisive, super organized, and highly tough. Roy, who taught school in Fresno, collaborated with Alan in the CDC days and served as an inheritance tax appraiser when Alan was controller.

Alan often summons Roy, Murray Flander, Allyn Kreps, Jonathan Steinberg (whose field of responsibility is veterans' affairs), Kathy Files (agriculture, farming, conservation), Carolyn Jordan (banking), or other staff members to talk over complex problems. Visitors who chance on these sometimes heated sessions are often shocked by the abrasiveness of the senator's cabinet. They wonder how he survives. But Alan thrives on these free exchanges. At times a conclusion is reached that will offend some individual or force in the constituency. Someone always pointedly reminds Alan of that before the meeting breaks up. "So be it," he often says.

Paul R. Clancy wrote an article in the *Washington Monthly* about the informal relationships in Alan's office:

> In Cranston's office he is not referred to in reverent tones as "the Senator," as so many others are, but simply as "Alan." Having an interview with him is more of an informal dialogue than a press conference and, more than likely, friends of Cranston who happen to have dropped by will gather around to listen. You get the feeling that he, his staff, and friends are all part of a big family, and if you want to come for dinner, there's always a place.

Alan's first serious problem as a senator was handling the incredible volume of his mail. Soon after he was sworn in, he began receiving ten thousand letters, cards, and telegrams a week. He came to dread his trips to California and the confrontations with angry constituents and supporters whose letters had not been answered. My husband, Jack, wrote him a personal note and got back a form letter. Eventually, Roy and Anne Ainsworth (a warm, talented, former federalist activist who later served a stint in President Carter's White House mail office) managed to organize the mail department and deal effectively with the paper tide. The mail ebbs and flows, and sometimes the flows are overwhelming. When President Nixon ordered troops into Cambodia, ten thousand angry letters poured into Alan's office every day for six weeks. Unopened mail bags piled up and spilled out into the halls.

While managing to be on hand in the Senate for more than 90 percent of all roll-call votes, Alan flies back to California at least eighteen times a year. Originally he would settle down beside an empty coach seat and turn it into a makeshift desk for the huge amount of paperwork he carries in an outsize briefcase. He views long air flights as a marvelous, undisturbed opportunity to catch up on reports, documents, mail, and other work. Now, however, he has learned to juggle all the papers on his lap and between his feet, and he shuns any empty seats. They proved too inviting to citizens who couldn't resist the opportunity to sit down by a senator and present their views for five hours. Once a lobbyist, after several drinks too many, sat down next to Alan right on top of his papers, and proceeded to harangue him about a legislative problem. After listening a while, Alan politely tried to free himself. He failed. He tried a bit less politely. When that failed too, he grabbed an air-sickness bag, opened it hastily, and held it expectantly in front of him. The lobbyist fled.

There was one visitor to the empty seat whose visit Alan appreciated because of the fascinating nature of the conversation that ensued. Boarding a plane at Washington, Alan encountered Richard Kleindienst, who some time before had served as Richard Nixon's attorney general. The two had developed a friendly working relationship when, together with Senator John Tunney, they had successfully negotiated an understanding regarding the method of appointing federal judges in California. They exchanged pleasantries and separated. Alan entered the coach section, and Kleindienst headed for first class.

A while later, Alan was working away when Kleindienst, quite a large man with a ruddy face and a breezy manner, loomed over him and plopped heavily down in the empty seat beside him. Kleindienst was in a remarkably ebullient mood. Clearly he was celebrating something. Having had a drink or two in first class, he was very expansive, delighted to discuss any topic, and seemingly pleased to answer any question.

Alan delicately brought the conversation around to Watergate — delicately because Kleindienst had suffered personally in that travail, winding up resigning under fire as attorney general. But Kleindienst didn't recoil from this sensitive subject. Alan started asking questions, and Kleindienst answered them all, one way or another. One of Alan's questions was: why didn't Nixon destroy the tapes?

He answered that when the White House learned that Alexander Butterfield was going to reveal the existence of the tapes in an open session of the Ervin Committee, the president, Ehrlichman, Haldeman, himself, and perhaps one or two others held a meeting in the Oval Office to discuss this unexpected and unpleasant development.

Was there any way to stop Butterfield? Clearly not.

Was there any way to deny the existence of the tapes successfully, somebody wondered. No.

The discussion centered upon how to explain why the tapes were made and what reasons should be given for refusing the inevitable demands that they be turned over to the investigating committee or made public.

They agreed that the best course was to claim executive privilege and assert that it was necessary to protect the privacy of people who had spoken freely to the president without knowing they were being secretly taped.

"At no time did we discuss doing away with the tapes, because nobody there thought we'd be compelled to give them up," Kleindienst said. "Nobody even brought up what would happen if they got out."

"Why not?" asked Alan.

"Power," replied Kleindienst. "Too much power — or illusions of power." He explained that the men in the White House still, at that stage, felt so powerful that they automatically assumed they could control the tapes — along with a great deal more that turned out to be totally out of control.

"Looking back", said Kleindienst, "it probably should have been handled like Harry Truman would have done it. He'd have piled all the tapes on the White House lawn, called in the press, and let them photograph him tossing a match and setting them all on fire, explaining with a defiant grin that he'd turned pyromaniac to protect the privacy of all the unsuspecting folks who'd been taped — declaring, of course, that it was never intended that the tapes would land in anybody else's hands. And admitting, probably, that it was a mistake to have made them in the first place.

"If that had been done, Nixon would still be president, and I . . ." Kleindienst's voice trailed off.

The next day, reading the morning paper, Alan learned why Kleindienst had been so ebullient and expansive. An hour or so before he got on the plane, a panel of the U.S. District Court had decided not to take any disciplinary action against him for his part in Watergate. Thus he was permitted to keep his license to practice law.

Alan's first close friendships in the Senate were with three other freshmen, Republicans William Saxbe of Ohio and Richard Schweiker of Pennsylvania and Democrat Harold Hughes of Iowa. All four were intensely frustrated by the Senate's ancient, arcane ways. Hughes and Saxbe were mavericks who had little patience with the system, and both were to leave the Senate voluntarily after one term, Saxbe to become Nixon's attorney general and then his ambassador to India; Hughes to devote his life to religion and a crusade against alcoholism.

Hughes was a former truck driver, an alcoholic who had gained control and who had become governor. He was Alan's best first-term friend — tall, ruggedly handsome with heavy black hair and a radiant smile, yet often darkly somber like Lincoln.

Early in 1969 Alan suggested the four team up to streamline and speed up the work of the Senate. They consulted widely with other freshmen as well as with the most seasoned of senators, drew up a blueprint, and finally, with some trepidation, laid out their suggestions to Majority Leader Mike Mansfield. They knew how Lyndon Johnson in his iron-fisted dictatorial days as majority leader would have responded: with fury, scorn, and ridicule. The taciturn Mansfield was blessed with a tolerance never discovered in Johnson — but the four freshmen were uncertain how far that tolerance extended, and they were, they feared, being somewhat presumptuous. Mansfield heard them out mostly in silence, puffing on his pipe. He asked a few questions, phoned the parliamentarian to clear up a fine point on the sacred Senate rules, and then dryly and with great succinctness said, "Well, this and that and this other won't work, but these ideas make some sense, if you'll straighten out this aspect and that. So why don't you work your ideas over and come back. New looks at old ways of doing things never hurt."

The four freshmen went back to the drawing board, came back to Mansfield, paid a visit to Hugh Scott of Pennsylvania, who had just succeeded the late Everett Dirksen as minority leader, and soon several of their suggestions were adopted. These first changes were far from revolutionary, but they were not insignificant. One change affected Senate procedures at convening time each day, saving inestimable time and making a good part of each day far more predictable.

In succeeding years the four drew all other incoming senators, Republicans and Democrats alike, into a powerful bipartisan coalition to improve the Senate's functioning, its rules, procedures, budget, staffing, space, and equipment. The group — like CDC in its early days — wisely steered clear of ideological concerns that could have broken up the alliance. As the years went by, they came to comprise a working majority of the Senate, able to accomplish almost any reasonable goal upon which they could approach unanimity. Senator Lloyd Bentsen of Texas, who came to the Senate in 1970, became the group's formal leader. Alan served as its informal co-leader until he was elected majority whip in 1977.

One reform that was relentlessly pursued by the group was vigorously opposed by most of the more senior senators and later became controversial far beyond the environs of the Senate: the matter of staffing. Most, but not all, of the newer senators — particularly Mike Gravel of Alaska and Bill Brock (now chairman of the Republican National Committee) of Tennessee — felt that they specifically, and the Senate generally, needed more staff assistance.

Individually, the members of the coalition wanted more help with workloads that were ever rising because of the array of complex and controversial issues demanding attention and because of the increasing tendency of constituents to look upon their representatives as ombudsmen who should be able to solve their personal problems with the federal bureaucracy. They particularly wanted help with their committee assignments. Also new members of the Armed Services Committee and the Finance Committee complained bitterly that they weren't allowed to bring staff assistants inside closed committee sessions.

Most importantly, they were concerned by the erosion of the power of Congress vis-à-vis the executive branch as President Johnson, Democrat, and then President Nixon, Republican, sought and asserted and exercised more and more power — ignoring, bypassing, outmaneuvering, and overriding the Congress. They felt that to compete effectively with the executive and to preserve the system of checks and balances within the government — one of the essential foundations of individual liberty in our country — more staff to aid in research, analysis, planning, and effective action was an absolute necessity.

"If we don't watch out," grumbled Harold Hughes, "the Senate will go the way of the House of Lords, and the imperial presidency will sweep us on to one-man rule in this country of ours."

The new senators won their way over the objection of the older senators, most of whom were quite adequately staffed due to the power of seniority, as far as their personal needs were concerned. Committee sessions hitherto closed were opened to the new staff aides.

Later on, after Nixon had been driven from office by Watergate and the beginning of the impeachment process and when Congress reasserted its rule and authority in the Ford and Carter presidencies, the press and public voiced concerns that the pendulum had swung back too far and that an independent and recalcitrant Congress was frustrating executive decision-making beyond the point of reason. This led to complaints about "overblown and expensive hill staffs" and "senators who are run by their power-mad aides."

Meanwhile, the reformers were strengthened with the arrival of newcomers like Lawton Chiles of Florida, Dick Clark and John Culver of Iowa who began to play leadership roles in these efforts. The group tackled seniority — and reduced its potency; attacked the method of assigning Democrats to committees — and democratized the process considerably; took on proxy voting in committees — and modified it greatly; and declared war on secret, closed meetings — and opened all of them up to the long-excluded press and public save for sessions dealing with sensitive national security and personnel matters. Subsequently, Alan worked very closely with Senator Walter Mondale, Democrat of Minnesota, and Senator Charles Mathias, Republican of Maryland, on changing the rules to make it easier to break filibusters.

Alan was the first member of the class of 1968 to move into the majority leader's chair and handle a piece of legislation on the Senate floor. This happened in May 1969 and came as a consequence of his first significant break with President Nixon, who took office seventeen days after Alan was sworn in. Alan, a new senator, was determined to try to find common ground with the new president, and in March he told columnist Nick Thimmesch:

> I've been on the other side of the fence and been engaged in political combat with Richard Nixon for a good part of my political life, but we've had some experiences that are in some ways common to both of us. We both went through two straight defeats and then returned to victory — he to the White House and I to the Senate. Oddly enough, I now hold the Senate seat that he once held. Another coincidence is that he is the thirty-seventh president of the United States and I am the thirty-seventh senator from California.
>
> Now that he has been chosen to lead our nation, I propose to do all I can to help him lead. I will not oppose him on a strictly partisan basis, and I will do all that I can to support what he seeks to do. When I oppose him, it will be simply because I feel that he's wrong.

Alan had then cited as an example his support of David Packard's nomination for undersecretary of defense. "I know Packard. We lived in the same part of California. He's a man of total integrity and great ability, and I did what I could to insure that he was approved."*

Congressional Quarterly reported that Alan scored a 70 percent rating for his support of Nixon on nineteen key roll-call votes on foreign policy in 1969. Republican George Murphy supported Nixon only 55 percent of the time.

*From "West," Los Angeles *Times,* March 2, 1969.

CHAPTER 24

★ ★

Senator Cranston in Action

★ ★

We must have a policy of peace to match our policy of power.
— Alan Cranston

One of President Nixon's first moves was to attempt to abolish the Job Corps, a project of LBJ's Great Society designed to provide job-training opportunities for disadvantaged youth. The Job Corps had become unpopular in some communities, and no one else on the Senate Labor Committee was particularly eager to defend it. So Alan, though a new and junior member of the committee, took on the task. Jonathan Steinberg, a brilliant and aggressive young attorney who has played a major role in developing much of Alan's domestic legislative program, helped draft a resolution to defer shutting down Job Corps centers and camps until the congress had reviewed the whole matter.

The committee approved Alan's resolution. Determined to go all out for victory in his first Senate legislative effort, Alan sought an appointment with every senator of both parties to present his case. No one can remember another freshman having done anything quite like this before. The Job Corps issue wasn't exactly earthshaking, and many of the senators Alan visited in their offices no doubt wondered why he was going to so much trouble. His approach enabled him to become personally acquainted with every senator at the outset of his Senate career — something that some senators don't do for years.

In one office, that of Russell Long of Louisiana — the powerful chairman of the powerful Finance Committee — Alan struck gold. Not many weeks before, on the opening day of the Ninety-first Congress, there had been a close hard-fought contest for majority whip. Alan had voted for the challenger, Ted Kennedy, over the colorful incumbent, Russell Long, who was ousted four years after succeeding Hubert Humphrey in the post. Right after Long's defeat in the Democratic caucus the Senate was scheduled to convene. Its first order of business was to swear in the new senators. As Alan approached the swinging doors of the Senate, about to walk on the floor for the first time, he was savoring this historic moment, consciously intent upon recording every aspect of it indelibly in his memory. At the precise moment that he stepped through the swinging doors of the Senate, he was swiftly distracted from his contemplations of the exalted nature of the occasion by the sudden realization that he was entering in virtual lockstep with Russell Long. He turned to him impulsively and blurted: "I hated to vote against you that way, Russell."

"Oh, that's all right, Senator," replied Long nonchalantly, with a broad grin, putting an arm around Alan's waist and giving him a fast hug. "It seems to me we just oughta have a rule that you new fellahs don't vote till you've been around here a while and gotten the hang of the place."

Now, Senator Long greeted Alan cordially in his office, sat down as if he had all the time in the world and a lot more besides, and soon became engrossed in Alan's effort. He riffled through some Job Corps documents Alan had brought along, quizzed him on his strategy, and made suggestions.

"We've got to help these poor people," he said, "and some of the contractors running these camps are good people. I know some of 'em."

When Alan left two hours later, he had a new and unexpected senior partner in his save-the-Job-Corps enterprise.

Soon the issue was joined on the Senate floor. Alan had secured a good many pledges of support, but most senators — including all the Republicans, among them his good friends Saxbe and Schweiker — had remained noncommittal, so he had no idea how he would do.

It was a chaotic, exciting, fascinating but frustrating exercise — reminding Alan more than anything else of a day he had played third base in a high-scoring Little League practice game with Robin, and every hit and a countless stream of runners came his way.

Alan stood up, called up his amendment, spoke for it, answered questions from other senators, and — yielding the floor — sat down in the majority leader's chair. Jon Steinberg sat beside him in a staff chair that had been brought in by a page. Staff chairs are smaller than senators' chairs and are armless. Staffers are *never* allowed to sit in senators' chairs.

Other senators spoke for and against Alan's position. Russell Long and Gaylord Nelson of Wisconsin were his principal supporters. His California colleague, George Murphy, was among his vocal opponents. Finally there came the first of three roll calls on a Republican motion to recommit the resolution to committee. Alan and his allies defeated the motion by a single vote, forty-seven to forty-six. Senator Jack Javits, Republican of New York, then offered an amendment that would have eviscerated the resolution. It was debated at length and voted down, fifty-seven to forty.

Through these roll calls and in between, Alan roamed about the floor, a three-foot-long tally sheet in his hand, which had his notes about the anticipated vote of each senator, trying to corral enough support to win. He was getting a great deal of support from his fellow Democrats, but not a single vote from the Republicans. When he crossed the aisle to the minority side and beseeched his Republican friends, Saxbe and Schweiker, to help him, they were still noncommittal. The minority leader, Everett Dirksen, had apparently made the issue a matter of party discipline and of loyalty to the new Republican president.

By the time the Javits amendment was voted down, everything that might reasonably be said on each side of the issue had been repeated several times over, and the Senate was ready to vote on Alan's resolution. Nonetheless still more was said, and then came the final roll call. Every Republican voted against the resolution. All except eleven Democrats voted for it, and it was defeated, fifty-two to forty. Every Democrat except Herman Talmadge of Georgia had voted with Alan on at least one of the three roll calls, but Alan's failure to hold enough of them with him on the final critical vote—he could only afford to lose four Democrats—made defeat inevitable.

The moment the final vote was announced, Russell Long sought recognition, got it, and moved to reconsider the vote that had just defeated the resolution. He then began to speak—and speak—and speak. About the president, "It is my hope and my sincere prayer that President Nixon will be one of the greatest presidents in the history of our country. I do not say that because necessarily I am in favor of Richard Nixon. I am in favor of America." About the Republicans, "If the Republicans think they are getting some 'Brownie points' by voting with the president on this, they can just forget it. I would like to plead with my Republican friends. Please do not ruin this sanctuary of the wretched and the poor." About the senator from California: "He is asking for nothing more than the right to have the case heard. He is saying, 'Just hear my case.'" At times Long somehow projected the innocent demeanor and appearance of a choir boy. At others he was pugnacious and argumentative.

It became evident that the senator from Louisiana was launching a filibuster that might go on endlessly. The Senate grew restive, and Alan grew uneasy. He wasn't overjoyed with the prospect of his first big effort on the Senate floor winding up as somebody else's filibuster. He didn't see how the filibuster would work. He saw no way to pick up any Republican votes, and he doubted that enough Democrats would switch to pass the resolution. He wanted to talk it over with Long, but Long was talking nonstop, so how could he?

Alan asked a Democratic senator if he would interrupt Long with a lengthy question, providing Alan with an opportunity for a fast consultation with Long, who wouldn't really have to listen to the query. The senator declined. So Alan sidled up to Long, who was speaking at the moment in a loud voice, with great emotion, waving his arms, about youth, crime, jobs, opportunity.

"Russell . . ." Alan whispered.

"I would like to urge senators," Long shouted "if you have never been there and slept on the ground with these boys, if you have never seen what it means to take a boy potentially dedicated to a life of crime and make him a good citizen of the United States, you should, at a minimum, be willing to consider the program."

"Russell . . ." Alan whispered.

Long paused, his attention momentarily diverted, and glanced at Alan, who whispered rapidly, "Russell, I'm not sure it's wise . . ."

Instantly Everett Dirksen and several other senators sought recognition, hoping to seize control of the floor from Long. They shouted at the presiding officer, "Mr. President! Mr. President!"

Long swiftly swung his eyes back to the chair and thundered, "Mr. President, I have not yielded the floor! My friend from California simply wants to whisper to me."

He turned back to Alan and shouted at the top of his lungs, "Now you keep whisperin', and I'll keep talkin'."

The cadence of Long's delivery then ground almost to a halt. He shouted one word, paused four or five seconds, shouted another word, paused again. Alan filled the pauses with whispered thanks for Long's help mingled with pleas that he stop helping. This strange dialogue went on for what seemed an age to Alan. Eventually Long responded in a hoarse stage whisper, "All right, it's your resolution."

Then addressing the Senate, he said, "The Senator from California has made a noble effort on behalf of the poor and the tempest-tossed, those people who are lost as a part of our society. He has persuaded me that we have been defeated. Therefore, I will not press the issue further. I withdraw my motion to reconsider."

Alan spoke briefly, saying:

Mr. President, I want to express my gratitude to the Senator from Louisiana for all the valiant work that he has done on behalf of this resolution. I thank all others who supported the resolution which I introduced. I also thank those who opposed it for their fair play and sportsmanship during this entire debate.

I regret that it did become a partisan effort. I think all those on the Republican side of the aisle know that I did my best to prevent this. I talked to the minority leader and the minority whip and to every other Republican senator about this resolution stating why I was proposing it and urging that it not become a partisan battle—which it would not have become, of course, if they supported me in my efforts.

We won two victories this afternoon. I recognize that we are not likely to win a third. I am reluctant to see the Senate tied up for a substantial amount of time in a losing battle for reconsideration.

But we do want to impress upon the president and the secretary of labor the position of the Senate. It is a position shared by every senator, that the people in the Job Corps be taken care of to the maximum degree possible and those who were about to enter the Job Corps be taken care of to the maximum degree possible.

I urge the president of the United States, on behalf of all here, to do all that can be done through his administration to aid these young people.

Senator Javits responded for the Republicans, saying:

Mr. President, I should like to express my appreciation to the senator from California. He was very effective and gallant. May I assure him that I will join with him in every effort to see to it that the administration will do everything it has said it will do and that the maximum solicitude is shown for these young people. I have deep faith that the secretary of labor and the president will join us in doing just that.

And Majority Leader Mansfield wound up the debate with these words:

> I wish to add my commendation to the warm expressions of praise already extended to the senator from California. The flawless manner in which he presented this measure to the Senate certainly points the way to what I am sure will be a number of outstanding contributions by him in the future.
>
> This first effort by Senator Cranston has already demonstrated that in choosing him to represent their state, the people of California have selected an advocate of exemplary skill and ability. In the final analysis, the vote may have been against the resolution bearing his name; but there is no mistaking the fact that he made his position clear; he urged it with great persuasiveness, and his views with respect to the Job Corps, I am confident, will be taken by all with the deepest consideration. Senator Cranston has certainly marked the beginning of his role as a leader of legislation with great distinction."

It was early evening, and the Senate soon adjourned. Afraid that he might have ruffled Long's feelings, Alan had wanted to thank him when the debate ended, but the Senator from Louisiana had vanished. Now Alan launched a search and finally found him in his "hideaway" office in the Capitol. Long was sitting there with an aide who was correcting the transcript of the debate. The Senator rose, greeted Alan warmly, and exclaimed: "Well hello, Alan Cranston, you put up a great fight. But why'd you throw in the towel? We had the ball right in our hands. Right in our hands! We could have worn 'em down."

Alan, settling down for a drink, explained his reluctance to impose on the Senate during his first foray on the floor and why he didn't think they could have prevailed anyway. Long disagreed, and there ensued a long discussion of Senate tactics and strategies, parliamentary maneuvers, and filibusters, laced with reminiscences of one-man filibusters carried on by "My Daddy"—Russell's famous father, Senator Huey Long. The aide left. Alan stayed. In the course of what turned out to be not only a long evening but a very long night, the conversation drifted to other topics; Alan and Russell adjourned to a downtown restaurant where they joined a table full of exuberant Louisianans. They finally wound up together in Russell's apartment at Watergate.

There they examined populism, the vagaries of Louisiana and California politics, welfare, taxes, friends, foes. They traded stories about campaigns and exchanged theories about campaigning. Alan told of his efforts to establish that Max Rafferty was not to be believed. Russell responded with a tale about one of his Uncle Earl's campaigns.

"Uncle Earl wanted to get it across that this opponent he had on his hands was a downright liar. So he said in all his speeches: 'My opponent is a prevaricator. Day and night, he tells nothing but lies. You want to know how you can tell if he's lying? Watch his lips. If they're moving — he's lying!' "

Russell told of another time when Uncle Earl was short of campaign funds in his race for governor, and he promised to do "some impossible fool thing" in return for a handsome contribution. After Uncle Earl was elected, the contributor repeatedly tried to see him, but Uncle Earl consistently refused to grant him an audience.

"Came a Sunday when Uncle Earl was relaxing in the governor's mansion in Baton Rouge. A highway patrolman who doubled as bodyguard came to inform the governor that this same man was at the door again demanding to see him, knew the governor was there, and flatly refused to leave.

At that, Uncle Earl blew up and shouted at the trooper, "You go down and tell that son of a bitch I said I lied!"

Sometime in the course of the rambling talk, Russell asserted that no member of the Long family had ever lost an election in Louisiana.

"Didn't Uncle Earl lose a race for Congress once?" asked Alan.

"Oh, yes," expostulated Russell immediately, "but that was his own fault."

Later on that night a sharp difference developed between the two — Alan can't remember just what. Russell made no effort to conceal his view that Alan was not only dead wrong but had revealed unpardonable political stupidity. A stocky man with wavy brown hair who resembles his father physically, Russell scowled and took on the expression and appearance of an angry, ring-wise prize fighter. Suddenly, resorting to the Southern habit of calling people by their full names — as he frequently did — he blurted out with a mixture of impatience and scorn, "Alan Cranston, you'd better enjoy yourself around here because you are a one-term senator!"

"Maybe yes, maybe no," replied a startled Alan.

"What's your middle name?"

"What's that got to do with it?"

"Alan Cranston, *what* is your middle name?"

"MacGregor."

"Alan *MacGregor* Cranston," shot Long triumphantly, "*You* are a one-term *senator*."

Soon Long regained his choir-boy appearance and, sometimes amiably, sometimes with passion, talked about his "Daddy." It was past two in the morning when Alan suggested that perhaps he should leave. Russell said it was early. Alan said it was late. Russell accompanied him downstairs to bid him farewell at the front door of the apartment building. Only then did he discover that Alan wasn't really going anywhere — that he was staying in Ray Lapin's apartment in an immediately adjacent building in the Watergate complex, just across a courtyard.

"I'd like to see where you're staying," said Russell. So Alan invited him up; up he came, and they sat around talking some more. Somewhere around three, Russell decided it was time to return to his apartment. Alan accompanied him down in the elevator to the front door.

Russell said: "Why don't you come on back to my place, and we'll have some coffee?"

With visions of drifting back and forth everlastingly from one apartment to the other, like the Marx Brothers in *Room Service*, Alan demurred, and the two senators finally parted. After he had taken a few steps across the court, Long turned back and got in the last word: "Alan Cranston, if you hadn't thrown in the towel, we'd a spent this night talkin' on the Senate floor for posterity and those poor people, instead of talkin' to ourselves all over this dang town."

That was the beginning of a relationship that flowered. Alan and Long began to team up every now and then on legislation. Alan was particularly important in helping preserve the oil depletion allowance for small independent producers — a move Long also favored — when Congress voted to take it away from the major oil companies. Long has been important to Alan in helping senior citizens with medical care and social security problems and in straightening out inconsistencies in federal tax laws and regulations that were adverse to California. They also worked together in 1978 to reduce the capital gains tax rate. When Alan was elected to Long's old position as whip in 1977, and again when Alan was reelected in 1979, it was Long who seconded his nomination.

Russell Long is not the only storyteller in the Senate. One of Alan's very first conversations on the Senate floor was with Barry Goldwater. For some reason they were discussing haircuts, a subject that may be of great interest to the white-maned senator from Arizona but is of no particular interest to the quite-bald Alan, who seldom finds time to have anybody cut the scant hair he still possesses.

Goldwater said that when he first ran for the Senate he was told that senators were entitled to free haircuts. That rubbed him the wrong way — sounded like socialism. When he was elected, Goldwater investigated. He went to the Senate barbershop for a haircut and, to his surprise, found it quite good. Even more to his surprise, he found himself going back for more. This bothered his conservative conscience, and after four or five of these free haircuts, Goldwater asked the barber, "Isn't this just like socialism or even communism, you drawing down a government check for all those haircuts? Wouldn't it be better if you got paid for each haircut and maybe worked a bit harder and earned more money?"

The barber replied, "Senator, you're the only man comes in this barbershop doesn't pay me for these haircuts!"

Later Alan and Goldwater joined in several projects, including a bill relating to the latter's hobby — ham radio. Together they wrote an important letter to the attorney general regarding the need for a special prosecutor during the Watergate affair who would specifically have authority to investigate the activities of the plumbers in the Ellsberg break-in.

Alan has been able to find common ground with other conservatives as well. He and Jesse Helms joined in a bill to protect the integrity of state highway funds against a federal law mandating motorcycle helmets. With Howard Baker — Republican from Tennessee who subsequently became minority leader — Alan drafted and pushed through the Senate a resolution favoring detente with the Soviet Union. With Jim Allen of Alabama, Alan negotiated a settlement of George Wallace's concerns that permitted passage of the bill — a pet project of Russell Long — that produced the revolutionary concept of public financing of presidential campaigns.

Alan worked intimately with conservative Gordon Allot of Colorado, chairman of the Republican Policy Committee, against the draft and for a bill to raise military pay, and with Bob Taft, Ohio Republican, on many Banking Committee issues.

He worked with Sam Ervin, Democrat of North Carolina, on free press legislation, and with Henry (Scoop) Jackson, Democrat of Washington, on verification of SALT in June 1977.

A month after the Job Corps resolution died, a newsman who chanced upon Senator Walter Mondale outside a Capitol Hill restaurant asked him, "What do you think of the latest Cranston resolution?"

The Minnesota Democrat gaped in mock horror, "Don't tell me there's another Cranston resolution!"

There was indeed. He had introduced a resolution, sponsored by George Aiken of Vermont, dean of Senate Republicans, seeking to move a keystone of American foreign policy—established by Thomas Jefferson but changed drastically by Woodrow Wilson—back to its original Jeffersonian principle:

> Resolved, that it is the sense of the Senate that when the United States recognizes a foreign government and exchanges diplomatic representatives with it, this does not imply that the United States necessarily approves the form, ideology, or policy of that foreign government.

This resolution, which passed the Senate overwhelmingly, helped pave the way for President Nixon's new approach to the China question.

A capital reporter, Jude Wanniski, in a feature article for the *National Observer* on June 2, 1969, remarked:

> One of the biggest surprises to Capitol Hill veterans is Senator Aiken's cosponsorship of the resolution. "Aiken almost never cosponsors a resolution, and here he joins up with a freshman Democrat, a nobody," says a staff member of the GOP Policy Committee. "I don't get it." But having the company of the seventy-six-year-old Mr. Aiken gives Mr. Cranston a running start at making history in his first year as senator.
>
> For all his boldness, Mr. Cranston's popularity with his colleagues seems astonishingly high, but that may be because he does not exude charm and brashness.

In October 1971 the Senate was in a furor over the expulsion of Nationalist China from the United Nations. Alan signed up seventy-two senators as cosponsors of still another resolution of his calling for fairer national representation in the U.N.—and a fairer way to apportion the cost of its operation.

Senator Tom Kuchel, Alan's able Republican predecessor, had left behind an important piece of unfinished California business—preservation of beautiful Point Reyes on the rugged north coast. Kuchel had worked long and hard to establish a Point Reyes National Seashore. Alan was determined to finish the task and did. The necessary legislation was signed by President Nixon on April 3, 1970.

This was the first of many conservation measures designed to save rare and unique parts of California forever that Alan has shepherded through Congress in cooperation with various California representatives, most often San Francisco's Phil Burton, a House magician on such matters. Probably no other facet of Alan's service will leave a more enduring impression on his state. The list is long: Redwood National Park, Golden Gate National Recreation Area, South San Francisco Bay Wildlife Refuge, Santa Monica Mountains National Park, Mineral King, California Desert National Conservation Area, twelve wilderness areas, and much else. Two items in particular are now on Alan's own list of unfinished business: preventing the over-development of the two places he loves the most — Lake Tahoe and Big Sur.

Another of Alan's concerns with conservation was illustrated during a meeting with an editor of *Pravda*. "What do you think are the outstanding issues between the U.S. and the U.S.S.R.?" the editor asked.

"Arms control," said Alan. "The SALT talks, the prospects for increasing trade, immigration, human rights."

After a long discussion of these matters, Alan threw in, "Of course, there's whales."

"How's that, Senator? *Whales?* What is this 'whales'?"

"Those big things that swim in the ocean."

"Oh, *whales!*"

"Your country is killing them all," said Alan.

The editor was so dumbfounded at Alan, considering this a vital issue that it took a while for him to grasp it.

Constituents often wonder if the letters they write to their representatives have any effect. The fact is that they do, sometimes to a profound degree. At the very least, they help tell a senator about public opinion among his constituents. If Alan has a strongly held view, based upon principle, careful thought, and what he believes to be the underlying facts, he won't change his position to please his constituents — although he may take great pains to find ways to explain his views in a manner that could make his stance more acceptable or at least understandable. If Alan is uncertain about something, he'll be strongly influenced by his constituents' apparent desires—but he'll also seek guidance from other sources.

One of Ralph Nader's *Congress Projects* sent a questionnaire to every senator early in Alan's Senate career. One question was, "Generally, what are the factors that influence your vote and how do you rate their relative importance?" Alan answered, "In order of importance: moral principles—what's right and wrong; needs of California and our nation; my political philosophy (minor); and Senate interrelationships (only if nothing else matters)."

Sometimes letters bear information or an idea that triggers far-reaching consequences. One of the latter sort reached Alan in the first few weeks of his first term. Shortly after he had become chairman of the subcommittee responsible for veterans' affairs, he received a letter telling of the plight of patients in the Bronx Veterans Hospital in New York. The letter claimed that the Veterans Administration was underfunded, understaffed, and totally unprepared to cope—not just in the Bronx—with the flood of shattered youths coming home from Vietnam. It urged Alan to investigate and to find a remedy.

Alan set out to ascertain the facts and found that Vietnam survivors and other veterans were indeed being inadequately cared for in the huge, far-flung VA system.

The Vietnam War had created a horrible paradox. High velocity bullets, napalm, and land mines were causing wounds that would have proved fatal in previous wars, but the victims of these were surviving—even paraplegics and others who had suffered multiple wounds—because of prompt medical attention on the battlefield, miracle drugs, helicopter evacuations to nearby field hospitals, and vastly improved medical techniques. But once the victim was back in the states in a VA hospital and the time of crisis over, he was often neglected and the quality of his care was indifferent. Staff problems and low morale, stemming in part from budgetary limitations, had an effect.

The remedy lay in beefing up the VA medical staff across the board, creating a new and more compelling sense of compassion and concern in the system. More paramedics and technician specialists had to be added, as well as psychologists and psychiatrists because of the problems arising from the unprecedented unpopularity of the Vietnam War. Relationships between veterans' hospitals and nearby medical schools had to be expanded and improved. It took substantial time, but these remedies were largely achieved. Alan became chairman of a full standing Committee on Veterans' Affairs in 1977. Senator Strom Thurmond of South Carolina was a key Republican member of the committee, and Alan developed an effective relationship on veterans' issues — and eventually on some other matters — with this mellowed one-time champion of strict segregation who has served in the Senate longer than all Republicans save one.

Many members of Congress are effective only in their own body, only to see their legislation vanish in the other house or die in conference committees between the two. Alan, however, knows more representatives than some House members do. On veterans' affairs he worked up a warm relationship with the chairman of the House Veterans' Affairs Committee, Olin (Tiger) Teague of Texas; and when he left, Alan already had formed a great relationship with his successor, Ray Roberts of Texas, as well as with others influential on the committee. Alan also has warm relationships with staff members all over Capitol Hill, who can be influential in determining the fate of a bill.

The work on veterans' health matters, together with concerns in the keen minds of Jon Steinberg and an assistant of his, Louise Ringwalt, led Alan to be interested in a broad range of health issues. He co-sponsored Senator Kennedy's national health insurance legislation, worked with Senator Tom Eagleton to establish a new Institute on Aging, pushed through a bill to focus efforts on the sudden-infant-death syndrome, and helped pass the National Arthritis Act — to bolster arthritis research and to establish prevention and treatment centers across the country to deal with our number one disabling disease, affecting thirty-one million Americans. Alan steered a bill through the Congress during his first term establishing an Emergency Medical Services Program — based upon knowledge he'd gained about battlefield emergency care — to promote development of medical communications networks and the training and use of paramedics in ambulances and in hospital emergency rooms.

All this led Alan on to a deep interest in biomedical research and in what can be done to increase the human life span and to hasten the day when cancer, cardiovascular disease, and other less widespread afflictions are more understood, better controlled, and possibly conquered.

All, of course, was not sweetness and light in Alan's first legislative efforts, nor has it ever been. President Nixon, for example, vetoed two of Alan's health bills and other of his initiatives have been thwarted. But Alan has always had so many efforts under way that some are succeeding while others were failing, so he rarely feels frustrated. Even on days when nothing goes right legislatively, he can be comforted by the knowledge that his staff is busy helping Californians with problems that they often consider — and which sometimes really are — matters of life and death.

Alan worked for Senate rejection of two of Nixon's worst nominees to the Supreme Court: Clement G. Haynsworth, Jr., and G. Harrold Carswell. Alan admits to a misstep, however, in the Carswell case. He charged that the Nixon administration had pressured a black attorney in the Justice Department to support Carswell, who was accused of racial bias. The lawyer denied the charge, and Alan conceded that though his staffer had talked to the attorney, he had not. When a conflict of interest charge was leveled at Haynsworth, Alan sent Democratic Senator Fritz Hollings, who was leading the support for Haynsworth, into gales of laughter with a *bon mot* he had heard: "Shall his honor be without profit in his own country?"

Former Senator Roman Hruska, Nebraska Republican, undid Carswell — who was considered too mediocre a jurist to be on the Supreme Court — with his remark that even mediocre people are entitled to be represented.

Alan subsequently received a letter from a constituent who complained: "I can't get my kids to study any more. I think they're aiming for the Supreme Court."

It was in the anti-Vietnam effort that Alan first put to use the vote-counting techniques he had developed over the course of his long earlier experiences around Congress and the California legislature. On Vietnam and on other issues that particularly interested him he kept a constant, running, everchanging tally of how he knew each senator would vote, how he thought each senator might vote, and whether a given senator was likely to be present or absent when the roll call actually came. There would be a question mark by the names of those whose views were indiscernible. On other scraps of paper, or in his head, Alan kept endless details about why senators appeared to feel as they did about an issue, what senator would be most likely to have impact on another senator's vote, and every other conceivably relevant fact, opinion, tidbit, sign, token, and omen.

Other senators were surprised to find Alan willing to do the nose-counting on their own bills or amendments and perfectly content to let them do the speaking on the floor, while he advanced the cause behind the scenes. One night he phoned Senator Mondale and offered to help out on a defense budget amendment the Minnesotan was planning to offer. Mondale said it was the first time another senator ever offered to help him like that.

After Alan had helped Gale McGee of Wyoming with a bill to facilitate voter registration, McGee praised Alan as:

> the senator from California (Mr. Cranston), who receives no acclaim in any public way, who runs around with a pencil and a computer — which is his mind — and keeps a complete record on everyone's past voting record, future voting record, and apparently even their innermost thoughts, as we have sought to try to understand the misgivings some senators had and the inclinations to voting that they ultimately expressed. Without that kind of total, energetic, and tireless involvement, it would be very difficult for anyone in this kind of undertaking in legislation to try to move on.

Not all senators were pleased by Alan's eager and early activities. Spencer Rich, who covered the Senate for the *Washington Post*, noted in a generally laudatory profile: "He buttonholed undecided Senators and sought to persuade them to vote his way. Sometimes he annoyed them exceedingly by speaking to them openly on the floor or repeatedly asking them to change their minds."

Senator John Tower of Texas, a conservative Republican leader, said openly that he thought Alan was "too pushy." Senator Alan Bible of Nevada, a Democrat who had come to the Senate in 1954, refused to give Alan any clue as to how he might vote on any issue. Once, perhaps mellowing a bit, after a bill dear to Alan's heart had been approved, he approached him.

"I voted the right way, didn't I?" he asked.

"Yes," nodded Alan, not sure what would follow.

"If you had pressured me, I would have voted the other way," said Bible, grinning.

Alan's most spectacular nose-counting feat occurred in connection with the controversial Lockheed loan. Lockheed, the nation's largest defense contractor, based in California and facing bankruptcy, had requested a $250 million loan guarantee from the federal government.

Alan at first was uncertain whether or not to support the loan guarantee. During the Banking Committee hearings he decided to go all out for it. After all, thirty thousand jobs were at stake; Lockheed, though a defense firm, planned to diversify into commercial aviation. Alan lobbied senators for their support.

When the time came for the Senate vote, Alan—who had collaborated on this issue with John Tower of Texas who was floor managing it for the Republicans—sat down beside Senator Lee Metcalf of Montana.

"Lee," he said, "you're going to decide how this vote comes out."

"No, I'm not," replied Lee. "You've got five or six votes to spare."

"Nope," said Alan, "look at my tally."

He handed him a well-worn tally sheet listing the one hundred senators by name. He had penciled a plus or minus by each name to indicate how he thought they would vote. By Metcalf's name he had placed a question mark. If Alan's vote count was accurate, the vote would indeed be so close that Metcalf would determine its outcome.

Lee held the tally and checked on its accuracy as each senator called out his "Ayes" or "Nays." The vote count was going exactly as Alan had predicted when the clerk reached the middle of the alphabet and called out: "Mr. Metcalf?"

Senator Metcalf did not respond. Alan was encouraged. Metcalf wanted to wait before casting his vote, a good sign.

The clerk reached the end of the alphabet. He then recognized senators who hadn't been in the chamber when their names were originally called. So far Alan had turned out to be wrong about two senators, but his total was still correct because they had canceled each other out. One yes had voted no; one no had voted yes. There were still a few minutes left on the fifteen-minute roll call, and some senators had not yet come in to cast their votes. Then Metcalf, finally convinced, turned to Alan and said, "I'm not going to be the one to put thirty thousand people out of work, Alan." He stood up and voted "Aye."

Metcalf's vote was the margin of victory. The bill passed by one vote—forty-nine to forty-eight. The government, incidentally, wound up making more than $31 million in loan fees on the guaranty.

In opposing Supersonic Transport (SST) Alan tangled with California's aerospace industry, its unions, and subcontractors all over California. But Alan joined Senator Bill Proxmire against the SST.

Proxmire engaged in some well-timed filibustering and spoke out constantly in committee and on the floor, while Alan nose-counted. They
both doubted the economic viability of the supersonic aircraft, saw no
reason for United States taxpayers to subsidize faster-than-the-speed-
of-sound flights around the world for a select few, and worried about
the environmental impact. The SST went down to defeat despite
assertions by its supporters that the consequence would be loss of the
United States lead in flight technology and claims that the rival
British-French supersonic Concorde would lead to European domina-
tion of the industry. Vindication came late in 1979 when the British
and French abandoned production of the Concorde and admitted that
not one was ever sold in a normal, competitive business transaction.

Alan had been expected to gravitate naturally to the articulate but
often powerless, liberal wing of the Senate. His talent for maintaining
good relations with conservatives and becoming a deal-maker when he
sensed that compromises could be struck surprised many observers. By
the end of his first term he had won the reputation of being the best
vote counter in the Senate. Majority Leader Robert C. Byrd of West
Virginia said, "He has the best vote count of any senator I know."

Charles Farris, at that time Majority Leader Mansfield's principal
floor aide, told Congressman Phil Burton, "When Cranston really
works on an issue, he's good for ten or twelve extra votes."

In an analysis of the hundred senators published in August 1972,
in Ralph Nader's *Congress Project,* the report on Alan said:

> Cranston is a man whose star appears to be on the rise. In the political juggling
> before the Democratic National Convention, Cranston's name was suggested as a
> vice-presidential possibility. Today Cranston is being discreetly mentioned as a
> possible majority whip of the Democratic party, a job held until recently by
> Edward Kennedy.

Alan had been in the Senate three and a half years.

CHAPTER 25

★ ★

"The Loneliness of the Long-Distance Runner"

★ ★

> "I think that you'll go very far," I said. "You'll be one of the world's big men."
>
> "I shall be alone though."
>
> "All the people who do big things are."
>
> "You think so?"
>
> "I'm sure of it."
>
> "I'd rather have had — the other."
>
> —From *The Man in the Brown Suit*
> by Agatha Christie

On the personal side, an ebb tide set in for Alan after his election to the Senate. When the house on the Bel Air hilltop slid downhill a few inches in a mudslide, cracked, and was rendered practically valueless, it was a minor setback.

Real sadness came with the realization that our mother's health was failing. Increasingly frail, in her ninety-first year, she died peacefully on March 26, 1969, in her small gray-shingled house among the trees at Los Altos — having lived just long enough to see her love and hopes fulfilled in Alan's election to the Senate.

Ray Lapin, in whose Watergate apartment the Cranstons stayed, was illegally removed from the helm of Fanny Mae (Federal National Mortgage Association) by President Nixon whom Ray proceeded to sue. When it became obvious that Ray's term as Fanny Mae president would expire long before the lawsuit was over, he gave up and returned to his business in California.

Alan and Geneva moved into their own five-room condominium on the first floor of the Watergate. Their book-filled living room overlooked the garden, and their upstairs bedroom gave them a view of the river and the trees along its banks. Sunsets and moonsets and the passage of boats were a changing delight. Perhaps they were drawn there, too, by Alan's knack for being where things happen, for Watergate — the site of Nixon's downfall — soon became a household word.

Geneva, who would not have chosen to live in Washington, was finding the adjustment hard. The fortresslike Watergate was, to her, "a concrete cave." Outdoors, mugging was a constant threat. Indoors, the security system was so rigorously enforced that it was intimidating in itself. Besides being a nuisance, the four locked doors on the way to the garage testified to the possibility of danger.

The mechanics of living were difficult. Driving the car out of the cramped, dark, cement-pillared Watergate basement was a feat.

Kim came for a visit. He fetched groceries from the Watergate underground Safeway and accompanied Alan from Watergate's basement garage to another at the Senate Office Building. Racing after his father through the rabbit warren of tunnels and hallways, he took the underground Senate subway to the Capitol, and exclaimed, "You live like moles in this place!"

Geneva told friends wryly, "We love California so very much that we're willing to live *here!*" Fortunately she found in Senator Saxbe's attractive wife, Dolly, a friend who shared her heretical views of life in the capital.

That December (1969) Geneva suffered a stroke. She persevered in therapy and refuted the conventional wisdom of doctors who told her there was no possibility of her making further progress. Though she made an excellent improvement, Washington life seemed even grimmer. As Alan began to prepare for his 1974 campaign, she decided to move to Palm Springs. She had friends there. Kim and Robin would be near, and year-round sunshine, swimming, and freedom offered a strong attraction.

The prospects for Alan's first reelection campaign were bright. Though he was often on the liberal side of issues, he was always willing to listen to, and often advance, the cause of the state's business interests. "When we agree on an issue, he goes all out," said Vincent Bordelon, executive director of the Los Angeles Chamber of Commerce.

His voting record was rated highly by organized labor, and he was on good terms with all major elements of the state's usually faction-ridden Democratic Party. He had maintained close grass roots ties with Democrats working in the vineyards ever since his CDC days. And every two years since he'd come to Washington he had campaigned vigorously throughout the state with Democratic candidates who could use a helping hand from a United States Senator. These efforts had their lighter moments.

Once Alan was walking precincts in San Diego with Assemblyman — now State Senator — Bob Wilson. In front of one house they approached a car was parked bearing a faded Nixon bumper strip. A harassed woman answered their knock on the door. Wilson said briskly, "Hello, I'm Assemblyman Bob Wilson, and this is Senator Alan Cranston, who's helping me in my campaign. I hope you'll vote for me." He handed her a campaign leaflet, and turned to leave. He and Alan were halfway back down the walk when they heard a shriek: "Wait!"

The woman dashed out of the house holding the brochure as far away from herself as possible — as if Democratic literature were deadly poison.

"Take this back!" she shouted.

Just before she reached them, a fox terrier rushed out and charged down the walk in her wake, barking shrilly. The woman turned and issued a stern command: "Checkers, go back! Checkers, go back!"

*   *   *

As the 1974 election approached, Alan once more attracted considerable Republican support in addition to his strong Democratic backing. He had developed a personal relationship with a great many of California's Republican leaders. This stemmed partly from an unorthodox move Alan made when President Nixon asked the Senate to approve the nomination of House Minority Leader Gerald Ford for vice president after Spiro Agnew's forced resignation. Alan proceeded to communicate, through several hundred phone calls and meetings, and a great many letters, with virtually every Republican leader in California. He talked to fifty-six of the fifty-seven Republican County Central Committee heads, to leaders of the official and unofficial statewide GOP organizations, and to major Republican office-holders and contributors. He wrote to every delegate to the 1972 Miami Republican Convention that had nominated Nixon and Agnew.

His message to them was a simple one: "I'm facing a unique and unprecedented responsibility. Although I'm a Democrat, I must pass judgment on a Republican nominee for vice president. Normally, you'd be doing this, as Republican leaders, and I wouldn't. You probably know more about Ford than I do. What do you know about him, good or bad, that I should know? How should I vote? For him, or against him?"

Surprised Republicans responded to Alan's inquiry freely, some with a measure of scepticism, most with genuine enthusiasm. Only two were strongly against Ford and urged his rejection. A good many said they would have picked someone else, but since Ford was nominated, they'd vote for him. Most felt that, given the circumstances, he was a good choice. Typical was the comment of a rural Republican County Committee Chairman: "He's probably as straight a guy as I've known, or ever known about, in politics. He won't do badly." A man who had dealt with Ford on legislation over the years said, "He's not an equivocator, or a liar, or a slip-around-the-corner guy." One of the curtest comments came from the then Governor of California. "He's a very religious man," said Ronald Reagan. After soliciting the insights not only of California Republicans but of colleagues of Ford's in Michigan, business leaders, labor leaders, Democrats, Independents, Alan reported the results of his survey in detail to the Senate in a floor speech, and declared, "I support the nomination of Gerald Ford to be Vice President of the United States. I vote for Gerald Ford with trust in his trustworthiness, with faith in his fairness, with sufficient confidence in his ability, and with great hope."

It wasn't long before Nixon resigned, Ford became president, nominating Nelson Rockefeller to succeed as vice president — and Alan went through the process all over again.

When he called a woman, who chaired the Republican County Central Committee in a small county in the Sierra Nevada foothills, to ask her what she thought of Rockefeller, she said, "I was waiting for your call!"

Alan encountered much more Republican opposition to Rockefeller than to Ford. But no one made a compelling case against him, a majority supported him, and Alan voted for him.

Alan's greatest asset as he mounted his campaign in 1974 was that to a lot of people he looked, acted, and spoke like a United States senator. Ten years after the Salinger campaign, he had a superb TV presence.

"That's what finally comes through about Alan—that he's the senator," Lu Haas, Alan's California staff chief, remarked out of his long experience with the media. "It's a process of development. In 1964, against Salinger, and in 1968, in the Rafferty campaign, he was *aspiring* to be the senator. Now Alan *is* the senator. The TV doesn't lie."

None of the strong and widely known potential opponents who had been the subject of speculation decided to run against Alan in 1974. His actual opponent was a state legislator who had dissented—from further off to the right—from many of Governor Reagan's programs. Senator H. L. Richardson was chiefly an enemy of gun control.

Again, Allyn Kreps was Alan's campaign chairman, Mickey Kantor became state campaign manager, and Bob Girard northern manager. Alan himself campaigned strenuously on weekends and slow business days in the Senate. Kenneth Reich of the *Los Angeles Times* accompanied him for two days and wrote:

> He demonstrates great stamina. At the end of a sixteen-hour working day that included numerous meetings, two speeches, television and radio interviews, and hectic automobile and helicopter trips, he seemed fresh and relaxed.

The 1974 campaign had its inevitable oddities. Once as Alan flew in a tiny helicopter to an event on a ranch in Riverside County, the pilot lost his way. Noticing a car parked on an isolated country road below, Alan suggested, "Why not land by them and ask directions?"

To his chagrin, when the helicopter landed, it threw up a vast cloud of dust from the dirt road. The car vanished from sight. The dust slowly subsided to disclose a horrified couple who had been making out in the car. From their shocked expressions, they apparently feared that an outraged husband or wife had landed beside them.

They were in no mood to give directions, and to Alan's further dismay, they were again buried in dust as the helicopter flew off to continue its search.

Nationally, Watergate dominated the news. In August Alan's old adversary, Richard Nixon, a leader who, in Lao-tzu's words, had failed "to honor people," resigned and went into exile.

In California the hot race for governor overshadowed the Senate campaign. Pat Brown's son, Jerry, was the Democratic candidate that year; Alan enjoyed his bright and original mind. One foggy night Alan encountered Brown and his chief aide, Gray Davis, in Capitol Park in Sacramento. Alan was alone and carrying his garment bag and briefcase, as he always does on trips. After chatting a moment, they parted. As he strode off into the fog, Brown said to Davis, "If Alan can wander around so informally, I guess we can get away with it too!"

In November, Alan was reelected with 63 percent of the votes cast, the biggest win for any opposed Senator of either party in state history. He won by the incredible margin of 1,500,000 votes, polling about 3,700,000 votes against Richardson.

After the election, Senator Russell Long came to Alan on the Senate floor to congratulate him on his stunning victory.

"I probably owe my election more to you than to anyone else in the whole country," said Alan humorously.

"How do you figure that?" asked the startled Long.

Alan reminded him of their night together after the Job Corps battle in 1969 and how Long had told him he was only going to be a one-term senator.

"I took that as a challenge," said Alan, "and decided to show you I could be a two-term senator and a three-term senator and a four-term senator!"

For a moment Long appeared nonplussed. Then he roared with laughter.

Alan's excitement and the joy of campaigning and winning were dimmed by the increasing distance between him and Geneva. She did not plan to return to Washington after the election. He sold the Watergate condominium and, after two moves from one small apartment to another, settled in a townhouse on the back of Capitol Hill. The marriage ended in divorce in 1977.

After the 1974 election, Alan plunged back into the never-ending job of representing California's diverse peoples and their myriad interests. The second term would be easier than the first in some respects: his staff was well organized; he knew all of his colleagues except for the newly elected and most of those too. He had established a great many close working relationships within the Senate.

However, the second term would be different in some ways. Murray

Flander, Alan's fiery and popular press chief, reports a staff meeting Alan called during which he stated that in contrast to his first term when he was all over the lot and involved in multitudinous issues, he wanted to concentrate more on the two issues that mattered most to him: the control of conventional and nuclear arms and the pursuit of human rights at home and abroad. Murray says, "That's when he really soars in eloquence—when he describes his dreams of world peace coupled with human dignity for each individual."

Despite Alan's resolve and true dedication to these problems, there were, of course, other demands. Countless California, national, and world issues, especially energy and the economy, commanded his attention. The strength and influence of his position as whip enhances Alan's ability to serve California's needs. He is the first California Democrat in history ever to hold a leadership post in the Senate. Only two California Republicans have done so—William Knowland and Tom Kuchel. That is partly due to a disconcerting habit of California's voters who have tended to trade in their sitting senators for new ones with great frequency, so California's senators seldom stay on Capitol Hill long enough to acquire institutional power. What Alan means for California was exaggerated by Walter Mondale when he listed all the levers of power in Alan's hands and asserted humorously that he had said to him, "You could abuse that power by doing more for California than it deserves. How do you face up to that moral challenge? Have you ever thought about it?"

As the vice president tells it, Alan responded by saying, "Yes, Fritz, I have. I've decided to do the fair thing. I take the nation's resources and divide them fifty-fifty. Fifty percent for California and fifty percent for the rest of the country."

Alan's participation in the "King of Capitol Hill" contest was one of the more interesting and satisfying diversions. It was an athletic event staged for the benefit of the Special Olympics, the international sports program for the mentally retarded created and sponsored by the Joseph P. Kennedy, Jr., Foundation. Two teams of senators, congressmen, and governors chosen on strict party lines competed in a series of events including tennis, golf, swimming, volley ball, track, a tug of war, and a bicycle race, among others. Alan was captain of the Democrats; his counterpart for the Republican team was Senator Lowell Weicker of Connecticut.

Although a pulled leg muscle prevented Alan from entering his favorite 100-yard dash (in which he once won a world's record for over-fifty-year-olds), he did enter three events: swimming, golf, and the half-mile bicycle race. He focused on the bicycle race and prepared so thoroughly that it was clear he had set out to win. He pedaled furiously round and round the running track at the University of Maryland and went long distances on country roads, seeking out steep and torturous hills. Jon Fleming, a staff aide who bicycled a long distance to work every day, trained with him and described with amusement the rigors of the experience.

"He raced me constantly, time trials every day, sought out racers, and pumped them about techniques."

Alan trained with professionals. One day at the Velodrome in Encino, where the banked curves are almost perpendicular, he got a youth who was a competitor in big time races to practice with him.

"What do you do if someone tries to pass you on the left side?"

"Ride him into the ditch," said the boy.

"What if someone tries to pass you on the right?"

"Ride him into the wall."

"Alan appeared to be digesting this idea," Jon concluded, tongue in cheek. Alan learned that wind resistance is the big thing. If you get about six inches behind someone, the competitor in front has to exert himself as you sail along in his wake.

Came the day of the race. There were six heats, then a final. Alan won his heat, but Senator Joe Biden of Delaware, in his early thirties and the youngest man in the Senate, won his with a faster qualifying time. The final became a two-man race between Alan and Walter Fauntroy, forty-two, the District of Columbia representative. Senator Biden and others were way back in the dust.

Alan got right behind Congressman Fauntroy, who took the lead at the outset. At the right moment, Alan shot ahead and away he went, and Fauntroy just couldn't catch up.

The key thing was in the completeness of preparation. Nothing was left undone that Alan could find to do. The pedal adjustments, the handlebar heights, the relationship of the seat to the central axis of the bicycle. Said Jon Fleming: "I'd been riding a long time, and Alan came up with things I'd never heard of!"

CBS covered the meet fully. Near the end, the two captains were interviewed. Lowell Weicker came first and made a few typical remarks. Alan said the two teams were tied and the meet depended on the last event, the tug of war. He added that the Democrats were winning all the street games — running, baseball, bicycling — while the Republicans were winning all the country club events — swimming, tennis, golf. "That's because the Democrats are out in the streets with the people while the Republicans stay in their country clubs!" Weicker's jaw dropped in surprise at this unexpected jab.

The Republican team won the tug of war and that gave them the championship. But it had been a marvelous two days for Alan: the victory in the bike race, the great TV exposure, and not least the comment of a Capitol Hill newspaper called *Roll Call*, "He put a lot of legislators half his age to shame." The same paper also observed that a Saturday-night buffet after the contest "was sparsely attended — probably because most of the exhausted athletes were recuperating at home. Senator Cranston, with his limitless energy and still in sports togs, chatted with reporters."

Another diversion that year was the revival at Palo Alto's Manhattan Playhouse of *The Big Story,* the play Lee Falk and Alan had written in 1939. It won favorable reviews and attracted enthusiastic audiences.

Of greater national importance was the distraction of the Democratic National Convention of July 1976. Almost a year before the convention actually met, Democratic National Committee Chairman Robert S. Strauss asked Alan to head the Credentials Committee, whose task is to certify delegates and investigate and make preliminary rulings on challenges. The Democrats have an unruly history of bitter controversies over the seating of delegates which customarily leave bruised feelings and dark enmities. Alan's ability to mediate and bring people together without rancor prompted Strauss to choose him, saying, "You will be a great bridge because liberals, conservatives, the north, south, labor, and Congress will trust you."

Before accepting, Alan attempted to phone every announced, potential, and hopeful candidate (about twenty) to see if any objected. They represented all the degrees of party philosophy from Morris Udall (who said, "There's nobody I'd rather have") to George Wallace (who said, "I know you'll be fair"). North Carolina's ex-governor Terry Sanford was even more favorable: "I'd rather have you than my daddy." The only candidate he couldn't reach was Jimmy Carter, who was too busy campaigning to take his call. Alan accepted the post with the understanding that he would not endorse a candidate until after his committee had finished its work. He did his usual job with fairness and good humor and, partly because there were new and improved rules and procedures, there were no floor fights over delegates. That duty done, Alan helped head off a potential clash between Jimmy Carter and Jerry Brown. He served as diplomat-negotiator, bringing together Mickey Kantor, representing California's governor, and Hamilton Jordan, whom Alan then met for the first time, representing Carter.

After the convention had nominated Jimmy Carter and Walter Mondale, Alan added active campaigning to his long list of tasks. In September he spent a day accompanying Carter and Mondale on the campaign trail. On the way from one appearance to another, he said to Carter, "After you're elected, I'd like to talk to you about foreign policy."

Carter quickly replied, "No, send me a memo right now because the next debate [on TV with President Ford] will be on foreign policy." He jotted down an address in Plains, Georgia, which would guarantee he would receive the memo personally. Just before he took off for Washington that night Alan phoned to tell me he was writing the memo. I was touched at his thoughtfulness because I had been urging him to talk to Carter about world organization, peace, and foreign policy.

This long day ended five or six hours later when Alan was mugged. Having returned to Washington and parked his car half a block from his house, he was walking toward his front gate when three young men accosted him. "Freeze!" commanded one, and Alan froze. The one who held a gun said, "Give us your watch and your wallet."

Alan stripped off his wrist watch and handed it over. He pulled out his wallet, but as he did so he thought with dismay about his driver's license, credit cards, and other items of no value to anyone else, but important to him. So he took out the money — about $70 — and held it out, putting the wallet back in his pocket and keeping his eyes fixed on the eyes of the man with the Saturday Night Special who grabbed the money and ran. The whole incident lasted no more than sixty seconds. "I didn't have time to be scared," he recalls.

Alan celebrated Carter's victory that November but was shocked and crestfallen that his colleague John Tunney, with whom he had developed a very close relationship, was defeated by S. I. (Sam) Hayakawa, the former president of San Francisco State University. The new senator was seventy, and thereafter when Alan was introduced as California's senior senator, he often responded, "I'm the junior senior senator. Hayakawa is the senior junior senator."

Once sworn in, Hayakawa proceeded to vote against Alan on almost every issue. That plus the differences in stature (Alan is six feet one inch; Hayakawa diminutive) and style (Alan is quiet; Hayakawa a flamboyant showman) causes them to be known as the "odd couple" of the Senate.

On a family excursion to Mount Vernon last summer, our daughter-in-law, Charyl Fowle, commented to Alan, "People keep staring at you. They're wondering if you're who they think you are!"

"Yes," said Alan with a grin, "They're wondering if I'm Senator Hayakawa."

In 1977 Senator Mike Mansfield had retired, and Robert C. Byrd of West Virginia was elected majority leader, vanquishing Hubert Humphrey, Ed Muskie, and Fritz Hollings, all of whom dropped out before the vote was held. In contrast to the desperate whip battles when Ted Kennedy overthrew Russell Long and was in turn unseated by Byrd, Alan was chosen unanimously as majority whip—the second most important leadership job in the Senate.

One of the first tasks of the new Congress was committee assignments, a complicated chore which could affect the efficiency of the Senate and the happiness of the senators. There was an impasse in the deliberations of the Steering Committee handling Democratic assignments which Alan finally broke, after hours of wrangling, with a list of compromises so nearly perfect that everyone was satisfied. At this point Russell Long remarked to Majority Leader Byrd, "Your new whip is as handy as an extra pocket on a shirt!"

As one of the official leaders of Congress Alan now attended meetings with Majority Leader Byrd, Speaker Tip O'Neill, and other Congressional leaders, as well as regular White House breakfasts with the president. He had new formalized leverage within the Senate as well as in dealing with the House, the White House, and all the departments and agencies. He was still independent, whip for the Senate Democrats, not for the new Democratic president. His role was to aid the majority leader, to help individual senators with their problems, and to throw himself into issues where there was a "leadership position" with which he agreed. He has allowed none of this, however, to interfere with his focus on California issues, and he has retained his freedom to go all out on whatever state or national issues he considers important. Thus he can seek to use power in the sense Senator Muskie meant when he said, "Power up there [the Senate] is the ability to change someone's mind." Power results from "mastery of internal maneuver"—one source of whatever power Alan has.

An unusual glimpse of Alan in action on the floor has been preserved in the *Congressional Record.* One of Alan's ongoing projects is Legal Services, a program which gives the poor their only access to our American legal system. Senator Byrd and Alan had agreed to ask the Senate to act on a long-delayed confirmation of the Legal Services Board of Directors at the end of a day's session, barely in time for the Board to submit a budget for the next year. Alan, who sat in the back of the chamber in those early days, suddenly realized that Byrd, who usually remembers everything forever, had forgotten this item of business.

Byrd was saying, "There being no objection . . ." on an irrevocable motion to adjourn. Alan broke the record for getting from the back of the room to the well, knocking over a chair on his way, and almost tackling the Majority Leader. Byrd immediately remembered and the nominees were confirmed. The *Congressional Record* states:

> MR. ROBERT C. BYRD. I have been pushed and pressed and put upon in a very nice way by the distinguished Senator from California and the Senator from New York to proceed as expeditiously as possible with the consideration of these nominations . . . I was half-way through my motion to adjourn when the Senator from California almost fell over the chair to my right getting to me in time to stop me. So I think he is to be congratulated, whatever his feelings may be at the moment.
> MR. CRANSTON. I thank my good friend from West Virginia. I am glad I did not push too hard, and I am glad I did not knock him down.
> MR. ROBERT C. BYRD. I am glad he did not fall over the chair.

The relationship between Alan and Byrd is quite remarkable. They come from totally different backgrounds. Byrd grew up as an impoverished orphan in the back-hill country of West Virginia. He didn't know his real name until he was a grownup. While Alan was becoming active in the World Federalist Movement in 1945, Byrd was resigning from the Ku Klux Klan. When Byrd first came to the Senate, he voted against all civil rights bills and launched a crusade against alleged "welfare cheaters" in the District of Columbia. He went to night school while in Congress and earned a law degree. His perspectives changed, his view broadened, and he was a middle-of-the-roader by the time he was elected majority leader by what the *Almanac of American Politics* called "the most liberal group of Democrats in history."

Byrd traveled to San Diego in 1974 to campaign for Alan, and he told of an incident that had something to do with the trust that developed between the two men. The West Virginian was then majority whip. Before he played his fiddle to an entranced throng at a garden party at Dick Silberman's, he said, "I didn't have to come way out here to help Alan. Alan didn't vote for me for whip. He voted against me. Some senators told me they'd vote for me, but they voted against me. Some senators wouldn't tell me how they were going to vote, and they voted against me too. Alan, he told me he was going to vote against me, he told me why, and he did vote against me. I respected him for that." Incidentally, Senate leaders are chosen on a secret ballot — but senators like Byrd and Alan possess an uncanny faculty for discerning who is voting how under every circumstance.*

The two share a deep devotion to the Senate and a commitment to make it work. They consult with great frequency, often a half dozen times or more in a single day. When they work together on an issue, Byrd is usually out front; Alan tends to act behind the scenes. Byrd by both inclination and necessity speaks very often on the floor; Alan, much more sparingly. Now and then on an issue important to the president, where Alan shares the White House viewpoint and Byrd either hasn't made up his mind or has other reasons for waiting, Alan openly takes the lead and speaks out strongly. Usually Byrd enters the battle before it's over, coming in with superb timing and added strength that greatly enhances the cause, as he did on Panama and SALT II. Both men support the president much of the time and give him the benefit of the doubt. But both feel perfectly free to differ with the president and do so when they choose.

They respect their own power and the power of the Senate itself and exercise restraint in the use of that power. They are aware of President John F. Kennedy's statement that he didn't know how important the Senate was until he was in the White House, and Vice President Mondale's remark that he has had precisely the same experience.

The job of a senator requires long hours of hard, sometimes tedious

*After his overthrow, Ted Kennedy told a group: "I want to thank the twenty-eight senators who promised to vote for me — and especially the twenty-four who actually did!"

work, especially for a dedicated workhorse like Alan. A Senate watcher observed that he makes better use of his "disposable time" than any other Senator.

James P. Gannon reported in a *Wall Street Journal* profile that Alan once discovered that he was scheduled to be in three different places at once: at a conference with three California mayors, at a meeting with Senator Byrd and ten freshman Democratic senators, and at lunch with British Prime Minister James Callaghan. Displaying his sense of priorities, he decided with a grin, "I guess I'll scratch the Prime Minister."

As Roy Greenaway says, "The workload's incredible!"

One Friday afternoon when he strode out of his office carrying his heavy briefcase on his way to California, he looked so carefree and cheerful that Roy called out, "Have a good time!" And Murray added, "Be good! Don't get in any trouble out there!"

Outside in the corridor Alan encountered a dozen uniformed policemen walking along. It was the changing of the Capitol guard. Alan stopped and said, "How about pretending to drag me back into my office!"

The men smiled, and two husky policemen each grabbed one of his arms and hauled him roughly back into the whip office. The other six marched in beside them, grim-faced. Mary Lou, Roy, Jan, Murray, Cleo, Peggy, and Kam stared in utter horror. They couldn't imagine what had happened. What had Alan done? Were the police seizing the Capitol? A *coup d'etat?*

During the hostage crisis in early 1977, when the Hanafi Muslim sect of the Black Muslims forcefully occupied three buildings in downtown Washington, D.C., no one knew who or what else might be targeted. That afternoon, a large Capitol policeman fell in step behind Alan as he raced down a Capitol corridor with Murray Flander, who took one look and said, "I think you've got yourself a bodyguard!"

"Are you supposed to be protecting me?" Alan asked. The man said he was and added that he had been instructed to stay with Alan wherever he went that evening.

Alan said he wasn't going out; he planned to be moving some things from the apartment he'd been renting to his new house. The guard said he'd accompany him. Later, as he carried a series of heavy boxes down some stairs and loaded his car, the guard stood around awkwardly and finally said, "I may as well help you." So Alan and he moved some heavier furniture than he would otherwise have attempted.

A police squad car was parked across the street keeping them under surveillance. Alan thought to himself that the neighbors were probably watching with interest, saying, "There's one more politician using public employees for his own needs!" Or perhaps deciding he was being carted off to prison: "Well, there he goes! We won't see *him* again!"

Senator Daniel Patrick Moynihan of New York acquired a guard the same day. He asked the same question, "Are you supposed to be protecting me?"

"Yes, sir."

"Do all senators have bodyguards?"

"No, sir."

"Why me? I'm brand new around here. I'm not important!"

"Sir," said the guard, "I think we're supposed to be protecting all the Jewish senators."

One of the great satisfactions in any senator's life is to be able to enact legislation that will make a difference in people's lives. One of the most satisfying for Alan was a forty-two-word amendment he wrote with four other senators—Jennings Randolph, Harrison Williams, Jack Javits, and Robert Stafford—which handicapped Americans have hailed as their Magna Carta. Jon Steinberg explains it:

> Its net effect was to prevent discrimination against handicapped individuals in *any* public facility or any facility receiving public funds—universities and everything else. That means discrimination in any way, the ingress and egress of buildings, stairs, ramps, rest rooms, and elevators and anything else like that. It led to the Department of Transportation designing buses with special elevated stairways and to most of the special curbs for wheelchairs we now see everywhere.

There was a long delay in issuing the regulations needed to implement the law. "I wasn't sure exactly how far the regulations should go," Alan remembers. "I was finally convinced when I had one of the most emotional meetings of my life with a group of handicapped leaders and activists over in the Labor Committee room—a dozen or so people who were blind, speechless, paralyzed or something else. They told me how our amendment had given them hope they'd never had before, that they saw the end of the long dark tunnel they'd been

in, but now the light was dimming. They weren't sure that strong
regulations would ever be issued, and then the law wouldn't be that
meaningful, and they weren't sure where I now was on all this. Everything was translated for the deaf, and everybody started to cry. . . .
One man in a wheelchair who looked utterly helpless and who couldn't
articulate wore a cap on his head with a stick on it. Somebody held a
square chart containing the alphabet in front of him and he communicated by leaning his head forward and pointing the stick from letter to
letter spelling out words and sentences that developed into one of the
most poignant, stirring, eloquent statements I've ever heard. It was
translated for me by someone who could speak, while someone else
translated that for the deaf. That was the clincher for me. I went all
out for strong regulations, and we got them."

In June 1975 a group of senators of both parties held a two-day
"Great Debate" in the aftermath of the Vietnam War. It was put together by Alan and Ted Kennedy with the help of Barry Goldwater,
with the Senate providing an ideal forum for an open and free-
swinging discussion of America's role in a changing world.

In early 1976 we were out of Vietnam but were in danger of inter-
vening in Angola in exactly the same small ways that led to our deep
and tragic involvement in Southeast Asia. Alan and John Tunney
talked it over one Sunday and decided it was time to strike against this
trend. They met the next day with Dick Clark of Iowa, who was
already working on the issue in the Foreign Relations Committee, and
with Ted Kennedy. The four senators devised a strategy that — after
a head-on collision with Henry Kissinger — kept us out of Angola.

The Soviets are now having their problems in Angola and are by no
means in full control there — and our country is at peace. Alan has
followed unfolding events in Angola particularly closely because he
recognizes that there were two sides to the controversy on American
policy there. He has been relieved by what he considers mounting evidence of the wisdom of the position he and the other senators took,
i.e., not only the Soviet Union's setbacks in Angola, but documents
that have come to light undermining Kissinger's case for intervention.

Alan is unwilling to act like an unswerving zealot on any issue. He
can see both sides and is ready to work out compromises. This quality
has led to some misunderstandings of Alan by his constituents and
some criticism by reporters who say he is too flexible. Alan rarely holds

out for absolute victories. He is convinced that few issues are a full 100 percent one way. If an issue seems to fall 90 to 10 percent, he will work for the 90 percent. But the 10 percent view is also entitled to consideration in his opinion. After all, perhaps the 10 percent are right.

More importantly, Alan believes that one of man's greatest weaknesses is his inability to foresee the consequences of his actions.

"People come up with a solution to one problem, and maybe it'll work and maybe it won't," he says. "The one sure thing is that either way it will provoke a brand new problem, perhaps two or three. Life's an endless series of actions and reactions, the reactions all too often totally unexpected."

One night Alan and Harold Hughes were ruminating in the cloakroom over this perverse quality of life. Hughes was in one of his brooding moods, and he said, "There are means, but never ends. There really aren't any solutions. So we should seek them lovingly."

Alan was deeply affected when long ago he encountered in *Principia Ethica* by George E. Moore (1903) and later found amplified in the writings of E. M. Forster the principle that since you can't calculate with certainty the final effects of any one act, you should take into account most of all its immediate and sure results. He was fascinated by Forster's application of this philosophy not only to a brutal or barbarous action like bombing or invading a foreign country, but also to every sort of unkindness or incivility.

A similar scepticism about absolutes affects Alan's attitudes toward his fellow humans. He knows no one is perfect, and he likewise believes that no one is all bad. So he searches for good in everyone. He considers no one an enemy. Many a foe has become a friend. I once asked Alan whom he dislikes. He thought a while, mentioned a few possibilities, and finally said, "I don't really dislike anybody." It's perhaps this trait and all that flows from it that led Bernard Asbell, author of *The Senate Nobody Knows,** to call Alan "the big peace-maker in the Senate," when describing senator-to-senator relationships.

Because Alan's extensive work in the Senate is beyond the scope of this book, I can only mention briefly a few highlights of his second term. Alan's part, on the side that was definitely unpopular with voters in California and everywhere else in the Panama Canal battle, may

*Doubleday, 1978, page 257.

have saved many American lives. On this matter he never entertained any doubts about the correctness of his course. Only one facet of this can be covered here.

In January 1977, just before President Carter took office, he held a meeting with Congressional and future administration leaders in the pink palace of the old Smithsonian. Its purpose was to discuss all the foreign policy and defense issues. Carter predicted that the Panama Canal Treaty would be the first major issue and the first crisis he would face in foreign policy. The military leaders described how very difficult it would be to keep the Canal open if hostilities broke out. Carter asked everyone to withhold judgment until a treaty could be negotiated.

Alan immediately dug up a resolution that had been introduced in the last Congress by Republican Strom Thurmond and by John McClellan, a powerful Democrat from Arkansas, that expressed firm and total opposition to any change of jurisdiction over the canal. Thirty-eight or thirty-nine senators had signed it—enough to defeat the treaty. Alan talked to every Democrat on the list and to most of the Republicans. He told them about the meeting and Carter's request. He described the difficulties the military foresaw in defending the canal, and he urged them to stay off the resolution this time and give Carter a chance to negotiate a treaty.

The resolution was never reintroduced. About half the senators who had been on it before declined to go on it again, and the leading opponents of the treaty didn't want to disclose the shrinkage in their list. This initial move made the subsequent drive to approve the treaty possible, thanks to hard work done by Alan and other senators—particularly Byrd, Baker, Church, and Paul Sarbanes, a remarkably able freshman from Maryland. The treaty was ratified with only one vote to spare.

In January 1978 Alan led a Congressional delegation on a fact-finding mission to China. He went with an open mind, though for a long time he had felt that our nonrecognition policy toward mainland China made no practical sense and was contrary to our national interest and the interests of world peace. After intensive study and long discussions with Vice Premier Teng Hsiao-Ping, U.S. Ambassador Leonard Woodcock, and many other leaders and experts, he concluded that it was in the best interest of the United States to recognize the People's Republic of China as expeditiously as possible.

The delegation returned a day early to attend Senator Humphrey's funeral. Afterwards Alan flew on from Minneapolis to Washington with President Carter. During that flight, climaxing one of the longest days he had ever spent — about thirty hours — Alan gave his impressions of China to the president and urged that he proceed to normalize relations in the course of 1978.

Virtually everyone told Alan on his return that recognition was politically impossible. He believed otherwise. On the morning after his arrival, he held a press conference and set forth his views. The treaty with the Republic of China on Taiwan remained an obstacle. Alan labored with people in the White House and in the State Department for weeks and months of work and study on this and other troubling and perplexing aspects of the matter. At year's end President Carter announced recognition of the People's Republic, and thus diplomatic contact was established between the government of the people of the United States and the government of what will soon be a billion Chinese people.

There was more of a furor in the Senate than in the country over this event. In order to maintain trade, cultural, and if necessary a military relationship with America's friends on Taiwan, it was necessary to enact legislation acceptable to them but not unacceptable to the People's Republic. A harsh debate flared in the Senate. Alan and Ted Kennedy helped resolve it with an amendment speaking to Taiwan's concerns that met the needs of all, or almost all.

A random selection of Alan's other efforts includes his earthquake prediction and mitigation bill; pushing solar, geothermal and other new energy sources; defending the first amendment rights of the press; promoting the Equal Rights Amendment; working for better housing and transportation, and steering financial institution legislation; supporting Headstart and human rights; establishing a system for the merit selection of judges in California.

He has played a part in reforming the Congressional budget system, in setting up the budget process, and in launching the new Senate Budget Committee, on which he has served.

Above all he has been a leader in the Senate for SALT, for arms control, and for grappling with the danger of nuclear holocaust. Should the SALT process break down, he will not abandon that vital struggle.

Recently when we had a talk, Alan said, "What I always try to do, but especially in the Senate now, is to pay infinite attention to detail but not to squander energy on small matters. I strive to focus on the heart of the more significant issues; hence, arms control in the nuclear age, the separation and balance of power in our government, human rights — essentially freedom itself — and health care, where my thrust is not just on one disease that hits many people but on basic biomedical research that relates to fundamental life processes, with emphasis on the secrets of the aging process — the one affliction that hits everybody."

On May 19, 1978, Alan married Norma Weintraub, a slender, fair-haired, brown-eyed woman of great gentleness and warmth, who has long been active in California politics. Norma is petite. Her size and apparent frailty belie the enormous spirit and energy with which she keeps up with Alan on his long days of travel throughout the state and even during his morning sprints. For twelve years she ran the Encino Chamber of Commerce in Southern California with a quiet efficiency and subtle strength. She has twin sons, Donald and David, both graduates of the University of California.

Vice President Walter Mondale said publicly in 1979,

> When I came to the Senate, Senator Phil Hart of Michigan was its saint. Tragically, he's gone. The saint of the Senate now is Senator Alan Cranston of California. He is the most decent and gifted member of the United States Senate. His commitments are in tune with the deepest values of our nation. There comes a time in almost every person's public life when you have to decide finally what's more important — your conscience and your nation, or yourself. I never worry where Alan Cranston will be on that decision. I remember Gaylord Nelson's great statement when he cast one of the three votes against the Gulf of Tonkin Resolution. He said, "I'm voting no because I need my conscience more than the President needs my vote." And that's the kind of person Alan Cranston is.

CHAPTER 26

★ ★
"In the Way of Things Happening"
★ ★

It seems appropriate to round this out as we began, with another glimpse of Alan, a month before his marriage to Norma, on a visit soon after he was elected whip. This time I visited him.

From my journal of April 1978:

TUESDAY.

Alan wakes me at seven in the morning, saying, "You need exercise."

Hurriedly I dress in the guest room upstairs, overlooking a tiny back garden and a school yard. The small house on the back of Capitol Hill is only wide enough for each room. Alan hurries me outside where tulips and azaleas blaze in the little ivied front gardens, and under the trees the old brick row houses are painted in pastel colors.

We walk, jog, and run from the house to the Washington Monument down the grassy mall and back — about five miles in an hour and a quarter. On each stretch of grass he runs ahead with long swift strides of almost machine-like precision and does exercises until I catch up. He takes delight in pointing out the old buildings and vistas, beautiful in the morning light. We walk a little way beyond the Washington Monument to view an old concrete marker on the site of what was once Jefferson's Pier, in the time when the Potomac came closer to the White House. As we run back the sunlight is just touching the gilded top of the Capitol dome, and the slim exotic spires of the old Smithsonian pink castle are in dark silhouette.

I am amazed at how far I have run. Alan laughs and says, "Everyone underestimates what he can do."

Few people would enjoy Alan's rigorous schedule. At six he gets up, brings in the *New York Times*, the *Washington Post* and the *Congres-*

sional Record and reads them in bed. Then he runs in his red warm-up suit. He has a breakfast of orange juice, fruit, sourdough toast, Sanka, vitamins, and oatmeal without sugar, salt, or milk. He generally follows a low-fat diet. Then he does paperwork and perhaps makes a few phone calls until it is time to go to the office.

When I start cleaning the house, he tells me gleefully, "You see, it only needs to be done every six months!"

A suggestion that he might get a haircut and assemble the laundry meets with an impatient, "I haven't got time!" Yet he takes time to bring me glasses of orange juice, clippings, and books, and three-by-five cards scribbled with the times and places of events of special interest.

Later we chat about discipline and time. He says, "I try to make decisions quickly though I know some will be wrong. Lots of things don't have to be decided. They'll decide themselves."

Walking to work he enjoys pointing out California Senator Hiram Johnson's historic four-story house with its fanlight and mansard roof.

After a series of meetings and hearings, we have lunch in the Senate dining room with tall, blonde Allyn Kreps, who has come on Alan's staff for the SALT struggle, and Bill Jackson, who was once on Alan's staff and is now special assistant to Paul Warnke, the United States chief of SALT negotiator at Geneva.

There is fascinating talk of the hope of arms control. "During the SALT negotiations," Bill Jackson says, "it's an unprecedented, absolutely extraordinary thing that Alan and other senators have sat in at Geneva on SALT discussions with the Russians. The Russians learn from them, and they incorporate some of the senators' ideas in their own positions."

Alan feels that SALT II is today's overriding issue. Luncheon is followed by a meeting in his whip office with Ted Kennedy to discuss health programs.

The three of us sit down by the fireplace and chat. The sunlight streams into the beautiful and historic room. The three-room office is hidden away on the ground floor of the Capitol near the rotunda on the west front of the Capitol. There the hill falls away, so that Alan can look out through a recessed window across a marble terrace to the mall below and to the Washington and Lincoln monuments — a view he cherishes.

The old mahogany furniture is on loan from a Capitol furniture pool, the landscape paintings from the Gallery of Fine Arts. Alan has added his pictures of Father and Mother and Grenville Clark and old prints of his own of Washington, D.C. and of San Francisco, Los Angeles, and Sacramento about 1840. In the reception room hangs a row of photographs of the previous whips—Robert Byrd, Ted Kennedy, Russell Long, Mike Mansfield, Hubert Humphrey, Lyndon Johnson. There are also likenesses of earlier occupants of this office, such as Daniel Webster and Hiram Johnson, whom Alan visited in this very place in the mid-1940s. Alan's improvements have included removing a lavatory once installed in a corner by Bobby Baker—it had made the spacious, chandeliered room look a bit like Grand Central Station.

The Senator from Massachusetts gestures with a cigar, laughs infectiously and exuberantly as he talks, a bit intensely at first. He rapidly unfolds a plan for advancing health legislation. Alan promises his cooperation and adds some ideas of his own.

Ted is heavyset with enormous broad shoulders. He has a mane of wavy dark hair, slightly graying, cut beautifully and quite long. His blue eyes twinkle gaily but shrewdly. People have called him "Bonnie Prince Charlie."

Finally Alan says, "Another thing. Don't you think that it might be helpful, with this new momentum we have, to bring up the idea of normalization of relations with the People's Republic of China *before* the SALT debate?"

Kennedy says very thoughtfully, "Yes, that would help in some ways." He adds, "I completely agree with you on normalization and so do others. But no one has expressed it quite so fully and frankly as you have!" He puts an ironic twist on his words and always seems close to laughter.

"Well," he says, getting up to leave and laughing once more, "I hope you can persuade the president!"

Alan now meets in rapid succession with the chief of police of Foster City, California, the Antelope Valley Board of Trade, and Jim Santini, Nevada's only congressman, for a discussion on saving Lake Tahoe. In the course of the meeting Alan phones the governor of Nevada, Mike O'Callaghan, a good friend.

The air is close in Alan's office. "We can't open the windows," says Roy. "The bureaucracy won't permit it. We even had six men up here for a discussion when we wanted to light a fire in the fireplace!"

Alan is next scheduled to meet with the Los Angeles Department of Airports, then to make a radio statement for KFI, then to attend a meeting on the budget in Senator Muskie's office, and finally to go to a reception of Du Pont plant sales managers at the Hyatt Regency.

All through the meetings he is dealing with constant interruptions, decisions, phone calls, visitors, and papers. Intermittently, he rushes to the Senate to vote when flashing lights and buzzers summon him for a roll call. Yet he stays relaxed and good humored.

"How do you stand it?" I ask.

"But it's so enjoyable," he says in surprise.

When things go wrong he shows his disgust with an audible sigh or a little downward turn of the mouth. He acknowledges that, "Three or four things, at least, will go wrong each day. I just tick them off as they happen." But his secretaries have told me that staff members are sometimes unnerved by those heavy sighs.

Anne Ainsworth, Alan's office manager, takes me on a tour to visit his staff. Besides the three-room whip office in the Capitol, Alan's staff works in a row of eight rooms in the old Russell Senate Office Building, including a private office and reception room. Six of these are called "pods," and each is the domain of a legislative assistant with a particular area of responsibility.

Alan has additional space in a somewhat ramshackle building two blocks away. His staffers there deal with immigration problems and the work of the child and human development subcommittee. There's a filing section and the mail section and its machines—with sacks of unopened mail still in the hallway (in the wake of the Panama battle when they received 75,000 extra pieces).

"We never finish our work," says the tall, dark-haired Jan Mueller, Roy's indispensable assistant, "but we try."

Alan's main reception room is momentarily a madhouse. Peggy Dondey, the gracious receptionist, answers the phone with one hand while dispensing tourist materials to constituents and their children with the other.

"Alan Cranston's office," she repeats. Then during a lull she complains humorously, "Alan doesn't want me to say 'Senator Cranston's office.' He says it's too formal. But sometimes people get confused. They ask, 'Is this the Senator's office? I want the Senator's office!'"

Alan and I meet again in the whip office; phone calls have accumulated in his absence from the vice president, the secretary of the treasury, and the secretary of defense. Photographs have been sent over from the White House showing Alan chatting with the president on the sofa in the Oval Office.

Mary Lou McNeely, Alan's secretary, says, "I like the one where you're both smiling."

Alan grins. "I like the one where I'm talking and he's listening!"

A gift basket from a grocery store has arrived from a friend — cheeses, candies, nuts — everything *not* on a low-fat diet. Alan says humorously to Mary Lou, "Everything *bad!* Whom can we give it to?"

Mary Lou, who always works late till businesses shut down in California, laughs and says, "Give it to me!"

"No," he says. "You're nice. Somebody *bad!*"

In the end Mary Lou divides it with the rest of the staff, persuading Alan to take home some brandied peaches. According to Alan, gentle, dark-haired Mary Lou can place phone calls faster than anyone he's ever seen.

Carolyn Caddes, a California photographer, takes Alan's picture for an exhibit of "Interesting Palo Altans."

"He has a wonderful face," she says, "especially the eyes, smiling or not."

That evening, instead of having dinner, we snack at a Wine Institute reception, at the Georgetown Club, made famous by Tongsun Park, honoring retiring California Congressmen Moss, Sisk, and Leggett. There Pete McCloskey, my Republican congressman tells me, "Alan has done more than anyone in the state to restore people's faith in politics and government because he is so effective."

I fall into bed at ten. Alan reads late and makes phone calls to California.

WEDNESDAY.

Another busy day for Alan while I visit with old friends. I arrive at the whip office to an end-of-the-day bedlam — phone calls, press calls, radio calls, constituents being ushered in to say hello and have pictures taken with the senator.

Alan tells a teenage girl, "Webster and Calhoun once had this office." She beams at him shyly. A group of young conservationists is ushered in and out.

A controversy erupts over an amendment to some banking legislation. The question is, who is liable, the banker or the consumer, if a new kind of credit card is lost and a crook cleans out somebody's bank account? Neither Roy, Alan's chief of staff, nor Carolyn Jordan, the counsel on banking issues, has a clear opinion on how to handle this. Should Alan, a member of the Banking Committee,* support an amendment setting a $50 limit on consumer liability that is strongly opposed by the banks?

Alan sighs and exclaims, "Why couldn't you figure it out before you brought it to me?" He questions them very closely and forces the way to a decision. He will support the amendment and the legislation.

The ambassador from Pakistan is ushered in. He is a fine looking raven-haired man in his forties with a long aquiline nose. He says that he has come to discuss the Bhutto affair. Ali Bhutto, the former prime minister, is held under sentence of death, following a *coup d'etat.* Bhutto's handsome young son, now an exile in England, recently visited Alan and appealed for his help. In the son's presence Alan signed a letter to the Pakistan government asking for clemency for Bhutto. The ambassador must surely be aware of this, for he states in a tense manner that he has come to tell Alan "the other side."

Ambassador Sahabzede Yaqub-Khan likens the affair to Watergate in its sad effect on his country, but he notes, "Fortunately for Nixon, he was not indicted for murder and conspiracy, as was Bhutto."

The ambassador describes the incident last year when machine-gun fire struck a car driven by a member of Parliament, killing the M.P.'s father. There was strong evidence that Bhutto had tried to have the M.P. assassinated on this and several other occasions. The military then overthrew the government. Bhutto was sentenced to be hanged. The ambassador stresses the belief of his government that accountability is important and that no one should be considered above the law.

Speaking still more tensely he adds, "Bhutto and I were very close, and this is painful to me. We know that representations have been made by senators to whom appeals have been made for mercy. But the Pakistanis are stubborn, and this may have the opposite effect of what is intended."

*Among Alan's present committee assignments, are the chairmanships of the Financial Institutions subcommittee of the Senate Banking Committee, and of the Child and Human Development subcommittee of the Labor and Human Resource Committee.

"The Supreme Court is considering an appeal of the case. It can decide whether to overturn, reduce, or uphold the sentence. The president—like Mr. Ford—would then have the option of pardoning Bhutto."

The ambassador speaks with extraordinary grace and eloquence. Alan listens carefully but very relaxedly, and I am astounded to see him smothering yawns in the close air of the room. Now Alan asks a series of pointed questions.

"How is your Supreme Court appointed?"

"All its members were appointed by Bhutto," says the ambassador.

"How was the president selected?"

"He was a general named by Bhutto."

"Why would the member of Parliament be a target of assassination attempts?"

The ambassador, perhaps relieved to have delivered his carefully prepared message, now bursts out, "Oh, he was a scurrilous, despicable man, greatly inferior to Bhutto! Yet Bhutto had considerable vanity and resented his attacks."

Alan says quietly, "You know I'm strongly opposed to capital punishment."

"Yes."

There are a few more exchanges. Alan makes plain his hope that Bhutto will not be hanged. The ambassador thanks him and takes a graceful and swift departure. He has made a smooth presentation though his hands were shaking. [A year later Bhutto was hanged.]

Back at Alan's house at last. To my relief, wind, rain, and darkness prevent us from running to the Washington Monument as planned. We have our first at-home dinner: frozen lasagna, frozen spinach souffle, and fresh fruit. We sit by the fire afterward while I read clippings and articles Alan has given me and he works on a speech on gay rights. This will be given Saturday night at the Hollywood Palladium to a branch of the American Civil Liberties Union. Staff controversy over the speech has caused it to go through successive drafts. After considerable changing, the draft finally seems a good one.

"One can only be sure of ensuring human rights in a democratic society by insuring that everyone enjoys them," he writes. "If even one individual loses them, or fails to gain them, the rights of *all* are endangered."

THURSDAY.

A rainy, cold, blustery day. Alan has a full schedule, starting with a meeting at nine regarding SALT with Dr. Wolfgang Panofsky of Stanford, a member of a presidential commission. Alan goes on to a series of meetings: one on the banking bill; one on energy; a lunch of the Policy Committee, a Senate Democratic leadership meeting to plan the legislative program; a meeting with Paul Warnke, the chief U.S. SALT negotiator; a meeting with Dick Nunez of Disney Productions; and a film show arranged by Max Palevsky, Ted Fritts of the *Bakersfield Californian*, and others concerning Huntington's disease.

The highlight of the week for me comes at five o'clock at a meeting in the whip office for Marshall Shulman, the State Department's top Russian expert who has just returned from Moscow. A pleasant-faced man in his fifties who looks like Jason Robards, he has devoted his whole life to studying the Soviet Union. Present are Senators Kennedy, Mathias, McIntyre, Leahy, Hart, Sarbanes, Bumpers, and Cranston and Allyn Kreps from Alan's staff. Shulman reports on his trip, noting a somewhat improved atmosphere in Moscow and remarking that the Soviets have made a number of concessions recently in the SALT negotiations. He feels they are anxious to conclude the SALT Treaty and thinks they are ready to make a few more concessions to bring this about.

The senators sit in an oval between the fireplace and Alan's desk drinking coffee and tea. About half-past six, at the end of an hour and a half of discussion, Alan suggests that these senators and a few others particularly interested in SALT start meeting every two weeks to prepare for the great struggle that will occur in the Senate when an arms limitation treaty is submitted for ratification.

The senators agree to start meeting regularly with the understanding that they're not committed to supporting the treaty till they know its final terms. They hope, and they expect, to be able to support the treaty. And if they do, they intend to be well prepared, and they intend to go all out for it. All agree that the fight will be formidable.

FRIDAY.

Today Alan and I are to fly to California in the early afternoon.

At 1:10 P.M. after a busy morning, he rushes into the whip office with three young Pennsylvania tourists in tow. He saw them leaning over a stairwell, peering at something. "What are you trying to see?" he asked.

"*Everything!*" they exclaim fervently.

"Then come along!" he said.

In his private office, he delights in showing them his old prints of the Capitol and his view of the Washington Monument, identifying with their excitement, as he shovels papers from his desk into his briefcase. He enjoys their comments as they roam about oohing and ahing, oblivious to the pressure of time.

Mary Lou lays a hand-written letter from President Carter on Alan's desk. Alan shows this to the girls, who gasp, "I can't believe it! I can't wait to tell Howard. He won't believe this," and so forth.

In his letter the president thanks Alan for his "personal demonstration of statesmanship and political courage" in the Panama fight. There is a scribbled postscript, "Alan, you did a great job," signed "J".

Alan's staff seems a little nonplussed at this odd moment for entertaining visitors, not even constituents. They want to break in with weighty problems, but Alan escapes and triumphantly strides out, smiling his good-byes.

On the plane Alan works his way through a great pile of newspapers. I fiddle with the vents and ask him if he wants that cold blast of air blowing on his forehead.

"I never notice drafts, smoke or dust," he says, flashing me a rueful grin. "If you do that you're not concentrating."

When the plane lands, we part, marking the end of my week.

Epilogue

★ ★ ★ ★ ★ ★ ★

January 20, 1980. The book is going to press. Alan and Norma spent the last three weeks crossing and crisscrossing California, talking and listening as people voiced their concerns and fears. Inflation. The energy shortage. Starvation and genocide in Southeast Asia. The hostage crisis in Iran. The Soviet invasion of Afghanistan. The collapse of detente. War?

On this day at a luncheon session of the Democratic State Convention at the San Francisco Airport Hilton, Alan spoke to a party torn with dissension. His subject was to be his theme for 1980 — a watershed speech. He seemed a little tense as he made his way through the jampacked lobby to the ballroom, assailed by queries and greetings.

His speech began ominously:

> We meet at a time of great world turmoil and peril. . . . If we fail to discourage further aggressions by the Soviets, the choice between war or peace could slip out of our hands. Clearly, there will be — clearly, there must be — increases in military aid and defense spending.

> In the course of this violent century, we have learned bitter lessons about power, and the abuse of power; lessons that others possessing and possessed by power taught us; lessons that we have learned about ourselves in Vietnam and elsewhere.

> The American challenge is to be prudent in the use of our vast power — avoiding its misuse — while finding ways to exercise it appropriately to protect our freedom, our security, and human rights in our strife-torn world. . . .

> A Soviet military move to seize or disrupt our Middle East oil supplies — presently indispensable to our economic stability and to military security for ourselves and our allies — could make a military countermove by the U.S. inevitable. . . . The

Middle East is . . . like a house of cards that could tumble in many different directions under the impact of the social, political and military forces now at work there. And the Soviet Union is—to everyone's peril—shaking up that house of cards. . . . I intend to go back to Washington when Congress reconvenes three days hence, determined, as I always have been, to take up again the long, always difficult struggle for arms control and for a peaceful sane relationship with the Soviet Union.

I do not know how that can be achieved. I only know that it must be achieved. . . . This is not a time for bluster. This is not a time for rattling nukes. . . . Is it safe to assume that there will not be a swift, strategic strike in the first moments of a U.S.-U.S.S.R. military confrontation? . . .

Is it safe to assume that nuclear war won't start by mistake?

That's the precise nature of the razor's edge upon which we and the Soviet Union are so precariously perched. . . .

The speech ended on a note of hope:

The United States has a new opportunity to stand tall in the eyes of the Third World. . . . In Iran the United States has given the world a lesson in how a mighty and self-confident nation behaves under pressure.

Despite intense provocation, we have behaved as we believe civilized nations ought to behave: reserving armed might as the last—and only last—resort. . . . The Soviet experiment is barely fifty years old, yet it is already geriatric, fearful, conservative. . . . By contrast, the American Revolution at age 204 is ever enlarging freedoms. . . . Our political system is alive and well. It works—for those who work at making it work. . . . The message to our fellow Californians and Americans should be:

We shall not lay down the burden of the battle for peace, and for economic and social justice here at home. . . . We shall not shirk from this nation's commitments around the world to nurture freedom and human rights. We shall fight for, and win, the goals and aspirations of all who believe, as we do, in the right of every human being to dignity and freedom.

The Democrats gave him a standing ovation. Norma reached up and kissed him. Then she fought to hold back tears. Seeing this, many in the audience were tearful. He was surrounded. The tears came not from despair or sadness, but from the wellsprings of a deeper emotion—a tribute in the face of all odds to the dauntless, questing resoluteness of the human spirit.

Postscript

Alan was on the threshold of an eventful year, a year marked by extremes of tragedy and triumph. The beginning of summer 1980 combined, within a span of fewer than three weeks, Robin Cranston's tragic death, after being struck by a careening car, Kim Cranston's wedding, and then, almost as though it were an irrelevancy, Alan's renomination for the Senate in California's Democratic primary. It would have been an extraordinary time in anyone's life, even for one as stoical as Alan, including as it did deep personal tragedy, a family event of singular happiness, and another political milestone.

In his reelection campaign in the fall, Alan warned that the eighties were off to an uncertain and dangerous beginning. The revolution in Iran and the seizing of the American hostages, the invasion of Afghanistan, the suspension of SALT ratification by the Senate, the energy crisis, the war between Iran and Iraq—all signaled a precarious position for the United States. Meanwhile, the nuclear arms race continued its ominous buildup.

The theme of Alan's campaign was a demand for "a resolute and creative struggle to achieve the safety and sanity of enforceable, verifiable, worldwide arms control and limitations."

Audiences were visibly stirred when he told them: "Freedom and human survival are at stake. . . . I am a futurist. I believe in a better, brighter, more tranquil future that has always beckoned. That's why I'm in the Senate. I will do my utmost there to provide wise and loving leadership for you, for our California, and for our America. God bless you all."

His schedule was augmented by radio and TV spots, one of which showed him in a bright blue jogging suit running with high-stepping grace and precision. It was to become the identifying motif of his senatorial campaign—and later his campaign for the presidency.

On election night Alan found it hard to detach himself from the TV screen. His face was somber as he watched friends and allies in the Senate go down—Senators Birch Bayh of Indiana, Frank Church of Idaho, John Culver of Iowa, George McGovern of South Dakota, Gaylord Nelson of Wisconsin. Their defeat showed the power of right-wing forces led primarily by Senator Jesse Helms of North Carolina. Ronald Reagan had defeated Jimmy Carter for the presidency, and the Republicans had captured control of the Senate, 54–46. The losses stunned the Democrats, who, prior to the election, had held fifty-nine seats.

On the other hand, Alan was reelected with the largest number of votes ever received by any U.S. Senate candidate in history—and with the largest number of votes ever received by a candidate for any statewide California office.

He was the first California Democrat ever to be elected to the U.S. Senate for a third term. He ran 1.6 million votes ahead of the Carter-Mondale ticket and nearly 200,000 votes ahead of Ronald Reagan.

"A bittersweet victory," Alan summed it up.

When he returned to Washington, he joined the Foreign Relations Committee and was for the third time unanimously elected Democratic whip. (He was elected for the fourth time in 1982, again setting new records.)

As Alan watched the performance of the Reagan administration his patience wore thin. In early March 1981 he blasted James Watt, Reagan's nominee for the Secretary of the Interior. Alan's hometown newspaper, the *Peninsula Times Tribune,* expressed its amazement in an editorial when "Cranston, a consistently careful conciliator, who seldom blows his cool," exploded against Watt's confirmation.

In Foreign Relations Committee sessions, he thundered against nuclear proliferation and the Reagan administration's apparent indifference to arms control negotiations with the Soviet Union.

In early April he wrote to me: "I've decided to take out after Jesse Helms." He attacked Helms at confirmation hearings on the nomination of Chester A. Crocker as Assistant Secretary of State for African Affairs. Alan accused Helms of harming the administration's foreign policy efforts by holding up nominations of key State Department personnel. "The fault lies here in the Senate," Alan exclaimed, glaring at the senator from North Carolina. "These are the president's men, and they are being held up." He likened Reagan's cautious treatment of Helms to the way Dwight Eisenhower used to tiptoe around Senator McCarthy. And, irked at Helms's use of roll call votes to hurt Democrats, Alan told newsmen, "Helms has introduced more meanness than I've seen in the Senate before. He may be the most dangerous figure in the Senate since the late senator from Wisconsin, Joseph McCarthy."

While Alan cooperated on routine appointments, some of the president's men were more than he could stomach. He led a successful battle against Reagan's nomination of Ernest Lefever as Assistant Secretary of State for Human Rights. And he was the only one on the Foreign Relations Committee to vote against Eugene Rostow's nomination to head the Arms Control and Disarmament Agency.

He also charged Reagan with repeating President Johnson's inflationary mistakes—spending for the military without raising taxes to pay the bills. Though Alan advocated stronger defense measures, he became the point man in the Senate, speaking out against big defense spending boosts made at the expense of social welfare programs. He voted against Reagan's budget, which called for huge tax cuts and huge defense spending with consequent monumental deficits, and he spoke out forcefully on the need for new strategic arms control initiatives.

Again he exploded against James Watt and demanded his resignation.

"Cranston has found his whip," reported Leo Rennert in the *Sacramento Bee*.

By the end of 1982 Alan had raised $3.4 million on behalf of the Senate Democratic Leadership Circle to aid Democratic Senate candidates in the upcoming election.

He attacked Reagan for giving up on his fight to balance the budget, and Alan called for curbs on the Federal Reserve.

He sent Israeli Prime Minister Menachem Begin a public letter holding him responsible for the safety of the Palestinian refugees who were massacred by Lebanese rightists.

He also led the dramatic Senate fight against the sale of Airborne Warning and Control System aircraft (AWACS) and defensive F-15 fighter plane equipment to Saudi Arabia, warning that the sale could upset the precarious balance in the Middle East, where the Israelis, vastly outnumbered by the surrounding Arabs, depended, he said, "for their safety not on quantitative but on qualitative superiority."

"If we make a serious mistake," Alan added, "Israel could perish—while we would remain. . . . The introduction of these sophisticated new weapons in the Middle East can only escalate the arms race, and place Israeli military forces on a hair trigger."

"Don't you feel frustrated at times?" I asked him later.

"No," he said cheerfully. "I'm fighting on so many fronts, when I lose on one, I'm winning on another."

He instigated Senate Foreign Relations Committee hearings in San Francisco and other cities (the first time this had been done) on a new proposal for negotiating an arms control treaty with the Russians, and he broke his own rule against taking stands on state propositions by endorsing the Nuclear Freeze Initiative in California.

In September 1981 he flew to Europe to discuss arms control with leading government figures in Russia, later reporting on these talks to government leaders in France, Poland, and West Germany. Norma, of course, went along, as did Gerry Warburg, Alan's aide, my husband, Jack, and myself (our three family members going at our own expense). Republican Senator Charles Mathias of Maryland, like Alan a member of the Senate Foreign Relations Committee, and his aid, Cas Yost, joined us later. This would be the first time since the inauguration of President Reagan that an American senator had gone to the Soviet Union.

A highlight of the trip was a luncheon in the Kremlin Palace of Congresses hosted by V.P. Rubin, Chairman of the Soviet of Nationalities of the Supreme Soviet, the parliamentary group that had sponsored our visit, now nearing an end. Seated next to me was Sergei Obrasov, the world-famous director of the Moscow Puppet Theatre, a charming man with white hair, a wide mouth, and sparkling wide-set blue eyes. Later Norma called him a "Christmas elf." He looked sixty, but he said he was eighty. When I expressed disbelief, he laughed and borrowed a term from nuclear arms control: "As usual, the problem is one of *verification!*"

He told me the medal he wore for his work with children was the highest nonmilitary decoration given in the Soviet Union. "It signifies that my country needs me; I believe the secret of human happiness is to be needed."

When the toasts began, Obrasov sprang up and spoke in a tense, husky voice of the need for peace, "because every leaf is different and every child in the world is different from every other. No child can ever be duplicated again."

Senator Mathias responded first to the welcoming toasts: "If man can survive in cold and airless space, surely he can find a way to survive here on earth."

Alan listened, his chin on his hand, his fingers spread along his cheek, his eyes dark and somber. Then he spoke. "I came to Russia because I believe that the effort to achieve peace through arms control is the most important work of my life." He outlined the reasons for the breakdown of the SALT II negotiations, then said, "Common sense must find a solution. Senator Mathias and I are leaving without optimism, but not without hope. . . .

"Perhaps the most moving experience of our week in Moscow," Alan concluded, "was our visit to the opening day of school, seeing those children just starting their education. It was unthinkable that they should be killed by nuclear weapons from our country, or that children back home should be killed by nuclear weapons from your country. Unthinkable that your children whom you love and our children whom we love— if we allow them to grow up—should try to destroy one another in war."

On our last evening we dined with our a group of Russian friends at a suburban restaurant. Just as we arrived, both Alan and "Mac" Mathias appeared on color TV in the bar, with simultaneous translation, from a program taped that morning. A Russian told us that their words of peace, obviously spoken from their hearts, were being carried to 80 million households, relayed by satellite through the nine time zones of the Soviet Union.

"Cranston has adopted open confrontation—and not quiet compromise—as the hallmark of his strategy in the Senate," a reporter wrote in the fall of 1981.

Alan had clearly changed. He was more confident and more fully realized, more strongly individual, more able to focus his talents. These changes had several causes. One was his overwhelming election to an unprecedented third term. And Alan's health and stamina were and are at high levels. With his usual zest, he has set out to conquer the process of getting old. He diets, runs daily, and participates in organized track meets.

But perhaps the most important cause is Norma, who despite her frail looks and Parkinsonian tremor, is steady, serene, supportive, and wise. She shares his love of politics, but all she truly wants is to be with him and for him to succeed in his goals. She understands his passion for peace and the volcanic forces that drive him. She is spiritually strong, sensitively tuned, but low-key, and she relaxes as well as he does throughout their long and chaotic days.

The other side of the coin is that through her he has found a role that helps him express his deep natural protectiveness. Their relationship, he has confessed, is not merely a warm companionship, but a love affair. This has made him reach outward more warmly and expressively to others. Being less vulnerable, he is more open.

Finally, the changed political situation in Washington has created a setting and given him a role in which he can be most truly himself, articulating his dreams, goals, and ideas for a better world—arms control and world peace, democracy and human rights, an improved economy and environment—while constantly flailing away at the obstructions and obfuscations in his path.

When Alan was first elected to the Senate in 1968, he had looked forward to the chance to deal with the major issues of war and peace, arms control, and human rights. His has been a steady voice. Fascinated with the Senate, its long history, its processes, and its many striking and interesting members of diverse backgrounds, personalities, and viewpoints, he worked hard and was unanimously elected majority whip. Fully sensing the Senate's role as a foundation of American democratic government, he found his vital purpose in helping to "make the Senate work."

But by the time his third term was under way, both his perspective and the Senate had changed. When he was first elected Richard Nixon entered the White House, and Alan's early legislative efforts were often frustrated by the man whose policies he had so often opposed. And the successive administrations of Ford, Carter, and Reagan seen at such close hand further diminished Alan's awe of the presidency. The overriding issues of our times were not being properly dealt with. The nation's priorities were becoming skewed. And now, Reagan's growing militancy and the ever-present threat of nuclear war—which has always concerned Alan—filled him with deepening alarm.

As 1984 loomed, he realized that he was only one within reach of the presidency who had devoted years of thought and effort to the matters

CRANSTON

of war and peace. He felt he was the only one with the passion and the capability to seek to halt the nuclear arms race and bring about an enforceable, verifiable arms control agreement. Effective arms control could bring about lowered defense spending and ultimately a balanced budget, more funds for rebuilding the nation's human and material resources. Alan envisioned an America of full employment, quality education, environmental safety, and less crime—an America of sounder values and new hope.

The next step was inevitable. In the fall of 1981 Alan set up a committee, chaired by Allyn Kreps, to explore the possibility of his running for president. He then proceeded to "test the waters" in thirty-seven states, and in less than a year he and the committee decided that the race was wide open and that he should run.

His Senate term ran to 1986, so a presidential race would not jeopardize his chance to remain in the Senate should he be unsuccessful. He felt he could raise enough money and organize a winning campaign. Above all, he had the passionate drive, competence, toughness, and vision to deal with the greatest issue of our times—the need for arms control and the prevention of nuclear war.

The co-chairpersons of the campaign are Harris Wofford, a Philadelphia attorney, former special assistant to President Kennedy for civil rights, and later the associate director of the Peace Corps, author of *Of Kennedys and Kings*, and from 1970 to 1978, president of Bryn Mawr College; Marjorie Benton, a civic leader in Chicago and U.S. representative to UNICEF; and Willie Brown, the California Speaker of the Assembly. The campaign manager is Sergio Bendixen, a handsome, soft-spoken, tremendously energetic, and skilled young Floridian veteran of the Ted Kennedy and Jimmy Carter presidential campaigns.

Alan's months of exploration climaxed at the California Democratic State Convention in mid-January 1983, where he won the straw poll with 59.2 percent.

On February 2, 1983, with Norma and Kim at his side, at a press conference in the historic Caucus Room of the Russell Senate Office Building so thronged that a reporter from *The Wall Street Journal* was unable to get inside, Alan announced his candidacy for president.

He spoke movingly of his decision to run and of his long history of interest in peace and world affairs. Then he said:

"The arms race can never end unless men are wise enough to call a halt or mad enough to destroy the world.

"I believe in the necessities of defense . . . but we have overleaped the bounds of reason."

He said the purpose of ending the threat of nuclear war would be the dominating goal of his presidency, taking precedence over all others.

"A president must concentrate the powers of his mind and his office on one or two principal purposes, else he will squander his strength and his substance on the demand of the moment and the crisis of the hour, and his years at the center will waste away."

It would not be easy to reach agreement with the Russians, he said, yet peace was in their interest as in ours. "At the heart of all my convictions always has been the belief that American freedom can only flourish in a world at peace. . . . The American people share my values and concerns. And, once united in purpose, they will be mighty—indeed, an irresistible force. I cannot forge that unity from my seat in the Senate.

"It can be done only from the White House.

"And so, today, I set out for the White House for the same reasons that, years ago, led me into public life.

"Some have said that my age—at sixty-nine—might be a handicap. I don't believe so. Principles and values don't decline with age. They just grow stronger."